"Roche and Burridge's book, *Choreography: The Basics*, is an insightful introduction to the theory and practice of choreography that is illustrated with current choreographic examples from diverse regions and cultural contexts. For anyone considering studying dance as a profession, I would recommend this book."

Professor Anna CY Chan, *Dean of the School of Dance, The Hong Kong Academy for Performing Arts*

"*Choreography: The Basics* is ideally suited to undergraduates seeking to better understand a multiplicity of approaches to making dances. Emphasising the social and relational aspects of choreography, alongside its craft and discipline, this accessible text is packed with insights and portraits of choreographic processes for the twenty-first century."

Professor Carol Brown, *Head of VCA Dance, University of Melbourne*

"Brought to life through diverse examples, *Choreography: The Basics* provides a road map of the experience, knowledge and contexts of making dances. I would recommend this book to all dance students and scholars eager to establish a sound basis to their choreographic studies."

Dr Jamieson Dryburgh, *Director of Higher Education, Central School of Ballet, London*

CHOREOGRAPHY
THE BASICS

This book provides a comprehensive and concise overview of choreography both as a creative skill and as a field of study, introducing readers to the essential theory and context of choreographic practice.

Providing invaluable practical considerations for creating choreography as well as leading international examples from a range of geographical and cultural contexts, this resource will enhance students' knowledge of how to create dance. This clear guide outlines both historical and recent developments within the field, including how choreographers are influenced by technology and intercultural exchange, whilst also demonstrating the potential to address social, political and philosophical themes. It further explores how students can devise and analyse their own work in a range of styles, how choreography can be used in range of contexts – including site-specific work and digital technologies – and engages with communities of performers to give helpful, expert suggestions for developing choreographic projects.

This book is a highly valuable resource for anyone studying dancemaking, dance studies or contemporary choreographic practice and those in the early stages of dance training who wish to pursue a career as a choreographer or in a related profession.

Jenny Roche (PhD) is a Senior Lecturer at the University of Limerick, Ireland. Having worked as a dancer for many years, she continues to collaborate on interdisciplinary arts projects as a performer, maker and arts practice researcher. Her book *Multiplicity, Embodiment and The Contemporary Dancer: Moving Identities* was published in 2015.

Stephanie Burridge (PhD) lectures at LASALLE College of the Arts and Singapore Management University and is a choreographer, performer and dance writer. She is Series Editor for the Routledge collections Celebrating Dance in Asia and the Pacific, and Perspectives on Dance, Young People and Change.

THE BASICS SERIES

The Basics is a highly successful series of accessible guidebooks which provide an overview of the fundamental principles of a subject area in a jargon-free and undaunting format.

Intended for students approaching a subject for the first time, the books both introduce the essentials of a subject and provide an ideal springboard for further study. With over 50 titles spanning subjects from artificial intelligence (AI) to women's studies, *The Basics* are an ideal starting point for students seeking to understand a subject area.

Each text comes with recommendations for further study and gradually introduces the complexities and nuances within a subject.

SOCIOLOGY (THIRD EDITION)
KEN PLUMMER

MUSIC COGNITION
HENKJAN HONING

PERFORMANCE STUDIES
ANDREEA S. MICU

AMERICAN STUDIES
ANDREW DIX

PHYSICAL GEOGRAPHY (SECOND EDITION)
JOSEPH HOLDEN

WORLD PREHISTORY
BRIAN M. FAGAN AND NADIA DURRANI

FRENCH REVOLUTION
DARIUS VON GÜTTNER

RESEARCH METHODS (THIRD EDITION)
NICHOLAS WALLIMAN

ARCHAEOLOGY (FOURTH EDITION)
BRIAN M. FAGAN AND NADIA DURRANI

REAL ESTATE
JAN WILCOX AND JANE FORSYTH

MANAGEMENT (SECOND EDITION)
MORGEN WITZEL

SEMIOTICS (FOURTH EDITION)
DANIEL CHANDLER

CHOREOGRAPHY
JENNY ROCHE AND STEPHANIE BURRIDGE

LANGUAGE ACQUISITION
PAUL IBBOTSON

CHOREOGRAPHY
THE BASICS

Jenny Roche and Stephanie Burridge

LONDON AND NEW YORK

Cover image: Images by Carol Brown, *Digital Dance* courtesy of the Victoria College of the Arts, Faculty of Fine Arts and Music, University of Melbourne.

First published 2022
by Routledge
4 Park Square, Milton Park, Abingdon, Oxon OX14 4RN

and by Routledge
605 Third Avenue, New York, NY 10158

Routledge is an imprint of the Taylor & Francis Group, an informa business

© 2022 Jenny Roche and Stephanie Burridge

The right of Jenny Roche and Stephanie Burridge to be identified as authors of this work has been asserted in accordance with sections 77 and 78 of the Copyright, Designs and Patents Act 1988.

All rights reserved. No part of this book may be reprinted or reproduced or utilised in any form or by any electronic, mechanical, or other means, now known or hereafter invented, including photocopying and recording, or in any information storage or retrieval system, without permission in writing from the publishers.

Trademark notice: Product or corporate names may be trademarks or registered trademarks, and are used only for identification and explanation without intent to infringe.

British Library Cataloguing-in-Publication Data
A catalogue record for this book is available from the British Library

Library of Congress Cataloging-in-Publication Data
A catalog record has been requested for this book

ISBN: 978-0-367-89615-7 (hbk)
ISBN: 978-0-367-89616-4 (pbk)
ISBN: 978-1-003-02011-0 (ebk)

DOI: 10.4324/9781003020110

Typeset in Bembo
by KnowledgeWorks Global Ltd.

CONTENTS

Acknowledgments	viii
Introduction	1
1 The journey begins	7
2 Choreographic notebook	37
3 Broader skills a choreographer needs	69
4 Choreographic (re)evolution, documentation and preservation	96
5 A choreographic voice	126
6 Choreography for sites, screens and community practice	157
Conclusion: next steps on your choreographic journey	185
Glossary	189
References	195
Index	205

ACKNOWLEDGMENTS

We would like to thank Brigitte Moody for her initial work on the proposal for this project and Yarra Ileto for assisting with the research and referencing.

The compilation of knowledge and experience from decades of choreographing, performing, teaching, learning, writing, researching and critiquing dance come together in this volume. We are grateful for the wisdom and inspiration from so many dancers, choreographers, academic colleagues, artists, friends and family who have supported our journeys in dance.

INTRODUCTION

If you want to train in and study dance at university level, you will also need to study choreography as part of your undergraduate dance studies. Choreography is a very broad term which covers a multitude of activities and descriptions. We use it to describe what happens when someone or something puts together actions in order or sequence. In other words, the term choreography refers to the structuring of movement. It can be used to describe well-executed and rehearsed set passes in soccer, the elegant patterns of flamingos on a salt lake in Africa, a sequence of Martial Arts moves, the precision of robots assembling cars in a factory. But of course, choreography is most closely connected to structuring dance in all its forms, styles and genres. Without choreography dance could not be presented or ideas communicated.

Choreography can involve using a set dance vocabulary like in ballet or inventing the actions to be performed (improvising) followed by the sequencing and progressions of that movement into a legible, communicable form. In other words, it's about what movements and phrases you choose and how you put them together. The eminent dance scholar, Susan Leigh Foster (2010, p.15) describes choreography as "a plan or orchestration of bodies in motion." There are as many ways of choreographing as there are people who do it. In the professional world of dance there can be a distinction between being a dancer and being a choreographer although in most small-scale dance companies you must be both. So, what does it mean to encounter choreography at university? Studying choreography in the twenty-first century means you will be equipped to make dances, be innovative, take creative risks and usually begin to develop your own approach to the creative process. More than this, choreography is now an established academic discipline being studied at PhD level and beyond. There are academic books about choreography and the act of creating dances. So, taking part in choreography classes at university is now part of a significant and recognised area of study.

There are no set rules about how to choreograph a dance as, ideally, each choreographer will develop their own style. Therefore, when you study choreography as part of your university dance course, you may be introduced to a broad range of methods that you can draw from. Often this will include viewing the work of various professional choreographers which will allow you to see the range of possibilities in this diverse field. It is also helpful to understand how choreography has developed over the course of the twentieth and twenty-first centuries, the time periods when the most significant innovations have been made in the choreographic field. The advent of YouTube as a means to view a range of different choreographic works from various periods has been of particular benefit for dance students to this end.

A choreographer brings a specific inner attitude to their work, a commitment to create, as a high degree of self-sufficiency, self-motivation and self-discipline are needed to develop your own approach to choreography so that you can become an innovative and reflective choreographer. Learning to choreograph takes time and a great degree of critical reflection to create a quality piece of choreography, requiring you to refine your ideas over time. Bear in mind that the process of choreographing, unlike that of a visual artist for example, is not a solitary activity but usually takes place with a group of dancers. Therefore, it is not enough to produce an idea, you will have to communicate this to your dancer/s and help them refine the movement so that it aligns with the vision you have for the work. This is one of the greatest challenges and (for many people) benefits of choreography, that is, the social and relational nature of the practice.

Aside from learning to choreograph within an undergraduate degree, many students continue to study choreography at MA and PhD level. Studying at this level usually requires students to have a good degree of experience as choreographers in the professional world as well as a grounding in the historical, cultural and theoretical perspectives that make up the academic discipline of choreography.

Along with training in dance technique and performance, every undergraduate dance studies course has choreography as a subject for you to study. It has many titles and can appear in course catalogues and programme structures on university websites as choreography, making dance, composition, choreographic processes, creative processes, fundamental principles of choreography, exploring choreographic genres, choreographing the body, choreography for different spaces and environments, choreography for live performance, choreography for screen and integrated choreography. The content and expectations will advance as you progress through your studies in choreography towards applying your developing knowledge and skills to final performance projects, production work, collaborative projects with other dancers and students studying other art forms such as theatre, film, music as well as arts management. You may also be prepared for choreographing for school and community groups in the local area for example working with integrated groups, cross generational, older adults and/or youth dance groups.

The largest proportion of time in the choreography class is devoted to developing practical skills. When you first encounter choreography in undergraduate dance studies you will be taught the basic tools for composing dances, experiencing the general stages of the choreographic and creative process from finding the right movement to designing and shaping the dance material, using increasingly inventive and sophisticated choreographic devices. Some students will enter a choreography class with considerable prior experience of composing dance and may be familiar with improvisations and creative problem-solving tasks. The difference at undergraduate level is that there will be opportunities to develop collaboration and communication skills, allowing you to work independently and in groups with other students coming from a range of different backgrounds.

There are many contexts in which you can practice choreography and this book will explore a wide range of these. You may have a particular interest in Hip Hop or Screendance, ballet or jazz dance, or be open to amalgamating lots of different influences. In all cases, studying the craft of choreography can only benefit you in developing your personal style. In many dance genres, dancers become choreographers without any formal training in choreography. For example, in ballet, until recently, conservatoire training did not generally include this as part of the teaching programmes. Dancers would learn through a kind of apprenticeship model, whereby they would experience a range of choreographic approaches through the choreographers they worked for. This continues to be the case in many major contemporary and ballet companies worldwide. Over time, this experience as a dancer might develop into an interest to make dances from the amalgamation of experiences accrued. Indeed, this could be said for other genres such as jazz dance, musical theatre, commercial dance and through crossovers from performers trained in physical theatre.

The development in teaching choreography as a distinct skill has mainly evolved through modern, postmodern and contemporary dance lineages, whereby at various stages, the methods used by choreographers have been identified and formalised so they can be taught to the next generation. This has resulted in a rigorous understanding within the field of choreography about what is innovative and new and what is a repeat of earlier ideas. As, famous choreographer William Forsythe (2011, p.90) says, "Each epoch, each instance of choreography, is ideally at odds with its previous defining incarnations." This quote captures how choreographers are always seeking innovation and to build on previous ideas to stretch the possibilities of the art of choreography.

The tools that have been formalised and taught in undergraduate dance studies courses are used by choreographers across the world and across different contexts and dance genres, including those with less formalised training traditions such as commercial dance and Hip Hop. Indeed, the choreographic tools you encounter through your dance course will be applicable across all dance genres. Even traditional dance forms, where dances are handed down intact from teacher to student over many generations, have seen an expansion of choreographic innovation through the development of hybrid practices. British choreographers such as Akram Khan and Shobhana Jeyasingh, for example, have extended the choreographic scope of the dance traditions they have trained in, South Asian Kathak and Bharatanatyam respectively, to present dances that contemporise these traditional forms and the subject matter they explore. Furthermore, choreography has extended into the digital arts, with the advent of Screendance as its own specific genre. In this context, there are many other considerations to think of than just filming a dance, such as framing the dancing bodies and how the editing process might influence the choreography, shaping it into a visually arresting piece of work. Within your undergraduate dance studies, you may encounter a range of these applications of choreography as well as creating specific projects to practice your skills.

Chapter 1 begins the journey and introduces some entry points for aspiring choreographers. What does it mean to be a choreographer and how do you begin? Common routes are through private dance studios, schools and community centres for example, as well as programmes aligned to professional dance companies. The role of social media in promoting dance and inspiring creativity in non-formal settings is also noted. Chapter 2 explores the structures, mechanics and tools of choreography and the fundamentals of reflection and analysis that are aligned to the creative process. Chapter 3 covers the range of additional skills that choreographers need to navigate the unpredictable working environment of twenty-first-century dancemaking. This includes information on independent dance, the various structures through which choreographers make work and how undergraduate dance programmes develop these skills. Chapter 4 explores the origin of the term choreography (writing dances), giving an overview of some key choreographic innovators who have influenced the teaching of choreography, spanning modern, postmodern and contemporary dance. The development of choreographic practice in intercultural contexts is explored, as well as the many ways in which choreographies are maintained, transmitted and circulated, including through online platforms. Chapter 5 brings exciting examples of dance as an agent for change and transformation. Choreographic exploration as a field of inquiry examines opportunities and models for higher degree study including practice-based, interdisciplinary and cross-disciplinary examples. Finally, Chapter 6 gives an overview of the fields of site-specific dance, Screendance and dance and technology, including software developments for interactive performances, motion capture and artificial intelligence agents. Additionally, this chapter charts developments in dance with disabled performers and gives an overview of key considerations when working in community dance practice.

This book will help you understand that there is far more to the study of choreography than just being in the studio on your own or with other dancers and making up dances. Learning to choreograph by experience is critical to success but developing your theoretical knowledge of choreography is equally important and this book provides a road map to help you take your first steps into the world of choreography beyond your school or dance studio.

A glossary of dance terms is provided on page 000.

REFERENCES

Forsythe, W. (2011) 'Choreographic objects', in Spier, S., ed., *William Forsythe and the Practice of Choreography*, New York and Abingdon: Routledge.

Foster, S. (2010) *Choreographing Empathy*, Abingdon and New York: Routledge.

THE JOURNEY BEGINS

Growing up in urban environments we experience many encounters with dance: street performances, dance studio and school shows, productions in theatres, gallery spaces, outdoors, and much more. Dance predominates in the digital arena from pop culture, informative dance classes in every genre on YouTube, and live streaming of professional companies that coexist in a crowded space. Added to this mix are television shows featuring many different acts and dance genres in an eclectic mix that entertains and excites.

Traditionally dance has an essential purpose for communication with ancestors, the worshipping of gods, and the retelling of myths and legends that are allegories for the mores and laws of the society. Universally the seasons, the lunar calendar, harvesting cycles and special occasions such as weddings, births, and deaths have been marked and celebrated through dance. Around the world, rich dance practices occur where the purpose, intention, and symbolism of every movement, gesture, prop, costume, and sound is meaningful. Complex rules of societies might require that parts of the celebrations are only known to individuals like priests and senior leaders of both patriarchal and matriarchal societies (see Glossary) while the audience, or participants, may be permitted to join in or watch some parts and not others.

Dance for public performances both locally and internationally prevails across cultures as contemporary artists work in hybrid forms that not only embrace their heritage with deep respect but re-imagine exciting departure points through choreography that is expressive of current times and human concerns. Choreographers throughout history have been at the edge, pushing forward with new directions, new concepts and creations that confront society, stereotypes, and preconceptions about dance.

This chapter introduces options to begin formalised training in dance and choreography. Beginning with dance schools in the private sector, the community and the education system it follows the progression from these first steps to options for furthering a career in professional dance and choreography. Choreography occurs within structures such as a dance company, a project for independent artists or collectives, in theatres, festivals or site-specific spaces. The mixing and interweaving of genres has made dance today exciting and innovative from classical ballet to traditional dance, digital dance, musical theatre and street dance. Key periods are important to understand this unfolding story and the role of individual change-makers who have shaped this evolution.

FIRST STEPS

Most young dancers take their first steps in a private dance studio, the school classroom, a community group or in non-formal settings such as with a group of friends who share a love of dancing. In the digital space, an interest in choreography can be inspired by watching movies, and pop stars in video clips; for instance, the dance routines of K-pop stars and other commercial groups have spawned a generation of dancers who copy the moves, adapt them and make up variations. Being engaged viewers and audience members is the first step towards a dance career. Pathways towards professional dance occur through taking classes to an advanced level, completing an accredited dance course as a school subject, auditioning for professional company training programmes, or succeeding through direct casting for a company or a production. While these avenues open up opportunities for emerging performers and choreographers, countless dance enthusiasts perform with community groups, university dance groups, in projects or simply enjoy recreational dance classes while maintaining their mainstay employment. Encountering the idea of choreography, and working towards making dances, occurs in all the above settings.

Private dance studios

A structured approach to learning may include attendance at regular dance classes to develop techniques and body training that enable skills of the genre to be honed. Some genres, like classical ballet, work through an internationally recognised grade system based on the completion of exams such as the Royal Academy of Dance (RAD), Commonwealth Society of Teachers Dancing (CSTD), the Cecchetti method and others. RAD states that

> Students start with the Dance to Your Own Tune curriculum, move through Pre-Primary and Primary levels and then into eight Graded and six Vocational Graded levels. Students can move from Graded Examinations to Vocational Graded Examinations at an appropriate time, or they can study both pathways simultaneously
>
> (Royal Academy of Dance 2021)

While private dance schools focus mainly on technique, students work with their teachers to learn repertoire for not only end of year shows, but events like eisteddfods, local and international competitions. Often the genesis of a choreographic career is a talented senior dance school student being asked to create a dance for the younger ones – sometimes this sparks a personal interest in choreography and, with an insightful teacher as mentor, the recognition of talent that can be nurtured and challenged. As ballet is a genre with a strong narrative basis, most ballet school concerts work within a plotline that can accommodate both young and senior students, giving everyone a chance to perform and play a part. Other formats are concert-style programmes where items are presented by each class – such shows offer a range of genres from ballet to contemporary, jazz and show dancing and may give opportunities for student choreography.

Although much of this story pertains to classical ballet training, other dance forms operate within similar structures. Street dance is thriving as young people respond to the images they view on social media, want to learn to dance and be part of a culture that not only embraces certain sorts of 'moves' but also fashion, lifestyle choices and the feeling of being part of a global 'scene' where they can express themselves and their voices can be heard. Private studios have tapped into this, and numerous brands are available worldwide with some even offering the promise of work in video clips with stars responding directly to a young dancer's dream. Millennium Dance Complex, for instance, founded in 2002, is an internationally renowned commercial dance studio in Los Angeles. The studio works with A-list clientele and employs the top choreographers of this generation becoming one of the biggest brands in dance and entertainment (Millennium Dance Complex n.d.).

In concluding this section, it should be noted that although most private studios create a nurturing environment for dancers, some still operate under a top-down authoritarian system (Lakes 2005) where students are pushed to an aspiration of perfection, are bullied and even abused. This negative side has been the subject of several national reviews resulting in organisations such as Ausdance National in Australia and One Dance UK implementing national guidelines for a Code of Conduct and Safe Dance Practices to address some of these issues.

Dance within the education system

The past couple of decades has led to realigning the arts as essential to the understanding of the world and our shared humanity. With millions of refugees on the move globally, the importance of dance has been recognised by UNESCO and other organisations as a non-verbal language that communicates through the body. It breaks down language barriers and can be a way of communicating across multiple borders (Burridge and Svendler Neilsen 2020). Dance educators have responded by promoting dance as a school subject at all levels of the curriculum and an increasing number of dance graduates from Bachelor, Master's to PhD level undertake careers across related fields. This is exciting but not without obstacles as dance juggles for space in the curriculum. A recent talk by Sir Ken Robinson claims that "Dance is as important as maths" (Robinson and Aronica 2018). This YouTube TED Talk gleaned millions of hits and sparked debate worldwide.

While dance in most countries at the primary and high school level is still part of physical education, dance at the pre-tertiary sector stands alone as a subject in many countries with an accredited curriculum and well-defined areas of study.

Accredited curriculum courses

Dancers might begin to consider dance as a career option while completing a two-year, pre-third level accredited dance course within the school education system at A-Level (UK), Junior College or Year 12 (Australia). Most courses are based on the three pillars of 'making, creating and reflecting'. These tenets, with some variations, can be found from Britain to Australia, New Zealand to Taiwan, European countries and the USA.

- **Creating**

    As a general concept, this incorporates the notion of a process rather than product orientation for problem-solving that includes experimentation, improvisation, defining, selecting, and the incorporation of a range of skills. In this process what may be termed 'breathing time' is essential – gestation that allows ideas to evolve and encompasses learning to ask better questions, and not simply finding solutions, is an essential element in this process.

- **Presenting**

    Multiple outcomes result from the creation process and individuals or groups could come to solutions via different routes; hence, they might present them in various ways and this should generally be included as part of the assessment requirement. For example, an oral presentation, a video, a folio of drawings, a dance or a piece of music could be presented – there are also interdisciplinary options such as using choreography to illustrate a science experiment or a mathematical formula. Presenting can encompass cooperative, collaborative approaches and include group assessment – recognising that there may be multiple variants to a choreographic assignment is part of the process and an invaluable learning experience.

- **Appraising**

    Appraising can include a variety of parameters that can incorporate summative and formative assessment, teacher and peer assessment. Problem-solving offers multiple choices, strategies and creative solutions with rarely a right or wrong answer. Appraising should incorporate the appreciation of difference, the imaginative way that students address the task and the methods they employed. These methods can both incorporate short activities and lead to long-term projects and explorations with a developmental focus and time orientation towards self-learning. Inherent in these strategies are opportunities for non-linear time frames, lateral and parallel teaching methods where 'connectedness' is elemental and team teaching encouraged.

Contemporary dance technique is typically the basis for training while most courses also offer street, jazz and other genres as part of the programme. The term 'contemporary', although contested by some dance scholars, is used as an umbrella term or catch-all phrase that involves a spectrum of movement styles activated in current (contemporary) times (Cenci 2018). Like all dance genres, a contemporary class begins with a warm-up that has reference to techniques. Once codified or structured techniques such as Graham, Limon and Cunningham were taught but more often today instructors typically tap into their own preferences, experiences and interests to teach a hybrid class. An essential part of any class is learning short sequences and phrases of dance that enable students to connect movement and express themselves through a longer sequence. Contemporary dance devours space and moves in a linear frame between the floor with grounded movements, medium and higher-level planes interacting with shifts in directions and dynamics. The flow and transitions between the set movements make contemporary dance not just compelling viewing for an audience but empowering and joyful for the dancer. The sequences learnt in the dance class are embodied and passed on physically from teacher to student. With some personal variations, this vocabulary usually forms the basis of early student choreography.

An essential feature of choreographic modules is the combination of theory and practice; dance history and learning about key eras and artists inform personal decision making affecting what approach a student might take. These journeys are exciting but also measured and calibrated incorporating specific tasks with explorations that move from building gestures to small phrases, working with partners and small groups and incorporating themes – these are the building blocks to making larger works.

Reflection and critical analysis occur through student journaling, discussion with peers and articulating choreography in terms of the intention, ideas and resolution. This holistic approach underpins pre-tertiary study and parallels the learning journey of making a dance through an active reflective approach. This process is an important stepping stone to a career in dance pre-empting study at third level (see Chapters 3 and 5).

Electives or co-curricular dance

Students in a school elective or co-curricular dance programme typically begin making dances by choosing music that the group would like to work with. In these early stages, they often work collectively, sharing ideas and making it up as they go along. There is usually a goal to work towards such as a concert, an inter-school presentation, festival or competition. Visiting professional choreographers could be hired by the school to work with the group and the outcome of this process has pluses and minuses – the plus is working with a talented, experienced artist who can collaborate with the students to help them articulate and synergise their ideas into a coherent, imaginative choreography.

Negative outcomes occur if the choreographer comes with a fixed idea, auditions the dancers and either eliminates or marginalises students who cannot execute the routine, and generally progresses without considering the educational context of participation and the value of encouragement and inclusiveness. In this scenario, the choreography is usually set on the dancers and practised for most of the class leaving little time for dance enquiry, reflection and individual exploration. Sadly, this process is common and driven by a 'win at all costs' goal for the status of the school in competitions that applaud winners rather than valuing taking part.

Community youth dance groups

Community youth groups come together around the world to dance, create and perform in platforms outside of schools and private studios. It is not uncommon for professional companies to have a youth wing and outreach programmes with the dual aims of nurturing talent whereby some dancers go on to become apprentices then full company members; and the prospect of growing future audiences who are loyal to the main company. Some community centres and organisations offer subsidised classes in a similar model to the private studio enabling children in lower-income families to come together to dance. Diverse ability dancers, church youth groups, marginalised youth-at-risk groups also make up this sector (see Chapter 6).

Choreography and performance for these groups is usually the main concern rather than perfecting techniques or taking up grade ballet or exams in other genres. Empowerment, building confidence, self-esteem and a strong social factor where students meet and share a common interest in a safe environment are equally important goals. Dances crafted around social issues give young people a voice to express their emotions. Some youth dance groups work with professional artists who assist in focusing ideas and shaping the choreography through a collaborative, collective process. Youth dance groups add a powerful, authentic voice to the arts scene. Australia's QL2 Dance (formerly known as Quantum Leap Youth Choreographic Ensemble) for example, is an artist development programme which aims to guide the next generation of creative artists in dance and to "believe in the power of young people to drive cultural change" (QL2 Dance n.d.).

Cultural dance groups

Community cultural dance schools serve multiple functions – primarily to learn traditional dances such as classical forms like Indian Bharatanatyam or the Balinese Legong, folk dances like a Polish mazurka or the Filipino *tinikling* dance between bamboo poles. For diaspora communities, it is an important link to their homelands and a chance to meet and dance with compatriots. While some of the dances are simple to learn and rely on basic steps and formations, the classical forms take years to perfect. Like the structures for Western classical ballet, students move through levels of classes towards performance. For instance, an Indian classical dancer achieving the *arangetram*, or solo performance, is a high honour like a graduation ceremony. Within the system of teaching and learning Asian classical dance forms the roles of masters and gurus are clearly defined – their authority is absolute, and traditionally the dancer moves through their career with allegiance to one teacher.

Like Western ballet schools, dancers from different cultural academies and genres perform at end of year concerts, community events and festivals and it is not uncommon to see, for example, a flamenco dancer exploring rhythms with a Kathak dancer on the same stage. This diversity is in the spirit of sharing and celebration and has led to innovation and hybridisation. However, in some cases, misuse of cultural material and insensitive interpretations has occurred. An interesting aspect of this issue relates to how traditional dance forms can be used as sources of inspiration for new choreography. What is appropriation? "Cultural appropriation refers to the use of objects or elements of a non-dominant culture in a way that doesn't respect their original meaning, give credit to their source, or reinforces stereotypes or contributes to oppression" (Cuncic 2020) (see Chapter 4).

A way forward for community cultural groups is by using their dance vocabulary to innovate and give voice to issues that speak of where they are in place and time. In Singapore, a doyenne of Indian Bharatanatyam dance and cultural medallion recipient Shanta Baskar has made dances about domestic violence and issues for women (*Maya Yatra*, 2018) when working with her Indian dance students at the National University of Singapore. This route not only makes the dance forms relevant in the present-day context but also enables some collaboration with students as they share their thoughts and experiences about the thematic sections while the vocabulary is designed by the guru. These opportunities empower the young dancers and give them a voice in the community.

To conclude this point, much of the innovation in contemporary dance in the present time is emerging from inspirational artists that are working with and across cultural material. The process is measured and proceeds with respect for the source vocabulary while incorporating an imaginative repositioning of the material through themes and narratives.

STRUCTURES AND OPPORTUNITIES

The previous section introduced some opportunities to create dance in the context of private dance studios, schools, community and cultural groups or simply for personal expression. Although these platforms may come with some guidance and mentorship, choreography is usually made under the pre-existing umbrella of the genre being taught – classical ballet, contemporary, cultural dance forms, street dance, musical theatre, among others. In all these genres, the relationship between dance training, technique and choreography persists with graduates from one genre typically choosing to work within the movement vocabulary of that form albeit with a few variations.

Curiosity and the blending of multiple forms come from a choreographer's ability to move across genres and generate connections between what the dancers know and innovative ideas that push boundaries. Present day companies require creative, 'thinking dancers' that can be collaborators and co-creators. In the current dance ecology, there is often a disconnect between the company requirements and dance training that discourages mind-body (somatic) connections and interplay of bodily movement with critical reflection as collaborators in the process.

Dance companies

Within the structure of a dance company choreography occurs in myriad ways. National and state-funded companies may have 60 or more full-time dancers with a well-defined annual calendar of events moving from classical repertoire to newly created ballets in a contemporary style. Such companies include American Ballet Theatre, English National Ballet, The Australian Ballet, Paris Opera Ballet, Stuttgart Ballet and similar large, subsidised companies throughout the world. Outside choreographers are typically well-known, experienced artists who are commissioned to create new works; however, sometimes opportunities for dancers within the company are offered and most choreographers for classical and neo-classical dance genres began their careers as company dancers.

Although contemporary dance companies have a smaller number of dancers, many produce seasons within a similar structure. Some works are created by the founding artistic director who is the main, and often the only, choreographer for the group. This cohort includes the companies of Pina Bausch, Merce Cunningham and Martha Graham. Established contemporary companies commission work on a repertory basis like Netherlands Dance Theatre, Sydney Dance Company and City Contemporary Dance Company in Hong Kong. Like the major ballet companies, company dancers might create choreography for mixed showcases or touring.

There are countless such companies internationally yet the opportunities for 'outside' choreographers are limited and a handful of 'in-demand artists' like Americans William Forsythe and Twyla Tharp, London based Akram Khan and Hofesh Shechter, Canadian Crystal Pite and Alexander Eckman from Sweden, to name a few, have works appearing in multiple companies. It is interesting to note that the once clearly defined demarcation between classical and contemporary choreography has been broken down in large part due to the eclecticism of Tharp. Tharp is well known for her curiosity and diverse body of work ranging from her company repertoire to pieces for American Ballet Theatre and numerous other companies, plus films like *Hair* (1979), *Amadeus* (1984), and *White Nights* (1985) throughout a long and illustrious career. Her determination to creatively cross the divide embracing both pointe shoes and sneakers is exemplified in choreography like *The Upper Room* (1986) with music composed by Philip Glass. She has opened the way for artists like Khan to create his version of *Giselle* with a ballet company and Eckman in his 2014 version of *A Swan Lake* to move between pointe shoes, bare feet and highly theatrical, absurdist elements juxtaposed in the same work. Prima ballerinas such as Sylvie Guillem and Natalia Osipova have also been instrumental in closing the gap as they sought to work with leading contemporary choreographers. They have moved fluidly between repertory performances with classical companies like the Royal Ballet, contemporary solo programmes and commissioned work.

Independent dance artists and freelance choreographers

The rise of dance artists in the 1990s known as 'independents' (Clarke & Gibson 1998) is driven by diverse factors. Generally working on a project basis, they pursue independently funded work or take on short-term projects commissioned from other dance companies, stakeholders such as art galleries, museums, or alternative public spaces. Many collaborate in a cross- or multidisciplinary process with musicians, visual artists, photographers, architects, fashion designers and multimedia digital companies. The scope of possibilities is a compelling factor for many choreographers to become independents. In 1997, Clarke defined the independent dance sector as

> ... [a]n extensive and mobile community of independent dance artists in the UK, with the largest concentration based in London. Through choice or necessity these dance artists work as freelance entrepreneurs, often juggling many roles simultaneously and taking their expertise into numerous communities through their performance, choreography, teaching and facilitation.
>
> (Clarke 1997, p.2)

On occasion, some independents may come together as a collective whereby they create shared platforms for their work and collaborate on a project. An entrepreneurial spirit, resilience and adaptability underpin success as an independent artist (see Chapter 3).

Commissioned choreography

The categories of 'independents' and 'freelancers' overlap as choreographers respond to a variety of commissions. These span a large area of activity including the commercial sector where possibilities include creating for musical theatre, theatre, opera, film, television, TV commercials, product launch events and fashion shows, to name a few. Major international companies such as Cirque du Soleil include complex choreography for aerial and acrobatic acts, including for *Ovo* (2009) by Brazilian choreographer Deborah Colker, while creating routines for competitive sports such as ice dancing, gymnastics, and dance sports are established fields. Olympic Gold medallist John Curry, for instance, commissioned Tharp to choreograph *After All* for a performance at Madison Square Garden in 1976 while ice dance luminaries Jayne Torvill and Christopher Dean worked with Sydney Dance Company artistic director Graeme Murphy in 1986.

Freelance choreographers in commercial work must be attuned to trends in dance occurring on social media sites such as Instagram and YouTube, be versatile and imaginative with the ability to collaborate and work with teams of production management, producers and directors as well as performing artists where dance may not be their primary medium, for instance, opera singers, theatre and visual artists. Some well-known dance choreographers who have transitioned most successfully to the commercial world include former London Contemporary Dance Theatre performer Anthony van Laast who is a British dance maker specialising in choreography for stage, musicals, concerts, film and television. His show credits include Broadway and West End musical comedies *Mamma Mia* (2001) *Sister Act* (2011) and choreography for the live-action film *Beauty and the Beast* (2017).

Arlene Phillips is another choreographer who can move between choreographing for artists such as Whitney Houston, to London West End musicals like *Starlight Express* and the inclusive UK dance company Candoco (see Chapters 5 and 6). In 2016 she created *You and I Know* for the company while the 2018 *Life on Mars* collaboration with the BBC television show *Strictly Come Dancing* gave the company worldwide recognition for a joyous expression of diversity through dance.

Festivals, art museums and site-specific dance

Often large national or state arts festivals will commission a choreographer to create an independent show, a collaboration or a specifically themed work; while smaller dance festivals provide important opportunities for young choreographers and emerging artists to present their work in mixed programmes. Typically, the required length is ten to 20 minutes and an individual's work is seen by an audience alongside that of peers in the context of new creations. These festivals are common around the world and are immensely important for artist development while introducing audiences to a new generation and fresh ideas. Such platforms are a springboard to a choreographic career path, with networking and interacting through shared classes, workshops and associated events.

Galleries, museums and public spaces often have a regular calendar of performances. Niche showcases at community events, and in alternative spaces, have also welcomed new work by young artists, recent graduates and collectives. Here dance might be experienced through an 'immersive' or 'participatory' experience where the audience becomes part of the show or is allowed to spend time with the work experiencing the process with the artist. Art galleries have often become sites for interactive dance-based performances like that of UK-born Tino Sehgal who calls his method 'constructed situations'. His 2010 *The Progress* showed at the Guggenheim in New York inviting a transformative response from viewers as they moved through the exhibition. Many people return over time and undergo different experiences through renewed interactions with an unstructured, fluidity that places the creator and viewer on the same footing.

"The term site-specific refers to a work of art designed specifically for a particular location and that has an interrelationship with the location" (Tate n.d.). Occurring in community spaces, dancers may engage with the structural components of a site or delve deeper into contextual issues that have impacted the history, heritage and community. US luminary Trisha Brown explored this genre in extraordinary ways during the postmodern era of the 1960s and 1970s in works such as *Spiral* (1974), *Roof Piece* (1971), *Man Walking Down the Side of a Building* (1970) with the dancers in harnesses. Kate Lawrence, artistic director of Vertical Dance, adds another dimension to site-specific work by incorporating rock climbing harnesses to create spectacular pieces that respond directly to the environment – sometimes soaring above it, other times exploring surfaces from rock faces of cliffs to broad expanses of open terrain. A vast, open sky submerses the dancers in a small human frame against the larger consequences of the universe inviting reflection.

Intrinsically this concept is not new as throughout history sites have been important places for communities to dance for ritual and religious purposes. Seeking resonance and purpose in urban landscapes, as well as discovering places of meditation and reflection, have a renewed purpose as the world is challenged by crowded living spaces, loss of community identity and natural spaces and habitat. The dancers leave traces through their engagement with a site.

Personal expression

Many choreographers are simply compelled to create – to express themselves through movement regardless of an audience, funding support for their projects, or a stage to show their work. Driven by passion, commitment to issues or the sheer joy of dancing, these individuals or collectives work outside of the platforms above and may be more interested in concepts, ideas and the process of creation rather than showing a finished product. Moreover, choreography by artists across genres finds its way to social media platforms such as YouTube, Instagram, and blog sites achieving large followings that generate an online career with the possibility of monetising their success.

INNOVATION AND NEW DIRECTIONS

Dance history serves to inform us of past and present choreography by not only introducing key artists and change-makers but also contextualising their work historically within classical ballet, modern, postmodern and contemporary periods from the East and the West. Selecting from the many choreographers, innovators and trajectories across multiple dance genres necessitates presenting a general overview with some examples.

At the turn of the twentieth century, dance responded to the pace and innovation of the second industrial age of automation, mass production and the harsh realities of urban living among political uncertainties in many countries. Embracing the European avant-garde in centres such as Paris, Berlin and Zurich it incorporated new ideas from fields such as philosophy, sociology and psychology. These explorations were led by artists across a range of disciplines from the composer Igor Stravinsky to the writer Jean Cocteau, fashion designer Coco Chanel and artists George Braque, Pablo Picasso and others. They opened the way for a new aesthetic that included cross-disciplinary collaboration, borrowing from other cultures, and responding to changing political circumstances in pre-World-War-I Europe.

At the same time New York heralded the jazz age and American artists such as Josephine Baker performed in Paris; most notable was Baker's famous 1925 'banana dance' in the *Revue Nègre* that made her an overnight sensation. As an artist of colour, she was embraced and adored in France in contrast to her own country that segregated African American performers and audiences on racial grounds. In her later years, she returned to the United States and became an activist to redress this situation.

These developments were in stark contrast to the existing highly romantic repertoire of classical ballet with its myths and fairy tales, themes of unrequited love that cast women as ethereal beings that were as unreal as the princes that pursued them, and the inevitable happy endings. The great romantic ballets such as *Swan Lake* (1877), *Sleeping Beauty* (1888), *Giselle* (1841) and *The Nutcracker* (1841) were still performed; yet it was the new wave of early modern dance artists who left a legacy that sustained contemporary dance today in its various configurations. Some influences are stranded in the examples that follow – they intersect, overlap and are philosophically and bodily connected through the practices of the artists.

Personal philosophy and free expression

What marked the choreography of early twentieth-century dance change-makers such as Isadora Duncan (1877–1927), Rudolf von Laban (1879–1958), Mary Wigman (1886–1973), Doris Humphrey (1895–1958) and Martha Graham (1894–1991) was a deep philosophical direction that underpinned their work. They believed in personal expression that was free from the restrictions of academic ballet training and the hierarchy of a company. They sought an individual path inspired by personal values, nature, issues of social justice, egalitarianism and gender equality. Duncan danced barefoot in flowing tunics that enabled freedom for the body in an age where women were restrained by the fashions of the day that demanded tightly laced corsets and multiple undergarments. She incorporated everyday movements like running, skipping and hopping in her creations, taking inspiration from nature, Greek pottery and the classical music she performed to.

Laban similarly worked with everyday movement, incorporating community dancers, factory workers and non-trained dancers in his 'movement choirs' that also celebrated men in dance. Laban Movement Analysis (LMA) is a comprehensive study on body movement (Davies 2006) and a legacy that is a fundamental tenet to dance composition as it is taught around the world today particularly within the education system. Similarly, Labanotation is an invaluable tool for the documentation, preservation and accuracy of recording choreography by companies, ethnographers, anthropologists, researchers and scholars throughout the world (see Chapter 4).

Mary Wigman is credited for sowing the seeds for German Ausdruckstanz or expressionist dance theatre. Her performances incorporated the use of vertical space from grounded movements on the floor in, for example, the 1926 *Hexentanz* (*Witch Dance*), to medium and higher-level planes. She danced in silence, with percussion instruments or minimal sound, and performed with an emotional intensity that was brave and connected directly with the audience. The Ausdruckstanz movement gathered momentum in Germany with variations of what is now a clearly defined strand of performance known as dance theatre or Tanztheatre. Pina Bausch extended this movement with powerful pieces like *Café Muller* (1985), *Rite of Spring* (1975) and *Nelken* (*Carnations*) (1992) for her company Tanztheatre Wuppertal. Her choreography resonates profoundly with the audience as it creates vast emotional landscapes juxtaposing imagery of the beauty of love, life and living against intense, stark realities.

Evolving movement vocabulary

Doris Humphrey and Martha Graham were two early modern dance artists with legacies that have some features in common although their choreographic repertoire is distinctive. Both emphasised an analytical approach to the body. Technique and choreography as the building blocks of dance were underscored by the use of the breath as the initiation and focus for body movement. Humphrey's 'fall and recovery' technique links to the release techniques that are part of training today where there is motion, suspense, falling and recovery. Graham devised complex exercise sequences based on the notion of 'contraction and release', 'spiralling' and travelling in classes that begin on the floor then move to standing exercises and locomotor runs, prances, small and large jumps. It is strong, contained and controlled in contrast to the flow of Humphrey's work. Other dancer/choreographers like José Limon, Lester Horton and Merce Cunningham contributed individual techniques that were tied to the physical, philosophical and emotional requirements of their choreography. This connection between the physical technique in the classroom and what we see on stage is incorporated into the classical ballet canon; however, the modern and contemporary choreographers' focus on motivation, intention and individual expression sets these genres apart.

The influence of other cultural dance forms on classical ballet

The Ballets Russes (1909–1929) led by impresario Serge Diaghilev (1872–1929) revitalised ballet by responding to the momentum of a new age that wanted a change from the fairy tales and myths of the older ballet narratives. Around the early twentieth century there was a curiosity about dance forms from other cultures and composers, visual artists, fashion designers and in particular, the Parisian audiences rode a wave of a love affair with the exotic. This period was rich with innovation and creativity as artists moved between Europe and America absorbing influences and reinterpreting them. American choreographer Ruth St. Denis (1877–1968) for instance, was fascinated by the dances from India that she encountered as 'exotic arts' in the high-class salons of Europe. She created large scale dance dramas for the burgeoning movie industry in Hollywood. Of Ruth St. Denis, author Joseph H. Mazo notes:

> St. Denis took what was handy – a contemporary interest in the exotic, the nation's delight in spectacle, its enjoyment of sideshow attractions… even its periodic religious revivals… The mind that revelled in mysticism and understood dance as a religious experience also had a remarkable appreciation of popular taste.
>
> (p.83)

Exposure to Asian dance forms was reinforced through events such as international visits by dance troupes from Cambodia, Thailand and Japan as part of expositions and trade fairs. An example occurred in 1906 when the Khmer Royal Ballet of Cambodia, under the auspices of King Sisowath 1, toured to perform at the Colonial Exhibition in Marseille. The dancers inspired a set of drawings from French artist Auguste Rodin in 1906 while resident Ballets Russes choreographer Michel Fokine made a collection of dance works based on his interpretation of some of the Oriental dancers he witnessed in Paris.

Exemplar 1 – Michel Fokine, Vaslav Nijinsky and George Balanchine

Russian virtuosic dancer Vaslav Nijinsky performed 'Dans Siamoise' choreographed by Michel Fokine for the Ballets Russes in response to viewing traditional Thai Khon dance. This choreography was part of *Les Orientals* (1910) by Fokine and was one of several choreographies in the repertoire of the Ballets Russes that adapted cultural material to the delight of Parisian audiences. Commentators on these works acknowledge their success was due to impresario Serge Diaghilev's understanding of prevailing audience interests, fashion and artistic trends. Roger Leong, curator of the 1999 National Gallery of Australia exhibition, *From Russia with Love: Costumes for the Ballets Russes, 1909–1933* notes:

> The success of the company's exotic productions can be linked to the Western European fascination with the 'Orient' as remote, strange and exciting. Tales of sexual passion, high drama and violent death were set in imaginary locations inspired by Persian, Indian, Central Asian and ancient Egypt cultures.
>
> (Leong 1999, p.8)

The use of parallel feet in Nijinsky's 1913 *Rite of Spring* followed after working with Fokine and contributed to a modern approach to classical ballet that we see again in *L'Après-midi d'un Faune* where unique, angular hand and elbow positioning occur. Choreographer George Balanchine also incorporated parallel feet in many of his ballets while giving a significant nod to the syncopated rhythms and complex patterns of jazz age music. Balanchine (1904–1983) was a dancer, choreographer, teacher and Artistic Director. His early career began in Europe, later joining the Ballets Russes before traveling to the United States in 1933. By 1934, Balanchine co-founded the School of American Ballet which eventually groomed dancers into his company New York City Ballet, founded in 1948. He had an influential role in the development of the American Ballet Theatre with both the school and company still in operation today. In his own words, Balanchine expressed "The important thing in ballet is the movement itself" characterised by his neoclassical form and at times plotless ballets

> (Ballet Theatre Foundation 2020). Notable works include *Stars and Stripes* (1958), *Firebird* (restaged with Jerome Robbins in 1970), and *Jewels* (called the first full-length plotless ballet, 1967). With choreography in the repertoire of all major ballet companies around the world, he was known as an extraordinary innovator of classical ballet, choreographing with minimal sets and costumes and creating simple, thematic threads relying on abstraction and the interplay of the dancers in space. Fokine, Nijinsky and Balanchine showed that ballet was flexible and could innovate its codified movement vocabulary as well as tackle a diversity of narratives and themes.

Postmodernism

An evolution of 'anti-establishment' ideas in the 1960s and 1970s occurred in response to the political landscape in America, and the disruption of societal mores that gathered momentum as disenfranchised young people protested for change. Alternative lifestyles, respect for race, diversity, an egalitarian society, civil rights and protests against the Vietnam war along with a longing for peace and spirituality underpinned the movement. Dance was part of this, and the focus was New York City at Judson Memorial Church. Yvonne Rainer, Meredith Monk, Trisha Brown, Lucinda Childs, Steve Paxton and others met to explore ideas about what dance could and should be in the present time. Although they came under the umbrella term of 'postmodern dance', each was individual in their approach, and although an aim was to reject codified forms of dance as elitist and begin with the democratic notion that everyone could dance, most came from various dance backgrounds including ballet and modern dance. In attempting to break free from preconceived notions they included everyday movements and actions in their choreography, opened the space to collaboration, improvisation, workshopping, and diversity incorporating trained and untrained dancers. Often there was no accompaniment and the participants worked in silence, to metronomes, used their voices or incorporated ambient sounds. By wearing everyday clothes and eliminating the need for theatre spaces by choosing to meet in car parks, on rooftops, art galleries and public spaces to show their work they democratised dance. In one sense this could be regarded as site-specific work where the location, its history and special features were partners in the choreography; in other instances, it was simply a convenient, low-cost option that embraced the philosophy of openness and inclusion.

Eclecticism, the mixing of genres, everyday movements and game structures all combined to close the gap between art and life. Lucinda Childs' *Carnation* (1964) where she sits in a perfect ballet second position then proceeds to put rollers into an upturned wire frame on her head and 'eat' a sandwich of cleaning sponges exemplifies the postmodern philosophy. The innovation and extraordinary surprise of this solo still reverberate today as dance makers seek new ways of working across the creation process. The movement lasted a few short years but the dancers at Judson Church changed dance forever and enabled alternative ways of seeing, learning, teaching and performing.

Two dance artists that were originally part of the postmodern group were the previously mentioned Twyla Tharp and Merce Cunningham. Cunningham is noted for many innovations in a career spanning over seven decades of practice; notably his work with composer John Cage, the notion of separating music from dance so that both occurred together only in space and time, chance operations so the structure of a dance might result from tossing a coin (see Chapter 4). Cunningham collaborated with many visual artists such as Jasper Johns and Andy Warhol and remained curious throughout his life experimenting with the latest technologies such as video, body sensors and motion capture (see Chapter 6). After the postmodern era dancers emerged central to the creative process as active contributors to choreography.

Contemporary dance

The barriers are down between classical ballet and modern dance with hybridisation, eclecticism and openness the norm. Choreographers and dancers work and train within these parameters through collaboration, cooperation, and sharing values of equality and egalitarianism. Diversity occurs across the makeup of dance where multiple nationalities work together in established, project and 'pop-up' companies while fields such as independent dance, interdisciplinary and digital dance, working with differently abled bodies, intergenerational and senior dance projects feature on the spectrum of professional dance today. This connectivity occurs internationally via multiple platforms enabling networking and cultural exchange. Research, innovation and creativity underpin these developments.

Choreographers such as Wayne McGregor have set up relationships for research across diverse sectors from science to digital arts through the Studio Wayne McGregor.

> Studio Wayne McGregor is the creative 'engine' that drives the research and conceptualization period of his works. This process involves creative partners across various disciplines in art, design, science, computing and many more, by conducting various experimental labs with the body in choreography.
>
> (Studio Wayne McGregor n.d.)

Dance training today requires a holistic approach whereby dancers articulate their practice and can critically reflect on the process in everything from a post-show dialogue, a studio work-in-progress sharing session, or a research project at a university.

CONTEMPORARY DANCE TRAJECTORIES

The development of new movement vocabularies arises from exploring within the traditions and philosophies that the region encompasses and combining these connections with personal interests and larger themes about the society and state of the world. Like all dance makers, choreographers working within Asian traditions seek to find a unique voice in concept and movement vocabulary – their creativity, virtuosity and perseverance has been the genesis of emerging and previous generations of contemporary Asian dance makers (Burridge 2021). Some examples follow that represent a small sample of important trajectories and activity around the region.

Japanese Butoh

The legacy of Japanese Butoh, pioneered by Kazuo Ohno and Tatsumi Hijikata, is profound and has had a lasting influence on theatre and dance practitioners. In a rejection of Western ideologies post the Second World War after the bombing of Hiroshima, it seeks to journey deep into the psyche, exploring what it means to be human. Through emptying the body of past experiences, embodied habits and preconceptions the artist taps the subconscious in a distinctive, aesthetic dance theatre form known as 'The Dance of Darkness'. Signified by white-painted semi-naked bodies partially draped in monastic robes or Japanese kimonos, the earthbound dancers reach out with clawed hands, turned-up toes and open mouths in a silent scream that reveals the inner self. There is a stark beauty in much of the work that is inspired by nature and often includes elements such as water, falling sand and light. Butoh can polarise audiences through its slow progression and trance-like state that some find hard to appreciate but equally enraptures others. In the 1980s Butoh underwent a 'Renaissance' in response to touring to Western countries that were unfamiliar with the form and demanded a more 'accessible' version of the slow pace and harsh realities of the original. Founded in 1975 by Ushio Amagatsu, the most well-known international touring group is the Sankai Juku Company whose works such as *Meguri* (2015) and *Umusuna* (2008) have astounded audiences and critics with their deep sense of beauty and shared human spirit.

CLOUD GATE DANCE THEATRE OF TAIWAN

The choreography of Lin Hwai-min, founding Artistic Director of Cloud Gate Dance Theatre of Taiwan, incorporates Asian traditions like qigong, martial arts and Beijing Opera with Western contemporary dance to create a new vocabulary deeply rooted in an Asian dance language. It directly responds to "the architecture of the Asian body." Lin notes:

> In the West, ballet dancers elevate, just like Gothic church attempts to reach the heavens. The Forbidden City in Beijing is very tall, but the emphasis is on its wide spread. ... I reasoned ... why don't we train ourselves in the disciplines created ... and passed on by people with shorter legs.
> (Wang and Burridge 2012, p.xi)

His choreography has deep resonance in Taiwan. Narratives respond to the local landscape and seasonal changes as a metaphor for the cycle of life in pieces like *Rice* (2013), or the elegant echoing of a calligraphy line in movement in the *Cursive Trilogy*; *Cursive* (2001), *Cursive II* (2003) and *Wild Cursive* (2005) while *Portrait of the Families* (1997) (see Chapter 5) makes a bold political statement. *Moonwater* (1998) exemplifies an East/West sensibility in an abstract treatise synergising the spirituality of tai chi inspired movement in harmony with Bach Cello Suite. Cloud Gate Dance Theatre has toured the world to critical acclaim and has secured its place among the most recognised dance companies of the world today.

Bangarra Dance Theatre in Australia

Indigenous dance in remote communities in Australia exists for ritual purposes connecting the community to the concept of the universe, 'the Dreamtime' and a history dating back 60,000 years. Ceremonial dance is underpinned by complex belief systems and protocols for not just the performers, but also the audience (Burridge 2011, p.35). Within this framework, one of Australia's most exciting contemporary dance companies has emerged. Bangarra Dance Theatre creates works that share the Aboriginal and Torres Strait Islander experience through contemporary dance. Founded in 1989, the company has forged an identity deeply connected to traditions of indigenous storytelling, embodied in contemporary expression. Bangarra always seeks permission from community elders whenever any traditional dance material is used, whether movement vocabulary or story. *Ochres* (1994) could be identified as an essential part of this journey. Beginning with a ceremonial tradition of an Aboriginal elder, Jackapura Munyarryun, dance artist and cultural consultant with Bangarra Dance Theatre since 1991, 'painting' himself with natural pigments from the earth then opening the space for the other dancers to emerge in animal-like gestures close to the earth, then moving into an innovative vocabulary of contemporary movement inspired by tradition. The dance was a revelation in Australia at the time and foregrounded a pathway of incorporating traditional elements into the contemporary language and storytelling through dance. Bangarra was a feature of the opening ceremony for the Sydney Olympics (2000) and continues to present indigenous dance stories, histories, and narratives that inspire audiences around the world.

Classical to contemporary Indian dance

The eight Indian classical dance forms include Bharatanatyam (Tamil Nadu), Kathak (Uttar Pradesh), Kuchipudi (Andhra Pradesh), Odissi (Orissa), Manipuri (Manipur), Kathakali, and Mohiniyattam (Kerala). These rich traditions have enabled choreographic explorations by artists who revisit the movement vocabulary and the narrative traditions to express themes of the contemporary world. Bharatanatyam and Kathak, for instance, underpin the choreography of two artists that embody their dance heritage in unique ways.

Exemplar 2 – Chandralekha and Akram Khan

Chandralekha Prabhudas Patel (1928–2006) was an Indian performer, choreographer and activist. Her movement philosophies challenged the conventions of traditional dances in India by fusing the classical style of Bharatanatyam with yoga and Kalaripayattu, a martial art from Kerala. Her works as described by Massey (2007) are "exemplars of modern Indian dance, based on her premise of the indivisibility of sexuality, sensuality and spirituality." The piece *Sri* (1990) for example was performed with dancers bending their spines reflective of an image relating to male dominance and suppression (Ananya 1998). Chandralekha incorporated the movement vocabulary of Bharatanatyam and the tradition of storytelling to make works that embrace contemporary issues particularly for women; the body was her canvas as she probed issues concerning the body – the feminist body, the sexual, political, the creative and resistant body. She states "My concern is with the body… where does it begin… where does it end?" (PSBT-India 2014). Her early work *Namaska* (1986) was based on a simple traditional greeting while her final, and most iconic *Sharira* (2000) exuded feminine power and overt sexuality defying the conventions of passive, beautifully costumed female dancers telling traditional tales through hand gestures and facial expressions.

British-born luminary Akram Khan unifies his Bangladeshi heritage of Kathak movement and storytelling with contemporary dance. An attribute of Kathak is the momentum of spinning, which has spiritual and ritual connections, combined with complex rhythms of the feet accentuated by the use of ankle bells (*ghungroo*). These movement devices can be seen overtly in works like *Ma* (2004) and *Sacred Monsters* with Sylvie Guillem (premiered in 2006 with the last performance in 2014) while other collaborations extend the storytelling parameters such as *Zero Degrees* (2005) with Sidi Larbi Cherkaoui. *Vertical Road* (2010) paints a large canvas of movement vocabulary as the dancers explore notions of identity and the search for spirituality in an increasingly chaotic and dehumanising world. His version of *Giselle* (2016) for the English National Ballet probes the underlying narrative of class stratification choosing to foreground the plight of migrant factory workers. From this position, the protagonist Giselle, like her classical counterpart, cannot move forward with someone from the upper classes of society. Khan's insightful storytelling, combined with innovative, dynamic dance vocabulary, propels his choreography into the lives of audiences around the world who resonate with the expression of deep human emotion. Such traction through choreography is transformative.

Thai classical Khon dance

Exemplar 3 – Pichet Klunchun

Pichet Klunchun is an internationally recognised choreographer from Thailand who trained in Thai classical mask dance (*Khon*) with a renowned master of the 'Giant' role, Chaiyot Khummane. Since founding the Pichet Klunchun Dance Company in 2007, his vision for Thai dance has expanded and diversified seeking to engage audiences internationally as well as in Thailand. Khon dance reflects the two-dimensionality of the Thai shadow puppets (*Nang talung*) that inspire clearly recognisable movements. Attributes include the square stance with knees in a deep plié, elbows framing the body often set parallel to the floor, fingers bent back, and head held erect as the dancers move in a lateral plane with small variations. However, such two-dimensional square movement of Khon is a challenge to fuse into a contemporary form. Klunchun experiments with this aesthetic in works like *Black and White* (2011) through an organic approach which allows the dancers to explore movement with the torso in multiple directions while the legs remain fixed in the solid traditional stance. *Black and White* is about balance – physical, spiritual, political and personal. This way of working is somewhat controversial in Thai society where the dance form is deeply revered and experimenting with new ways of moving within the framework of these traditions may challenge audiences. Klunchun's company has staged many new works and toured extensively while the artist has sought creative collaborative opportunities with luminaries like Jérôme Bel in the show *Pichet Klunchun and Myself* (see Chapter 4).

Another work to note is *Nijinsky Siam* (2010). Inspired by virtuosic Russian dancer Vaslav Nijinsky who in turn was inspired by dances from a Thai troupe visiting Paris in 1906. Klunchun states, "… the idea for 'Nijinsky Siam' first came to him when he saw some black-and-white photographs of Nijinsky in what looked like Thai dance poses" (Kolesnikov-Jessop 2010). The 1910 ballet *Les Orientales*, the dance created by Michel Fokine, included "Danse Siamoise" originally performed by Vaslav Nijinsky with the Ballets Russes at the Paris Opera. The ballet is believed to have been inspired by the performance of a Thai classical troupe, the Nai But Mahin Dance Company, that Fokine had seen in St Petersburg in 1900.

An interesting insight into such work comes again from the artist. In addressing the issue of appropriation of cultural material he expresses the idea of being in 'dialogue' with Nijinsky and states in the performance programme "I say to Nijinsky: 'You took what was not yours, but you made it yours.' I ask him: 'Now, let us come into each other's sensation, right here on stage, so I can co-exist with you'" (ibid).

Embodied cultural knowledge, and confidence in rich traditional dance heritages, underpin bold innovations by regional choreographers These initiatives have encouraged a thriving group of independent dance artists and small companies who are commissioned by dance festival curators to make new work. Recently formalised networks between regional centres have evolved and become essential players in enabling talented regional artists to tour and be seen outside their country. Dance curators, festival directors, dramaturgs, producers and independent dance centres are central to this story of the twenty-first-century dance ecology (Burridge 2021). Conversations about aesthetics, ethical considerations around incorporating traditional material and authenticity, parallel curiosity, innovation and risk-taking enable choreographers to move forward on their journey.

SUMMARY

This chapter has explored the intention of choreography, encountering choreography, training and philosophical shifts aligned to key moments in the evolution of classical ballet, Asian traditional forms and contemporary dance. Some developments are embedded within the context of indigenous, folk and royal court dance, and pioneering explorations are led by a generation of artists who embody a diversity of cultural backgrounds and training. They are making powerful, deeply human and complex creative work that has roots in traditional forms.

Other artists work within company structures to create work for audiences in conventional proscenium theatres or black boxes. The genres range from classical ballet to contemporary, jazz, street dance, musical theatre and others. An increasing number of independent artists seek opportunities outside of the mainstream to collaborate across art forms exploring new ideas in new spaces ranging from art galleries, alternative venues and site-specific locations. Immersive experiences are also part of the scene.

Social media and digital apps are essential components of dance now. Dance choreography has expanded to include anyone who wants to move, make up a dance and post a picture, from the highest-level professionals to hobbyists, community groups, front-line workers and more. The impact of this plethora of non-stop dance postings cannot be ignored and sifting through these offerings is time consuming while much is also lost in translation across the digital space. The number of choreographic opportunities is increasing across all these areas as they evolve and coexist in a sector progressively opening up to diversity, eclecticism, hybridisation, collaboration and sharing of experiences.

FURTHER READING

Burridge, S. ed. (2021) *The Routledge Companion to Dance in Asia and the Pacific: Platforms for Change*, New Delhi: Routledge India.

Butterworth, J. (2012) *Dance Studies: The Basics*, Abingdon and New York: Routledge.

Butterworth, J. et al. (2021) *Fifty Contemporary Choreographers* (3rd edn), Abingdon: Routledge.

Noisette, Phillipe (2011) *Talk About Contemporary Dance*, translated by Dusinberre, D., Paris: Flammarion.

REFERENCES

Akram Khan Company (2015) *Home*, available: www.akramkhancompany.net/ [accessed 26 April 2021].

Baer, N. (1999) 'Design and choreography', in Hall, S., ed., *From Russia with Love: Costumes from the Ballets Russes 1909–1933*, Canberra: National Gallery of Australia Publications Department, 40–55.

Ballet Theatre Foundation (2020) *Home*, available: www.abt.org/ [accessed 1 June 2021].

Bangarra Dance Theatre Australia (2021) *Home*, available: www.bangarra.com.au/ [accessed 20 April 2021].

Bangarra Dance Theatre Australia, Knowledge Ground (n.d.) *Home*, available: https://bangarra-knowledgeground.com.au/ [accessed 23 May 2021].

Clarke, G. and Bramley, I. eds (1997) *Supporting, Stimulating, Sustaining: Independent Dance*, London: Arts Council England, available: www.independentdance.co.uk/wp-content/uploads/2010/11/SupportingStimulatingSustaining.pdf [accessed 19 June 2021].

Cuncic, A. (2020) 'What is cultural appropriation?', *verywell mind*, available: www.verywellmind.com/what-is-cultural-appropriation-5070458 [accessed 4 June 2021].

Kate Lawrence (2013) *Home*, available: www.verticaldancekatelawrence.com [accessed 5 June 2021].

Kolesnikov-Jessop, S. (2010) 'Walking in Nijinsky's footsteps', *New York Times*, 24 June, available: www.nytimes.com/2010/06/24/arts/24iht-jessop.html [accessed 19 June 2021].

Lakes, R. (2005) 'The messages behind the methods: the authoritarian pedagogical legacy in Western concert dance technique training and rehearsals',

Arts Education Policy Review, 106(5), available: www.tandfonline.com/doi/abs/10.3200/AEPR.106.5.3-20 [accessed 19 June 2021].

Lin, H. M. (2012) 'Foreword', in Wang, Y. and Burridge, S., eds, *Identity and Diversity: Celebrating Dance in Taiwan*, New Delhi: Routledge India, xi–xiii.

Lucinda Childs (2021) *History*, available: www.lucindachilds.com/history.php [accessed 4 June 2021].

Marian Goodman Gallery (2021) *Tino Sehgal*, available: www.mariangoodman.com/artists/62-tino-sehgal/ [accessed 25 June 2021].

Massey, R. (2007) 'Chandralekha, controversial Indian dancer whose ideas challenged convention', *The Guardian*, 9 February, available: www.theguardian.com/news/2007/feb/09/guardianobituaries.india [accessed 30 April 2021].

Mazo, J. H. (1977) *Prime Movers, The Makers of Modern Dance in America*, Princeton: Princeton Book Company.

Millennium Dance Complex (n.d.) *Home*, available: https://millenniumdancecomplex.com/ [accessed 2 June 2021].

PKLifeWork (2012) 'Black and White' (Khon), *Pichet Klunchun Dance Company* [video], available: https://youtu.be/KlRfkTLSICM [accessed 3 May 2021].

PKLifeWork (2012) 'Nijinsky Siam', *Pichet Klunchun Dance Company* [video], available: www.youtube.com/watch?v=t2vgbYpo8Yc [accessed 29 July 2021].

PSBT-India (2014) *Sharira – Chandralekha's Explorations in Dance* [video], available: www.youtube.com/watch?v=vyXh_5dT0zw [accessed 5 April 2019].

QL2 Dance (n.d.) *Our Vision*, available: www.ql2.org.au/ourvision [accessed 4 June 2021].

Robinson, K. and Aronica, L. (2018) 'Why dance is just as important as math in school', *TED Conferences*, 21 March, available: https://ideas.ted.com/why-dance-is-just-as-important-as-math-in-school/ [accessed 3 June 2021].

Royal Academy of Dance (2021) *Home*, available: www.royalacademyofdance.org/ [accessed 28 May 2021].

Studio Wayne McGregor (n.d.) *Studio Wayne McGregor*, available: https://waynemcgregor.com/about/studio-wayne-mcgregor/ [accessed 4 June 2021].

Trisha Brown Company (n.d.) *Home*, available: https://trishabrowncompany.org/ [accessed 23 May 2021].

Twyla Tharpe (2021) *Home*, available: www.twylatharp.org/ [accessed 5 May 2021].

Wang, Y. and Burridge, S. eds (2012) *Identity and Diversity: Celebrating Dance in Taiwan*, New Delhi: Routledge India.

CHOREOGRAPHIC NOTEBOOK

Success as a professional choreographer requires formulating and sustaining a personal identity – a signature that marks your work and makes it unique. A strong intention, clear idea and dance philosophy underpin this. Eclecticism, multimedia, interdisciplinary arts with collaborations that extend outside of the arts sector have redefined what dance can be in the present time. Multiple decisions come into play in the generation of movement and thematic material adding complex layering to the development of a new creation. In this chapter, these points will be unpacked with examples and suggestions to support the way individual creative artists map their choreographic journeys. Imagination and passion in tandem with belief in the concept are crucial; however, many tools and devices can help bring an idea to fruition and craft an original dance. It should be noted that internationally there are various methods adopted to teach the elements of composition across the education system and tertiary dance courses.

The components defined in this section emphasise form, relating to what the body is doing in space, time and energy; content, including the components such as structures, themes, narratives, episodes; and context, involving multiple interconnected aspects such as the dance genre, the intention, cultural traditions, the site or performance platform and more. While they are noted sequentially in a linear structure the intention is non-hierarchical and each category is both independent and interdependent.

FORM

Body awareness

Choreographic building blocks for dance at the most basic level begin with understanding space, time and energy, known as the elements of dance. These terms have been introduced and expanded on by movement analysts including Rudolf Laban, Irmgard Bartenieff and later choreographers like William Forsythe and Merce Cunningham. A dance class for very young children begins by understanding the body and how it moves – wriggling knees, elbows, fingers, shoulders then moving on to the larger groups of the torso, arms and legs in fun, exploratory activities. Focusing on specific body parts enables children to experiment slowly and find their own pathways. Usually, the activity starts in a static position, either standing or sitting on the floor, and variations can be added such as instructions to move slowly, like a snail, or fast, like a soaring bird. This language imagery utilising metaphor, or even metaphors that open out into other metaphors (Foster 1997, p139) is a common tool for teaching dance and evokes the imagination to initiate individual responses and meaning-making. The lesson builds to incorporate larger locomotor tasks involving moving around the space, interacting with others, and generating small phrases of connected movements.

In recent years teachers and choreographers have developed multiple movement languages that combine material gleaned from their dance training and participation in choreographic repertoire and workshops. Synthesising these influences with their personal philosophy and studio experimentation has resulted in hybrid forms and methods that may be passed on to others. The section on developing movement vocabulary also gives some examples and throughout this chapter, the connection between dance training and choreography becomes clear.

As discussed, there are various options for structuring explorations in choreography. Another useful approach is the methodology 'Viewpoints' that has gained traction across international institutions of performing arts since the 1970s. Originally developed by American performing artist and educator Mary Overlie as the six viewpoints theory, in essence it addresses the divisions prevalent in teaching theatre practice and dance composition whereby the former favoured the elements of story and emotion, while dance emphasised shape and movement. By opening a fluid dialogue between the elements that can be addressed and deconstructed at any point in the process, all are equal partners in the creation process rather than the notion that the story predominates, and the movement is a response.

> Viewpoints are a non-hierarchical approach to movement that provides a vocabulary for thinking about and acting upon Time and Space. Using the tools of Tempo, Duration, Kinesthetic Response, Repetition, Spatial Relationship, Topography, Shape, Gesture, and Architecture Viewpoints is a practical approach to creating choreography with performers.
>
> (Bogart and Landau 2004)

Another practice is 'Flying Low', a technique initiated by Venezuelan born dancer, choreographer and educator David Zambrano (see Chapter 3). The class moves dynamically and fluidly around the floor with the body flung freely, opening and closing, spiralling and connecting with speed. Instructors often incorporate popular music, making this a fun, individually focused training method for all levels of experience. Contemporary dance has always embraced the floor incorporating the vertical space and this method takes an in-depth approach to movement close to the ground and reconstructs the material around personal physicality and preferences.

For the artist, the current approach to body awareness and generating innovative movement vocabulary is individual and philosophically based. Through continual interaction, observation and participation in the creative process choreographers and dancers collaborate throughout rather than working in a hierarchical model whereby the choreographer stands outside and imposes a predetermined structure. Reflective of postmodern approaches to collaboration and collective creation, this strategy resonates with current expectations of the critically responsive and somatic thinking dancer.

Shape and structure

Structured individual and group work can develop through a kinaesthetic understanding (Laban 1960) of bodies in space; that is the points we can reach in multiple directions scaffolded within a spatial volume termed an icosahedron (see Chapter 4). Hence Laban was opposed to dance classes with mirrors as this tended to occupy one lens and point of focus for the dancer rather than working across multiple directions. Doris Humphrey is credited with writing the first book to codify choreography, *The Art of Making Dances* (1959) linking the 'fall and recovery' technique to her choreographic method that unifies the body and the psyche (see Chapter 4). Among Humphrey's legacy were specific considerations about the interplay between groups and individuals in the space, and importantly, the notion of asymmetry for modern dance. While this might seem a small point to note, it revolutionised the design of past choreography that relied heavily on a frontal focus, symmetry with synchronicity. Asymmetry enabled the breaking up of the space into different zones of action and emotion, and the connection between individual reflection and group action at the same moment – devices that are common practice in choreography today.

A partner in choreography is time. Time can denote the length of the choreography, the parts within, and the dynamics/effort. In some cultures, dance as ritual practice might go for many hours or even days. The segments are clearly defined, each with its purpose. Within the spectrum, there is always a 'choreographic arc' (Humphrey and Pollack 1959) that encompasses a beginning, middle and end. Within the 'arc' there might be many episodes and phases that the choreographer can map out either in terms of real time; for example, making ten one-minute sections for a ten-minute piece, or creating a seamless flow from beginning to end. The intention, meaning, or thematic aspect is important to pace for maximum impact such that the climax occurs at the correct moment, and the build preceding this, and the following reflective phase, makes sense.

Movement vocabulary and sequencing

The notion of initiating movement from parts of the body through task-directed improvisation will assist in generating a personal movement vocabulary. For a choreographer, the observation of the dancer's improvisation is key to understanding how individuals like to move.

Exemplar 1 – William Forsythe, Ohad Naharin and movement initiation

Body awareness can be extended into structures that focus on multiple points of initiation for movement. William Forsythe is an American dancer and choreographer who was the Artistic Director of Ballet Frankfurt (1984–2004) and The Forsythe Company (2005–2015). Forsythe developed a 12-point process for movement initiation, believing that any point in the body can begin a dance. The resulting choreography is free from pre-determined ways of moving and frees the choreographer from formulaic structures. Even in a work like his 2021 *The Bar Project*, a short film of five episodes created during the COVID-19 pandemic, the artist incorporates innovative ways of working with a ballet barre despite it being a fixed point in the space. As a ubiquitous prop that has sustained many dancers throughout the pandemic, it suggests familiarity and the fixed ballet vocabulary. Yet using his methodology the movement extends into quirky, unusual tangents that connect the dancers and create a mood of social interaction and dependency as thoughts and feelings are divulged through the process. The episodes were created through Zoom sessions with the dancers; hence time and distance add another layer of complexity. As a metaphor for stability and sustainability, the ballet barre symbolises a safe place that Forsythe cleverly juxtaposes with playful, freer movement indicative of a way forward.

Many choreographers explore extending the parameters of movement vocabulary through task-based approaches to choreography; one of the most significant is Israeli dancer, teacher and choreographer Ohad Naharin. In a different, less conscious way from Forsythe, Naharin seeks to break down pre-learned ways of moving such that dancers, and non-dancers, are free to make their connections between their body and inner self. While serving as Artistic Director of Batsheva Dance Company from 1990 to 2018, Naharin developed the movement language known as Gaga technique (see Chapter 3), a methodology designed to discover freedom and pleasure through physical sensations, multi-layered movement tasks and inner groove (Batsheva 2015). The repertoire of Batsheva is distinctive and highly original, typically juxtaposing a large group dance against individual explorations. Images stay with the audience over time, for example, the iconic circle of chairs

> in *Decadance* (2000) where dancers fling themselves back and forth, while others hit the floor only to be driven back to the chairs in a relentless cycle. Such confidence by company dancers to express themselves individually and respond to the tasks within the choreographic vision can be directly attributed to Gaga training.

Introducing the notion that movement is constantly changing and can begin at any point moving in an ebb and flow around and through the body, gives a sense of freedom and specially personalised vocabulary. Forsythe and Naharin sought to develop and exploit these skills in the dancers they worked with to make exciting, highly individual choreography,

Part of this process is working with impulses that provoke action through voice, sounds, music and metaphoric imagery. These processes rely on improvisation (Banes 2003; Smith-Autard 2010; Kloppenberg 2010), an intuitive, democratic method whereby there is no right or wrong way to resolve the task. This reflects current trends whereby individual responses to movement by the dancers build and cohere into a larger choreographic vision. The purpose of improvisation in this context is as a 'process' rather than a performance device. It should be noted that contemporary choreographers often leave space in their work for segments of improvisation to encourage the flow between formal choreography and the immediacy of spontaneity achieved through improvisation.

The next stage is selecting some of these moments, re-working them into short phrases or sequences. This 'raw material' can be revisited in multiple ways; for example, trying it in slow motion or at a faster pace, beginning on the floor then moving through different levels, changing up the dynamics so it could be sharp and percussive, or smooth and flowing. Overlaying the material with an emotional quotient such as anger, fear or joy enables expression as each dancer draws on their personal feelings and experiences. In a composition class an instruction could be to deconstruct a phrase; that is to rebuild it in a different order, take it apart, or reverse it by playing it backwards. Reinvention, repurposing and remaking intertwine here. A master of these methods is Twyla Tharp and evidence of her skill in rebuilding and reconstructing dance material is epitomised in her iconic *The Upper Room* (1986) with music by Phillip Glass.

Group choreography

Thus far the process has involved individual practice. Developing personal vocabulary through constructing phrases and manipulating sequences enables a transition to work with other dancers in duets, trios, or small groups. Returning to examples of dance games with young children, a couple of ways to pass on dance material from one body to another are either through 'mirroring' whereby two dancers face each other, and one will follow the other; or by 'shadowing' with one dancing behind the other copying the movement, similar to the method teachers commonly use to pass on dance techniques to students. The deconstruction/reconstruction model previously mentioned allows the group to use the source material to build their own phrases, thereby further increasing the number of variables for the group to work with. Emanuel Gat, an Israeli choreographer currently based in France, uses game structures to develop how the group of dancers interact in his group pieces. In an online interview he explains that often a very simple task or underlying rule, such as each dancer choosing a distance they want to be apart from another in the group at all times, can create a very complex choreographic outcome. By setting these simple rules in motion, he can focus on discovering and shaping what is there, rather than creating all the group interaction from scratch (Emanuel Gat n.d.). An example of this in action is his piece *Brilliant Corners* (2017).

In managing a large group of dancers, important decisions will involve the integration of solos and duos, the arrangement of the group in the space including entrances and exits, plus noting sections of unison dancing that should be synchronised. Many choreographers who have a long experience of working with students, community and mixed ability groups know that these segments require a lot of practice and it is a good idea to begin rehearsing them first.

CONTENT

Dance history reveals a spectrum of approaches by choreographers to narrative and ways of creating 'meaning' in dance. These range from the literal recounting of myths and legends to the complete rejection of storytelling via the use of abstraction – there are many places in between.

Narratives and storytelling

Incorporating themes and stories in a choreography underpins traditional dance involving large narratives, such as the *Ramayana* story that extends from India, across Indonesia, and into Thailand and Cambodia and is frequently performed either in full or more commonly by presenting smaller sections. It recounts the stories of kings, queens and gods at a surface level but provides complex allegories about the universe, moral tales of good and evil told through symbolism involving intricate hand gestures, facial expressions, masks, costumes, props and settings. The narrative is familiar to audiences who anticipate favourite characters and sections they have witnessed many times as they follow the story of Princess Sita, King Rama, gods and demons along with the faithful, ever-present white monkey god Hanuman. Similarly, Western audiences can recount the tale of annual renditions of the *Nutcracker* ballet staged at Christmas around the world and follow the story of Clara, the Nutcracker Prince and the Sugar Plum Fairy.

Many contemporary choreographers have chosen to rework these classical narratives in new ways to not only give a personal twist to the tale but probe underlying issues to achieve current resonance. Swedish dancer and choreographer Mats Ek, who led the Cullberg Ballet from 1985 to 1993, reinterpreted the classical repertory with wit, humour and a dark touch of surreal pathos. With an artistic vision that is "distinctive for its imaginative interpretations of storylines, in combination with a lyrical approach which conveys through movement the underlying emotions and feelings rather than just the narrative detail" (The Dance Consortium 2012) Ek made versions of *Swan Lake* (1987) and *Giselle* (1982). In the latter, he places the jilted peasant girl Giselle in a mental asylum, while a 2018 reinterpretation of this classic choreographed by Akram Khan locates Giselle as a refugee migrant worker. While these choreographies might introduce new scenes and add variations to the original, they maintain a 'linear narrative' – that is a progression from beginning to end following a central character.

Matthew Bourne's 1995 version of *Swan Lake* broke down gender stereotypes by introducing male swans and overlaying the piece with male sexuality. Sir Matthew Christopher Bourne OBE is an

English choreographer and Artistic Director of New Adventures, founded in 2002. He is well known for working in the genres of contemporary dance, contemporary ballet and dance theatre across stage shows, musicals and film earning him Tony awards (1999) for Best Choreography and Best Director of a Musical for his 1995 production *Swan Lake* (New Adventures Charity 2021). South African choreographer Dada Masilo has created contemporary versions of various ballets from the classical repertory, including her own version of *Swan Lake* (2010) that confronts two major taboos prevalent in her native land:

> Between arabesques, bare feet striking the floor, clapping hands, swaying hips and voices punctuating the rhythm of the dance, she employs the metaphor of Tchaikovsky's homosexuality masked behind the impossible love of the original version and introduces the theme of AIDS at the end of the piece.
>
> (Danse Danse n.d.)

Other ways of using narrative include a 'non-linear' approach whereby the story builds through a series of scenes and episodes that are inter-connected. Akram Khan and Sidi Larbi Cherkaoui's *Zero Degrees* (2005), in collaboration with sculptor Antony Gormley and composer Nitin Sawhney, incorporated this idea by paralleling a clear story of arriving in India with the inner journeys of each man seeking an identity as depicted through dance – Kathak and contemporary. Dualities of darkness and light, joy and sadness, anger and acceptance permeate the collaboration about 'otherness' as they seek to find connectivity.

Collage

A collage mapping of a theme can open many options enabling tangents to come into play and offer various twists to the logic of the central story giving it a surrealist element. Swedish choreographer Alexander Eckman achieves this through a mix of devices such as introducing eccentric characters, use of repetition, suspending objects in space so they lose their solidity, architectural features such as shifting spaces by using moveable screens and apertures in the floor; plus an overall juxtaposing of reality and fantasy. Eckman's works are renowned for extraordinary sets and production elements like the 2014 film, *A Swan Lake*, which paints a rich, emotional canvas as the dancers skim through water, and *Midsummer Night's Dream* (2015) where they frolic in bales of hay in a paganistic nod to the summer solstice.

Dance theatre

An important development in contemporary dance that incorporates narrative is the dance theatre genre that has its roots in the work of Mary Wigman and the German expressionist Ausdruckstanz dancers (see Chapter 1). Pina Bausch and her company Tanztheater Wuppertal created vast canvases of human emotion that transport the audience on a roller coaster ride between pathos, comedy, pleasure and sadness as lives are relived and revealed through her insightful, deeply human artistry.

Exemplar 2 – Pina Bausch

Pina Bausch was the Artistic Director and founder of Tanztheater (Dance-Theater) Wuppertal (1973–2009). The company is currently led by Bettina Wagner-Bergelt (2019 – present). Intense and complex, these visceral works created in collaboration with the dancers occur within the backdrop of familiarities, like a café with tables and chairs in *Café Müller* (1985) or the vast crumbling earth walls of a massive grave in *Victor* (1986). The images are palpable and memorable; disturbing yet human and generous. Emotions fluctuate between immense sorrow with moments in the choreography paralleling a larger reality that is fluidly paired with quirky foibles that we all recognise. Choreographic devices such as repetition are crucial to the power of the artist's work along with spectacular settings that serve as small worlds within themselves that the dancers frequently enter and exit. The music selection is diverse and supports the atmosphere, often shifting from bittersweet popular jazz ballads to sweeping classical excerpts and full-length pieces such as Stravinsky's 1913 *Rite of Spring* for Bausch's choreography of the same name from 1975.

This style of dance theatre choreography depends on highly skilled dance artists who share their vulnerability as they work through the creative journey with authenticity and honesty. At its best, the genre can profoundly illuminate the human condition. A strong conceptual underpinning is essential and a team of dancers that are willing to share their thoughts, experiences, and feelings to the process. Dance theatre performers are multi-talented, required to dramatise strong characters, sometimes sing, play musical instruments, and contribute to the performance in many different ways that dig deep into their psyche and emotional history.

Conceptual choreography

A dance work could begin with a simple overarching concept – for example, loss. This central theme can be approached in myriad ways to underscore sections and subsections, moving between personal accounts and wider, global issues. As a frame, it can move in time to include past, present and future considerations and overlay literal and abstract renderings. These transitions enable an 'inner' and 'outer' reading of the choreography that connects in the same space harmoniously or in opposition. Often minimalistic choreography uses everyday movements like running and walking mixed with gestures and phrases, repetition, and striking imagery. Belgian choreographer Anne Teresa De Keersmaeker with Rosas & De Munt/La Monnaie (Brussels/Bruxelles) *Rain* (2001) is a mesmerising response to the hypnotic music of composer Steve Reich and includes all of these components in a work that parallels the precision and structure of the music.

Another choreographer who creates conceptually with a minimalist lens is French choreographer Jérôme Bel whose work might exist as a conversation as in the 2004 *Pichet and Myself*. The piece is performed to words spoken between Bel and Thai dancer/choreographer Pichet Klunchun. Bel challenges the parameters of what might be considered dance in much of his work and his role in the current dance ecology as a provocateur, albeit with self-depreciation and humour, promotes mixed responses from dance audiences. Conceptual work requires brave innovation and a precise structure and theme that is personally felt and genuine (see Chapter 6).

Abstraction

Dance that might be termed 'abstract' occurs where the process involves working solely with the body and movement. It could be argued that as soon as human bodies are in space there is a story going on, and as an audience, we relate to the dance through shared sensory experiences bringing our own perceptions and emotions to what we are viewing. While choreographers like Martha Graham are famous for stating that everything has a meaning and "movement never lies," Merce Cunningham denied this thesis and sought the opposite by deciding the order of events, for example, through the toss of a dice, or by chance. While these strategies offer a method to begin anew with each work without reference to past themes and material, a strong point of view is essential to affect the process.

To conclude this section, while the use of narrative might be considered literal and restrictive by some contemporary artists, the examples above illustrate a rich diversity of approaches. All incorporate what could be termed an 'emotional narrative' that immerses the audience, enabling them to respond, and reflect on their own experiences as they share in the dance.

PRODUCTION ELEMENTS

This section examines key components of staging a performance. As outlined in Exemplar 2, the use of appropriate production elements is connected to dance history, genres and philosophies of dance.

Props, set pieces and costumes

Classical ballet has a rich history of costume design ranging from the classic tutu and pointe shoes to character costumes, lavishly painted backdrops along with set pieces. Costumes for traditional dance are historically pre-set by character and colour, often incorporating multiple layers of material, elaborate makeup, masks and accessories. To this day, forms such as classical Cambodian Khmer and Thai Khon require the dancers to be sewn into the costumes, adding considerable time to the pre-performance preparation. Costumes for classical dance from the East and the West define gender, wealth, status and the attributes of the characters; for example the use of gold for princes and princesses, accessories of jewellery and rich fabrics. Ballet costumes leave an invaluable legacy and during certain eras in dance key artists of the day have been involved in the design. The Ballets Russes (see Chapters 1 and 4) commissioned such luminaries as Pablo Picasso, Henri Matisse, and Léon Bakst to create extraordinary costumes that stand alone as artworks and appear in the collections of national museums and art galleries (Van Norman Baer 1999).

In Chapter 1 we noted how Isadora Duncan dispensed with lavish costumes and danced barefoot in free-flowing robes. She was not only creating a new beginning for what a dance costume might be but importantly, was rebelling against the fashion styles of the day that restricted women. A decade and a half later the Postmodernist movement rejected elaborate dance costumes as elitist, opting for comfortable, non-gender-specific everyday clothes so that there was no separation between dancer and non-dancer, male and female.

Budget is also a consideration and professional ballet companies have large funding allocations for production staff and materials. Smaller contemporary groups work with designers to create unique looks for their choreography while others may use readymade high-street fashion clothes such as dresses, pants, shirts or singlets. Costumes are essential to embodying the intention of the choreography and what is being portrayed either through characterisation and a strong narrative, or a more open-ended, abstract work where neutrality is important. Outfits for jazz and show dancing have added lustre through shiny fabrics, added embellishments while street dance performers favour signature brands and accessories like sunglasses and baseball caps.

To conclude, shoes or no shoes have always defined eras in dance, from the role of the classical pointe shoes in complementing the image of a woman as a light, ethereal being to the earthiness of Isadora Duncan's barefoot dancing. Traditional dance is usually barefoot and in many cultures from Africa to Australia and throughout Asia, the direct connection to the earth is an essential element that aligns the dancer to the universe. Show dancing, tap dancing, ballroom and the sneakers of street dance all have a role in defining what the dance expresses, enabling styles of choreography and the development of movement vocabulary. Some skills are transferable but others, like dancing en pointe, take years of practice to develop the strength and correct technique.

Music

Classical ballet performances by top professional companies are usually accompanied by an orchestra while artists with a traditional dance background are also used to performing with live music. Dance forms such as classical Indian Bharatanatyam rely heavily on a dialogue between the dancer and musician as they transit between set pieces and variations that include room for some improvisation.

Working with a composer is part of dance history and has led to some extraordinary innovative collaborations including Tchaikovsky and Petipa, Stravinsky and Nijinsky, Philip Glass and Twyla Tharp, John Cage and Merce Cunningham, and others. This process is complex and varied from a composer offering a pre-recorded piece to the choreographer; a step-by-step method with the artists working alongside each other in the studio; the composer taking a storyboard from the choreographer as a basis for the composition; or the Cage/Cunningham model whereby time and place is the only connection between the artists. Cunningham purposely separated the relationship between music and choreography such that they were equal partners, and one form did not dominate the other.

As early as the 1950s choreographers such as Alwin Nikolais chose to compose their music in multimedia choreography. Embracing advances in twenty-first-century technologies, other artists are taking control of this aspect of the creative process by utilising new technologies that offer flexibility and can adapt as the choreography shifts and evolves.

Many contemporary artists, such as Mark Morris in his exquisitely timed *Falling Down Stairs* (1997) featuring cellist Yo-Yo Ma, work with musicians on stage. Mark Morris is an American dancer, teacher, choreographer and founder of the Mark Morris Dance Group (MMDG) since 1980. Morris is known for his musicality, as reported by The New Yorker is "undeviating in his devotion to music" (Mark Morris Dance Group 2021). Since 2006, Morris has conducted performances for MMDG and extends his choreographic works across major international ballet companies and operas. His works are known for their immense craftsmanship, with a touch of humour and controversy. Notable works include *The Hard Nut* (1991) – a retro-inspired version of *The Nutcracker* (1892) – and *Romeo and Juliet, On Motifs of Shakespeare* (2008).

While some choreographers commence with music that inspires them, others choose to begin with the concept then find music that works with it, or commission a composer as part of the creative team. A common question at choreographic dialogues is "what comes first… the music or the idea?" The answer can be either, but more commonly it is the overarching idea that inspires a professional artist. Music can guide the dynamics, force or energy of the action in dance, the choreographer should choose how the relationship will cohere. The use of silence, ambient soundscapes, voice or a mix of music are options; however, the choreographer should always be at the centre of these sources of inspiration rather than be driven by them.

Exemplar 3 – Relationship between music and choreographic structures: George Balanchine *Theme and Variation*

Many choreographic structures across cultural traditions and throughout history closely follow musical forms such as *raga* (mood) and *tala* (rhythm) sequences in Indian classical music (Vatsyayan 1963) and rondos, canons, and theme and variation in Western classical music. For example an A, B model can be termed a 'call and response'; a canon is where there is a sequential response to movement like singing a round, or an ABA design is termed 'theme and variation'. Here the theme is established in the beginning and then expands into variations while parts are still clearly recognisable, then finally returns. A beautiful example of this method is George Balanchine's (see Chapter 1) *Theme and Variation* (1947) choreographed to Tchaikovsky's Orchestral Suite No.3. It is redolent with the grandeur of Russian classicism and pays homage to Russian choreographer Marius Petipa. Stripped bare of the lavish sets and costumes associated with classical ballet, Balanchine exploits the purity of line, technical virtuosity, and precise formations that reflect the hierarchy of a company to

> create this signature work that exists in the repertoire of ballet companies throughout the world.
>
> In any of the above examples, the purpose of the music for the choreography should be clear. Is it to support the atmosphere, provide essential rhythms and phrasing, add lyrics that reinforce the theme, place it in a particular period in time or place? Minimalist sounds, silence, and soundscapes are also possibilities. Most choreographers switch between all these ways of incorporating music and dance makers should be open to all possibilities to explore and experiment.

Lighting design

Historically dance has always incorporated the innovations of the time and the use of lighting. For instance, Loïe Fuller (1862–1928) explored the possibilities of the new gas lighting inventions of her day by creating swirls of colour on a highly theatrical silk costume that included hand-held wands to extend beyond the shape of the body (see Chapters 4 and 6). This shape-shifting of bodies in space and time was grounded in an experimental, abstract sensibility that allowed the audience to engage in their own meaning-making with the performance.

A lighting designer is an artist who can create an emotional landscape for a choreographer by enhancing an atmosphere, shifting and exaggerating scenes and highlighting characterisation. Contemporary artists such as Alexander Eckman, Crystal Pite and Akram Khan (see Chapter 1) rely heavily on the latest design options to add layered complexity to their work. While established national theatres have the latest lighting equipment and staff to rig large productions, smaller black-box and community theatres have less to work with.

At a most basic level, lighting can support the production through adding general cover colour washes, side lighting for atmosphere, lighting corridors and special spotlights to focus the dancers and certain scenes. Emerging choreographers should be familiar with these lighting 'states' as for many showcases featuring shorter pieces (ten to 20 minutes or so) by several young artists in the same programme, managing with the limited scope is common practice.

Multidisciplinary focus

Merce Cunningham included multimedia work through collaborations with artists like John Cage (composer), Jasper Johns and Andy Warhol (visual artists) and new technologies. He embraced these as rapidly as they could keep pace with his thirst for innovation; for example, the motion capture technology of BIPED (1999) and movement generation software of Life Forms (see Chapter 6). From the early 1970s, Cunningham also used video projections both at the back and front of the stage juxtaposing backstage preparations with on-stage performances. These devices worked in tandem with his notion of dance occurring only in time and space independent from music, narratives and visual components.

American choreographer Alwin Nikolais incorporated multimedia into his choreographies, creating immersive environments where the dancers moved in collaboration with light, elaborate costumes, props and effects. Pieces such as *Tensile Involvement* (1953) and *Noumenon* (1953) 'disembodied' the performers in a process known as 'decentralization' that gave equal status to all the elements on stage, enabling multiple points of focus at any given time. Not without controversy New York critic Deborah Jowitt commented on this approach in a review of remounted works in the *Village Voice* (Jowitt 2010) reflecting on Nikolais comments from 1971:

> Nikolais – fuming over some people's charge that he "dehumanized" his dancers – wrote that he "wanted man to be able to identify with things other than himself. This is the day of ecological and environmental visions. We must give up our naval contemplations long enough to take our places in space."

It is interesting to note that in the present digital age contemporary choreographers like Japanese Hiroaki Umeda extend the Nikolais legacy of multimedia immersion of the dancer in pieces such as *Adapting for Distortion* (2008), *Haptic* (2010) through to *Medium* (2018). Chapter 6 in this volume looks at dance in the digital age and how this is incorporated in myriad ways by choreographers.

Staging a performance involves many people and skill sets at all stages of the process, from producers to marketing and human resources teams, medical staff, designers and backstage crew, front of house managers and more. Learning these roles and being able to liaise and communicate across areas is essential to a choreographic process – for instance, the choreographer would be involved in decision-making concerning promotional photographic imagery, programme texts and layout. Input into the lighting and costume design is integral to the choreographic process and knowledge of the basics of these fields is invaluable in bringing an innovative lens to the final production.

CHOREOGRAPHIC PROCESS

A choreographer proceeds through a structure that reflects the creative process not only in the arts but in all fields of research. The nomenclature might vary in different texts, but the four pillars identified are preparation, incubation, illumination and verification. First developed as a model by Graham Wallas (1926) the original four-stage model has been popularised with variations by, for example, motivational speaker James Taylor and others, who have applied them to business strategies, corporate planning, education, tourism, health and the financial sector with a wide range of clients. For choreographers, the stages are useful to note not only to track the development of the choreography but also in terms of how the different phases may relate to dance history, genres and contexts. The phases do not necessarily progress in equal measure in a linear timeframe and choreographers should move fluidly between them incorporating prior knowledge and certainty (convergent thinking) and originality, risk and spontaneity (divergent thinking). This model begins after a proposal, commission or contract has been approved and does not include advice on writing submissions or negotiations.

Preparation

Curiosity begins the creative process enabling some overarching themes to emerge. Strategies employed to flesh out these beginnings can be strategic, logistic, involve research, or rely on spontaneity through utilising task-based stimuli. A choreographic project needs components from each to move forward to the next stage. Some questions to consider include the following subsets.

Strategic planning

- Are you working alone, in a group, or with a company?
- Do you plan to choreograph and direct the project or work collectively?
- Is it a collaboration with other art forms?
- Does the context require specific considerations – is it a show for schools, the community, a special needs group, a digital platform, a festival commission, and more.
- Map out a realistic time frame for your commitment. This is particularly important for freelancers who are often combining a choreographic project with teaching commitments and other projects.

Logistic planning

- Who are the dancers and the company you are working with?
- What genre do they work in, what is their repertoire and history, and will the work be toured?
- What is the rehearsal period?
- Who are the production team and key collaborators – at what point do they become part of the process?
- Do you have a government grant, sponsorship, or other partners involved that require calibrated outcomes along the way?
- Do you need to plan for midpoint events such as a studio showing, film shoot of work in progress or dialogue-based lecture/demonstration for instance?
- Does the project involve cultural exchange and international collaboration? What are the processes and parameters for this?
- What is the venue, place or site? Is it pre-booked and the final performance date confirmed, or will you decide when the choreography is ready to be performed?
- Documentation of the rehearsal process and the final outcome – what is your comfort zone (and the dancers') for the flow of filming and photographing rehearsal material, and where will this be shared?

- Do ethical agreement forms need to be signed? For instance, are there children involved that need parental consent? Is it part of an academic study whereby student dancers become involved in a choreographic research experiment? As many choreographers now work as teaching artists or are undertaking practice-based choreographic degrees in an academic programme, these considerations are important.

Research

- Will you be working within a narrative, historical period, political or social issue?
- Do you need a dramaturg or a rehearsal director to work with you?
- Is it a concept that could be broken into components to be researched further?
- What resources are available?
- What experiential and immersive encounters could prepare the dancers to better understand the overall design and point of view? This could include a trip to a museum, inviting guest artists or speakers, acquiring materials, props and pieces to work with, to name a few.
- Stimulation from watching performances, clips of dance works, genres might be useful – although the purpose is not to be derivative, observations might confirm or clarify a direction.
- How do you plan to share and archive the research? Do you need permission from photographers, video recording artists to reproduce and use the images?
- If the project is part of an academic performance-based degree all the artists should be informed and be clear about their participation.

Task-based creation

This strategy is commonly used to generate ideas for dance making from young children to professional dancers. It uses stimuli through a set of tasks that require problem-solving through movement. The format might include brainstorming, games, workshopping, mind-mapping and free association methods. In planning this strategy the choreographer can decide if they will be the sole facilitator, if the group will take turns to share prompts or if there are going to be some pre-set tasks (homework) that everyone will have time to prepare for.

Multi-modal planning such as bringing in various drawing materials, large sheets of paper, coloured threads and pins to make connections contribute to making an interesting rehearsal session.

Examples of prompts include:

- Poems, music, use of imagery, words, props and costume pieces – the purpose of introducing these stimuli requires clarification and instructions for the dancers.
- Reading books, articles and viewing clips related to the topic.
- Creating a storyboard around the theme that everyone can add to as the piece progresses.
- Sculptures and environments that allow the dancers to interact with objects.
- Time-based tasks can be a task-based activity; for instance, move for 30 seconds, freeze in a position, create a flowing pathway for one minute, or create four 8-count phrases of dance.
- Other tasks might involve working with an expert in another field to explore further; for example, new technologies, martial arts, acting or singing skills, or learning another dance genre.

Tone, atmosphere, and collaborative strategy

This is an essential part of the planning that is often overlooked. Miscommunication and misunderstanding of each person's role in the project can be problematic. It should be defined at the outset and built into the project's 'tone' or working atmosphere. There might be a mismatch between the style of the project and the dancers' expectations of what they will be asked to do and vice versa.

- The choreographer should decide what level of dancer contribution the new work will need and have plans in place to facilitate the process.

- How the dancers want to be credited for their input should also be discussed; for instance "The choreography is created in collaboration with the dancers" is common practice for many projects.
- Does the time frame allow for fluidity of viewpoints and an experimental process?
- Does the project's brief and anticipated outcome enable process work?
- Often a choreographic commission requires the dancers to rapidly assimilate pre-set material, rehearse and perform it. Musical theatre and the commercial dance sectors typically work this way and selected dancers should be aware of this.
- Is it to be a collaboration (Knox 2020, pp. 46–50) where each participant has equal say in a non-hierarchical structure? If so, do they know how to collaborate?

A useful model to consider in this process is Butterworth's Didactic to Democratic process model (Butterworth 2012; Butterworth and Wildschut 2018) – defining and delineating roles and working relationships.

Incubation

The most exciting time of the creation process is when the concepts have been formulated in the preparation stage and are explored in various ways. Typically, this is facilitated by the choreographer or creative director who will plan a schedule of task-based activities for each rehearsal enabling the dancers to explore, connect physically

Table 2.1 Butterworth's didactic–democratic model

Process 1	Process 2	Process 3	Process 4	Process 5
Choreographer as expert	Choreographer as author	Choreographer as pilot	Choreographer as facilitator	Choreographer as co-owner
Dancer as instrument	Dancer as interpreter	Dancer as contributor	Dancer as creator	Dancer as co-owner
Didactic process ←				→ Democratic process

Source: Butterworth 2012, p.47

and emotionally to the component ideas, and dig deeper into the overall themes. Common practices include warm-up activities that correspond to the dance material being developed, improvisation, movement tasks given via verbal commands or inspired by music, stories or other means. Contact improvisation may also be incorporated whereby dancers intuitively work together exchanging impulses back and forth like a conversation, resulting in unexpected, spontaneous movement while fostering trust, cooperation and physical knowledge between the dancers.

Combining solo activity with work in pairs and larger groups widens the range of physical encounters, allowing the dancers to extend their boundaries to observe how others move – the shifts in dynamics, use of space and weight are crucial to the range of possibilities for developing a vocabulary for the group as they learn from each other in an ebb and flow.

Sharing personal experiences in more reflective sessions of the process enables embodied memories and individual expression to scaffold the wider general themes for the dance. Essentializing these moments that connect the body, mind and spirit through reflective practice relates to the wider philosophical field of phenomenology (Merleau-Ponty 2001). Revealing heightened emotional states through task building is essential to crafting a choreographic work that combines complexity with a unique aesthetic. A well-managed and planned platform for incubation will achieve such positive outcomes and lay the groundwork for progression.

Illumination

While the dancers have been working through many stages of task-based activities the choreographer will be observing and recording the material in various ways. Some choreographers ask the dancers to keep a journal to record their responses and add further thoughts and feelings about how the various sessions worked for them.

Recording material via video is a common practice allowing it to be instantly shared not only as a documentary of rehearsals but also as an important platform for dialoguing between the tasks and the dancers' responses. In this situation the atmosphere of the studio comes into play – will the choreographer have the final say in how the work will fit together incorporating the dancer's input or will it be an egalitarian sharing of material? Usually, a contemporary dance professional choreographic project comes together with a mix of both, albeit with the choreographer making the final decisions.

Illumination might not always throw out 'eureka' moments where the choreographic arc is clearly revealed. The process of making a final selection of material from the earlier stages takes place in this arena involving 'setting' the choreography on the dancers in an episodic timeframe where it incorporates a beginning, a middle and an end. Spending time on each of these components is important to ensure there is a logical progression and choreographic weight to the final work. The decision-making process is complex involving not only the selection of raw material and deciding how it fits in the overall work, but also who should dance it, what will be repeated, what are the best transitions and connecting sections, and overall, what should be retained and eliminated.

Commonly there needs to be a degree of flexibility such that sections can be re-worked, segments and even phrases and gestures exchanged and reconnected in different ways. These are the variables that should be open to change well into the process, as further rehearsal will reveal the best way to configure all the pieces.

Reflection is an essential component here. Methods include journalling throughout the process for personal contemplation, creating shared storyboards, look books, and online shared documents utilising the many digital tools that facilitate coordination of thoughts, rehearsal clips, stimulus in multi-modal forms, and dialogue chat groups between the dancers, the choreographer, and production crews.

During the COVID-19 pandemic from 2020, these digital platforms became invaluable and enabled choreographers to make works across distances working through innovative projects in new ways. Posting the process online, Zoom choreographic sessions, live streaming of classes and performances became the norm as artists grappled with ways to connect and keep working. Through necessity, the value of sharing, contributing, and evaluating dance material became inclusive, collaborative, and cooperative for many companies and projects.

Validation

The final part of the process for dance is often a studio or class showing, digital posting or performance for an audience. This section involves familiar components that apply to any staging of dance from a ballet school concert to a professional company.

- Rehearsals – practice sessions include a run of the whole dance for the company, taking sections at a time, coaching solos, duos and small groups.
- Familiarising everyone with the performance space – entrances and exits, location of the dressing rooms, marking where set pieces and props should be on the stage and where they will be stored backstage.
- Working with stage lighting, musicians and all the production elements.
- Acknowledging the etiquette and requirements of the theatre, the ethos of a festival, or other considerations such as post-show dialogues and aligned events.
- Digital platforms – will it be filmed, live-streamed? Are there other considerations for the dancers and production teams?

Summary

In summarising this section on the creative process, it is pertinent to look at how the model has been applied (consciously or inadvertently) in various eras in dance history and across genres.

The postmodern period (see Chapter 1) was predominantly interested in process; hence preparation and incubation were the most important phases as artists wanted to focus on experimentation rather than performance. In contrast, a musical theatre production would try to progress through the process to arrive at validation as soon as possible. Saving time and money are essential in putting on a commercial show and the time to experiment is limited.

Dance education has responded in diverse ways to the staging of school performances. Some dance programmes have a composition curriculum that encourages students to work through all of the creative stages to choreograph their work in a 'making', 'presenting', and 'reflecting' model found in the UK, New Zealand, and

Australia among others (see Chapter 1). Students engaged in electives have various experiences including learning just one dance created by the teacher or a visiting choreographer and spending their time rehearsing and perfecting it for a performance. Dance educators suggest strongly that this approach should be supported by holistic content including student opportunities to create, explore and reflect.

DANCE CRITICISM

This section examines the field of dance criticism. Components of this relate to personal reflection as a process that is explored earlier as part of the 'evaluation' stage of the creative process.

In the present time, newspapers and magazines are moving online worldwide, and the space given to critiques of dance shows has diminished. Well-known critics that can establish a track record through years of observing and writing about dance might be termed a 'dying breed' – it is the age of bloggers, opinion pieces and postings on social media platforms about shows by anyone who has seen them. The duality of this scene is that it democratises criticism to such an extent that everyone's a critic and multiple postings of a performance can generate a wide audience that extends far beyond the geographical site of the show and involve multiple thoughts and opinions. For companies and artists, sorting through to find valuable feedback from respected sources that are useful for future choreographic work is essential as this might be an important part of negotiating a tour and other engagements. Some structures and views to assist in validating the plethora of opinions can be sought from the fields of aesthetics and the philosophy of art.

A model for reviewing dance includes four considerations stated as describe, analyse, evaluate, contextualise. As seen in Figure 2.1, these should be seen as a cyclical framework that can be approached at any point interweaving each component throughout.

Describe

An essential partner in reviewing dance is 'visual memory'. Key moments, images, episodes, individual dancers, scenes and characters all constitute what could trigger 'memory points'. This

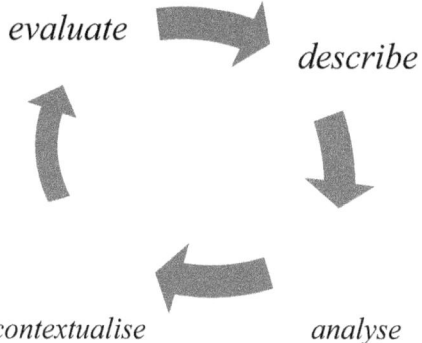

Figure 2.1 A model for critical review – enter at any point

ability to visually recall is crucial in beginning the process of reflection. A way to hone this skill is by playing simple memory games such as recalling the last 20 things you remember on the way to class or remembering 20 objects on a tray that you view for half a minute then writing down what you recall. Dancers usually have a heightened visual memory as their practice involves watching dance exercises and phrases in class, remembering them and bodily reproducing them; however, many top critics do not come from a dance background and bring a different lens to a performance.

A good review requires some description of the events. Articulating moments accurately and poetically enables the audience to imagine the show even if they have not seen it. The language of reviewing unfolds by incorporating a mix of information with imagery and metaphoric poetics that evokes the show. A wide and varied vocabulary can transit between what the bodies are doing in space, the dynamics, and the use of energy. In summary, 'describe' relates to what the dancers are doing.

Analyse

This part of a review is best intertwined with the description as it relates to why they are doing what is being described. The ways we understand the choreography can be complex from a detached perspective through to an intense, visceral experience. In responding to a performance, the interplay between the emotional/felt impact of the performance and judgments on how the physical movement choices and dynamics evoke a response can be articulated. The dancers' connections to each other and to the audience signal the viewer's reactions translating the intention and purpose of the choreography. Some works are simple to follow in terms of narrative, themes or scenes that are familiar; others require deeper reflection that might extend beyond the space of the performance. Words are important in transmitting these responses to a reader with expressions of nuance, ambiguity, and uncertainty valid in many observations of contemporary dance. Often a performance can be engrossing, insightful, provoking and beautifully executed yet you remain unsure of the central message and intention.

Evaluate

This section relates to personal perception, interpretation, taste and judgement of the performance and choreography. Part of how audiences respond to a live performance includes the shared experience that they enjoy – energy might build, and the audience can be caught up in an atmosphere of excitement and emotion. Individuals may find resonance with some of the themes that touch chords of memory, make them reflect and re-visit certain feelings such as anger or joy, or give them insights and a different way of seeing an issue.

Assessments of the skill of the dancers, the innovation of the choreography, and production values are based on the philosophical term of 'relativism'. Opinions that are made on a comparative basis are open to debate as some would argue these components should be assessed on a stand-alone basis while others favour a qualified response; for instance, if you have seen six versions of Petipa's *Swan Lake* by professional companies where does the performance you are viewing sit?

Contextualisation

Contextualisation is not always a consideration for some reviewers and is debatable among scholars of aesthetics and the philosophy of art. An opinion that it is an essential component is shared by renowned American dance critic Marcia Siegel as stated by Julie Van Camp (1992 n.d.).

> Siegel does not cite philosophers or theorists, but she works in a strong contextualist tradition. That is, a work simply cannot be understood or appreciated or evaluated independently of the historical, social, cultural, political and artistic context within which the choreographer is working.

The relevance of this remark might apply to a comment made by Deborah Jowitt on viewing a traditional Australian Aboriginal dance performed by a group from Arnhem Land, Northern Territory, Australia, performing in New York in 1985. Jowett states;

> Surrounded by contemporary American artworks that we understand – all having to do with disintegration, with incompleteness, with aborted goals – they [Aboriginal dancers] perform works about wholeness. The dancing, songs, and body painting preserve the myths. All seem cryptic.
> (p.251)

The body is a powerful means of dialogue that transcends verbal language and through embodiment, encapsulates signs and symbols of place and belief. Returning to the Bangarra Dance Theatre (Chapter 1) and their position as the foremost indigenous dance company in Australia with numerous international performances under their belt, the relevance of contextual knowledge in terms of understanding their performances is pertinent. The progression from literal to abstracted forms of narrative may enable dances in different contexts to take on different levels of meaning. While empowering and inspiring Aboriginal people, choreography created by Stephen Page can significantly change mindsets and educate non-indigenous audiences in a provocative and entertaining way. Context, in this example, is related to emic knowledge, or an 'insider' cultural perspective, of the intention and history of this form.

Similarly, other traditional dance forms embody this same knowledge and those familiar with the culture can recognise signs and symbols. When artists begin to combine these forms with contemporary dance, the artist might include some transitional material to assist the audience. A potent example is the narrative that Khmer classically trained dancer Chey Chankethya from Cambodia incorporates in her choreography *My Mother and I* (2013). The autoethnographic choreography about her life and relationship between her mother, her teacher, and herself as a young dancer conflicted by discipline and expectations of her dance teacher, the history of her mother who had survived living the brutal Pol Pot regime, and her identity as a contemporary woman working internationally, powerfully synergise and cohere. These tensions are played out with choreography that has the beauty, precision and rigidity of form juxtaposed with the loose, free flow of contemporary movement and a recital of anecdotes by the dancer that moves between poignant sorrow and wry humour in a compelling work.

This section has focused on context in terms of cultural material where the gap between the shared cultural knowledge of an audience and that of outsiders gives different points of access to interpreting the dance. While the term 'the other' might denote those on the outside and some critics might also take a 'hegemonic' (Bhaba 1994; Md Nor 2011) approach to critiquing such performances, in the current landscape of global dance these gaps have closed considerably as there is appreciation across genres and traditions of dance subverting a hierarchy that places one form above others.

Context can also apply to the genre being reviewed, the projected audience demographic (is it for young children, a school audience, or a community commission?), the location (site-specific, art gallery or museum), part of a festival, or season, and more.

SUMMARY

This chapter includes practical guides, structures and information to assist with making and reflecting on dance. The themes relate to creating choreographic content and moving towards staging and critiquing. The tools to work with encompass the elements of form, content and context that come under the larger umbrella of the creative process that involves preparation, incubation, illumination, evaluation and elaboration. Components of dance criticism – using the describe, analyse, evaluate and contextualise model to reflect on personal choreography and critique the work of others are also unpacked in this section. Examples of choreographers have been incorporated throughout. It is recommended to view some of these choreographies and check the websites of the artists.

FURTHER READING

Blom, L. A. and Chaplin, L. T. (1982) *The Intimate Act of Choreography*, Pittsburgh: University of Pittsburgh.

Burrows, J. (2010) *A Choreographer's Handbook*, Abingdon and New York: Routledge.

Humphrey, D. (1997) *The Art of Making Dances*, London: Dance Books.

Smith-Autard, J. M. (2010) *Dance Composition* (6th edn), London: Methuen Drama.

Sofras, P. (2006) *Dance Composition Basics: Capturing the Choreographer's Craft*, Leeds: Human Kinetics.

REFERENCES

Batsheva (2015) *Home*, available: https://batsheva.co.il/en/home [accessed 20 June 2021].

Bogart, A. and Landau, T. (2004) *The Viewpoints Book: A Practical Guide to Viewpoints and Composition*, New York: Theatre Communications Group.

Butterworth, J. (2012) *Dance Studies: The Basics*, London: Routledge.

Butterworth, J. and Wildschut, L. eds (2018) *Contemporary Choreography: A Critical Reader* (2nd edn), Abingdon and New York: Routledge.

Cloud Gate Culture and Arts Foundation (2020) *Home*, available: www.cloudgate.org.tw/en/cg [accessed 4 June 2021].

Cloud Gate Foundation (2020) *Home*, available: https://archive.cloudgate.org.tw/ [accessed 5 June 2021].

Danse Danse (n.d.) *Dada Masilo/Dance Factory Johannesburg: Swan Lake*, available: www.dansedanse.ca/en/dada-masilo-dance-factory-johannesburg-dada-masilo-swan-lake [accessed 15 July 2021].

Emanuel Gat (n.d.) *About*, available: https://emanuelgatdance.com [accessed 17 July 2021].

Jowitt, D. (1985) *The Dance in Mind: Profiles and Reviews 1976–83*, Boston: David R. Godine Publisher.

Jowitt, D. (2010) 'A look back at the work of Alwin Nikolais', *The Village Voice*, available: www.villagevoice.com/2010/05/18/a-look-back-at-the-work-of-alwin-nikolais/ [accessed 20 May 2021].

Mark Morris Group (2021) *Mark Morris*, available: https://markmorrisdance group.org/the-dance-group/mark-morris/ [accessed 23 June 2021].

New Adventures Charity (2021) *Home*, available: https://new-adventures.net/# [accessed 20 June 2021].

Smith-Autard, J. M. (2000) *Dance Composition* (4th edn), London: Routledge.

The Dance Consortium (2012) *Mats Ek*, available: https://danceconsortium.com/features/choreographer/mats-ek/ [accessed 24 June 2021].

The National Ballet of Canada (n.d.) *Alexander Eckman*, available: https://national.ballet.ca/Meet/Creative-Team/Alexander-Ekman [accessed 15 May 2021].

Van Camp, J. (1992) 'Dance criticism by Croce, Denby, and Siegel', *Dance Research Journal*, 24(2): 41–44, available: https://web.csulb.edu/~jvancamp/article6.html [accessed 20 May 2021].

BROADER SKILLS A CHOREOGRAPHER NEEDS

In the previous chapter we explored the technical skills required to develop a piece of choreography. However, in order to be in the position to create and stage a piece of choreography in a professional context, there can be many more skills required of an emerging choreographer. Fortunately, undergraduate degree programmes are integrating these skills into their curricula, so that graduates are more prepared to encounter the complex world of professional dance. First let us look at the landscape that young choreographers will enter once they have graduated.

TWENTY-FIRST-CENTURY CHALLENGES

As it is a vibrant and dynamic art form, dance is continually impacted by external societal factors such as cultural trends, arts funding and attitudes towards embodiment. These elements shape how dance artists can realise their creative work and the challenges they may face in developing a career in this field. The following section creates a snapshot of these challenges and the various opportunities dance artists may encounter in present times.

Dance-making: the current landscape

Over the first two decades of the twenty-first century, the environment in which professional choreography takes place has evolved considerably. This context is continually changing and is in no small part dependent on the arts funding structures of the country in which the choreography is being produced. For example,

DOI: 10.4324/9781003020110-4

the New York dance scene which was a thriving ecosystem of choreographer-led companies in the 1980s, was negatively impacted by the changes to arts funding in the 1990s, resulting in job insecurity for dancers and choreographers for the following decades (Dittman 2008). Indeed, shifts in general employment conditions brought about by technological advancements and the information age, often referred to as 'the gig economy', could be said to have currently come into line with the working patterns of freelance dancers and choreographers. State funding bodies are more inclined to support one-off dance projects and individual artists than to support the operation of a full-time dance company. This has resulted in many dancers and choreographers working nomadically in order to avail themselves of the possibilities that are afforded through commissions, artistic residencies and funding grants as mentioned in Chapter 1 when discussing independent dance artists (Roche 2018). Many independent dancers are required to work with multiple choreographers on a range of short projects over the course of a year. This can mean that scheduling can be challenging and it is often difficult to prolong the life of a choreography once the initial performances are completed due to the complexity in ensuring the continued availability of the cast.

Although it is not unique to this period, artist-led collectives are a popular way of enabling the development of creative work outside the structure of a dance company and building a community of support to help navigate a competitive professional sector. A collective is when a group of independent dance artists join forces to create training and performance opportunities that may be difficult for the artists to achieve individually. These can move from informal operational structures to become more formalised over time. Examples are ProDance Leeds which offers training and mentorship for recent dance graduates, and Birmingham Dance Network which is run "by a team of independent dance artists with diverse portfolio careers spanning performance, teaching, community dance, choreography and more" who provide support for dance artists in navigating the "tough" industry of contemporary dance (Birmingham Dance Network n.d.).

Another important development in recent years is the 'dance house' which is usually state funded and works within a remit to support the development of dance, choreographic experimentation, production and training opportunities. Dance houses are normally situated in economic centres or capital cities and have multiple dance studios and perhaps a studio performance space. Many dancers and choreographers will position themselves close to these centres as they can offer daily classes and workshops, artist residencies (which include free or subsidised rehearsal space) and opportunities to showcase choreographic works in progress. The investment in this grassroots development of choreographic capabilities is essential to ensure that choreography as a field continues to renew itself and to respond to new voices that are emerging with views on contemporary life and current social issues. These early developments bear fruit through other schemes such as the European Dance House Network (EDN), involving 22 dance houses from 15 European countries to promote and support the work of emerging choreographers through residencies and production support. These various pathways offer stepping-stones to independent dance artists to develop their craft and build their profiles within the industry. These models in some way replace the large dance institutions such as state-run or established national dance companies that previously might have fostered choreographic talent.

The multi-faceted role of the choreographer

To manage the complexity of the dance industry, choreographers require a wide range of ancillary skills beyond merely the capacity to choreograph. These skills can often include writing funding applications, negotiating with venues/festivals, managing budgets, auditioning dancers, contracting artistic collaborators, designing sets/costumes, hiring technical crew, developing publicity strategies and reporting to funders and other stakeholders. Depending on the level of financial support available for a project, these duties can be absorbed by other contractors, however many choreographers maintain involvement and decision-making roles across these various areas and therefore need to have some awareness of how these different components contribute to the production of a dance piece. The freelance choreographer's role is considered highly entrepreneurial and produces organisational structures that are emblematic of the creative economy, described by Melanie Bales and Rebecca Nettl-Fiol (2008 p.viii) in their book *The Eclectic Body* as "smaller, less permanent organizations that mobilise around talent," rather than more institutionally established dance companies.

Self-promotion

The proliferation of social media means that choreographers must manage their online image and be comfortable with promoting various creative activities to a broad public via the internet. In the early stages of a career, perhaps before they can garner support for these activities from other sources, choreographers will normally need to be competent in web design, creating online content to promote their work and writing promotional material for various marketing outlets. They may require video-editing skills to produce video trailers of their work, to promote it to programmers and to show samples of their work for funding applications. Overall, this requires a comprehensive approach to branding their creative work, or more accurately, to becoming a 'brand', so that they can start to build greater profile and gain more opportunities and support for developing their career. Engaging with social media on a regular basis is central to self-promotion in the arts. Whereas in previous decades, choreographic projects would create print materials, such as posters and flyers to promote their performances, increasingly marketing plans are centred on social media as a means of publicising the work. This means that a choreographer will need to develop a profile on social media that can be activated around an upcoming production. Since the beginning of the COVID-19 pandemic, this has become even more vital as many performances are live streamed online, rather than performed in front of a live audience. The quality of the materials presented through online platforms is especially important. Contemporary audiences are increasingly media savvy, and are used to viewing high quality images as well as responding to cleverly composed 'informal' footage from cast interviews or rehearsals. All of these complex elements mean that choreographers are rarely merely involved in just 'making dance steps'. The role requires an overarching vision, that can carry a project from inception through to performance and beyond. While the dancemaking process has become more democratic, in how dancers contribute creatively to the work, the choreographer must establish and maintain responsibility for the creative framework through which the dance piece is realised, so that all contributions can come together to manifest this particular vision. This extends to how the work may be publicised and the visual impact of all materials that are in the public domain.

Transferability of skills

As outlined in Chapter 1, beyond the professional dance sector, choreographers may work across a variety of contexts which require them to develop various other skills. For example, they may work in the professional dance world on their own projects or as part of a creative team in opera or theatre productions. Equally, they may be involved in site-specific or community-based environments, arts and health contexts or in collaborative, interdisciplinary projects working across various media platforms. They may also work as choreographers or teachers in the educational sector. These contexts may require them to work collaboratively with a team of other artists, or indeed with various public or private bodies (as with community-based projects, for example). A central skill required to manage these various contexts is the ability to transfer their skills as required in order to be sufficiently flexible to adapt to any challenges that might arise in each new environment. While many of these skills are developed over time and through experience, training institutions are taking into consideration the need for curricula to include them as part of a rounded dance education to make graduates more prepared for employment in the professional dance sector and applied fields. This is explored in more detail later in this chapter.

Structures of choreographic projects

As we touched on in Chapter 1, independents or independent dance artists now make up a considerable number of choreographers in the dance sector. Emilyn Claid (2006, p.133) defines the "independent dance culture" as "a framework for artists who direct, choreograph and perform their own project-based work independent of institutional companies and systems."

Independent dance practice varies from country to country often influenced by the funding structures of the context in which it operates (Roche 2018). As outlined above, this means that independent or freelance choreographers may work in various ways, depending on the project and how it is resourced. Even well-known choreographers may work sporadically between their creative projects, teaching and other paid employment which can come from other sources than dance.

So how might a regular mid-scale project be structured?

When working outside a dance company structure, choreographers can develop creative projects through a range of different pathways. To start a project, you will usually need funding to pay for rehearsal space, dancers, creative collaborators and production costs. Many festivals and venues will support the development and performance of new work either through cash support to pay artistic and production fees or through providing resources such as rehearsal/performance spaces and/or marketing. In many countries, government funding bodies such as arts councils or national endowments for the arts will support projects through an application process. The application forms usually require you to describe the project you are planning, the creative goals, the practical details such as venues and number of performances as well as all the personnel involved. You will also be required to give samples of previous work and a detailed budget that outlines all expenditure and income. Furthermore, you are often required to bring funding or in-kind support from other sources. This means that you need to develop partnerships with a range of different people and organisations. Many choreographers begin their professional work in this way, building up the scale and profile of their careers until they can access increased support for their productions. At the higher end of the spectrum, choreographers can receive large commissions or co-producing funding from various state bodies, venues or festivals to produce a new piece of choreography.

In a mid-scale dance project, four to six dancers might be brought together by a choreographer to develop a piece of choreography. As most of the dance movement is constructed throughout this process, the dancers and choreographers will work intensively to create the movement ideas, refine and rehearse them and then bring them to performance standard over several weeks. As outlined in previous sections, the processes of making will usually incorporate many creative contributions from the dancers, whose experiences can inform how the work develops. As these projects afford little time for working together, many choreographers struggle to develop distinctive movement languages in the same way that a choreographer with an ensemble may be able to achieve over time. Laurence Louppe (1996) describes how seminal choreographers such as Merce Cunningham, Pina Bausch and Martha Graham were able to develop distinctive and original choreographic styles because they worked with a stable ensemble of dancers throughout their careers. This is a luxury rarely afforded to choreographers in the twenty-first century, who often move between various working environments and must learn how to translate their movement ideas clearly and succinctly to new dancers over a brief period of time. Being able to communicate your ideas can be key to the success of a creative process.

Even very established choreographers do not always work with a stable ensemble of dancers. For example, Akram Khan will work with different casts of dancers for different productions. His work moves from small casts to larger groups, and like many well-established choreographers he may audition new casts of dancers for a particular production. This is not to say that choreographers and dancers do not work together over a number of choreographic projects but the challenges of freelance or independent working practices mean that it can be difficult for artists to commit to work together beyond the bounds of individual projects.

How do choreographers build their profile over time?

Many choreographers make work on the basis of a commission from a repertoire company or festival, for example, with funding provided through a series of partnerships. There are funding and presenting networks that allow choreographers to build on existing successes to grow the profile and performance opportunities of a particular dance piece.

Exemplar 1 – Oona Doherty and Reggie Gray

An example of the development of a choreographer's profile is the choreography *Hope Hunt* (2016) by Belfast born choreographer Oona Doherty. This work was presented in Dublin Fringe Festival in 2016, for which Doherty won best performer. Subsequently this work was chosen for the Aerowaves platform which is a showcase for emerging choreographic talent in Europe, founded in 1996 by John Ashford, then director at the Place Theatre, London (Aerowaves n.d.). With partners in 33 countries, Aerowaves nurtures and profiles new choreographic talent by presenting new works in the various partner countries. This can build a choreographer's international profile and open them to new opportunities for their work. Doherty went on to win further accolades for *Hope Hunt* including at the Edinburgh Fringe Festival (2017) and these successes led to the production of larger choreographic works, increased funding and commissions, including from Ballet Nationale de Marseille to create the piece *Lazarus* (2021) (Oona Doherty n.d.). This trajectory of a young choreographer demonstrates how essential producing partnerships, showcase opportunities and seed funding for choreographic experimentation are for the establishment of a career pathway in choreography.

Khan and Doherty demonstrate the reality of the entrepreneurial choreographer outlined above by Bales and Nettl-Fiol (2008), who develops a choreographic career outside of a fixed company structure. For both Doherty and Khan, their career trajectories have developed in professional training institutions in the UK (London Contemporary Dance School and Northern School of Contemporary Dance respectively) and along development pathways supported via public funding for the arts. There are other ways for choreographers to develop a career pathway, such as New York choreographer Reggie Gray who did not receive formal dance training but went on to develop a new genre of dance called Flex which led to an internationally performed production entitled *Flexn*.

A collaboration between renowned theatre director Peter Sellars and Gray, commissioned by Park Avenue Armory in New York, *Flexn* is a dance production that uses the vocabulary of the street dance form Flex, which "evolved from the Jamaican bruk-up found in dance halls and reggae clubs in Brooklyn," to tell the stories of the cast of dancers (Park Avenue Armory 2015). First performed in 2015 in the Park Avenue Armory, the publicity from the production describes it in the following way,

> Characterized by pausing, snapping, gliding, bone breaking, hat tricks, animation, and contortion… this electrifying phenomenon is showcased at the Armory in a new project that confronts issues of social injustice, with the dancers exploring personal narratives through their own unique movement vocabulary in post-modern dance.
> (Park Avenue Armory 2015)

Gray developed the dance form Flex, starting his own dance team called Hyperactive while in high school, going on to win many dance competitions and also performing for music videos, reality competitions and television (Sierra 2015). While the source movement vocabulary is Flex, the piece is drawn together in a theatrical performance context to speak to a wider audience on many of the social injustices faced by African American people through the justice system. *Flexn* was the largest production he had developed at that stage in his career and was a highly successful production that toured to major arts festivals internationally.

Marketing the choreographer

Choreographers developing their career pathway must become adept at managing the complexities of the arts marketplace to build networks and connections that may yield essential opportunities for their development. While choreographers may acknowledge the creative input of the dancers involved in their projects, to market themselves they may be required to cultivate an identity of a singular artist with a signature style and vision. In recent years, there has been more awareness of the collaborative process of making choreography as outlined in Chapter 2. Annie Kloppenberg (2010, p.189) identifies this as "post-control choreography" which draws heavily on the creative investigations of the dancers through improvisation to create choreography that will ultimately be set into a fixed form. Kloppenberg (2010) describes this as an opportunity for the choreographer to let go of controlling the whole work and to allow the dancers' agency to contribute to shaping the choreography. While the dance marketplace maintains the sense of signature choreographers (arguably, to effectively market a choreographer's work), in academic research there has been increased investigation into dancers' contributions to the choreographic process. This situation challenges the idea of singular authorship resting with the choreographer but has not impacted greatly on public or commercial perspectives of dancemaking.

Movement training for innovations in choreographic practice

In Chapter 2 you will have encountered perspectives that help you create choreography. Preparing the body to work creatively in dance is important because the daily training you practice can significantly influence the way you move and the kind of choreography you develop. Foster (1992, p.482) writes about this issue in her article *Dancing Bodies*, when she explains "the daily practical participation of a body in any of these disciplines makes of it a body-of-ideas." This was highlighted in Chapter 2 through the discussion of William Forsythe and Ohad Naharin's development of specific movement approaches. As mentioned above, the shift in practices of dancemaking has destabilised the canonical techniques developed through the modern dance era, such as Graham, Cunningham and Limon. Many of these early choreographic styles spawned dance techniques that have been widely used in the training of dancers and as a fundamental movement vocabulary in choreographing dances. However, perhaps due to the proliferation of many different choreographic languages and approaches to making dance, education and training in movement vocabularies has started to include new techniques which are less focussed on the form of the movement than the ethos behind it, such as Contact Improvisation, Release Technique, Urban Contemporary, Gaga, Countertechnique and Flying Low. As choreographers require dancers to be more inventive in their responses to choreographic tasks in the creative process, dance training in many contexts has shifted towards fostering individualism in dancers' personal movement styles. In the next section, we will explore some of these in more detail.

Gaga

There have been many challenges in how best to train dancers for working in twenty-first-century choreographic contexts, noted in Bales and Nettl-Fiol (2008, p.1) as "the apparent disjunction between technique training and performing or choreography." Consequently, a number of movement approaches have emerged to address this disjuncture, for example Gaga, developed by Ohad Naharin, Artistic Director of Batsheva Dance Company. As outlined in Chapter 2, Gaga was initiated by Naharin primarily to prepare his dancers to work on his choreography, however simultaneously he developed a system for non-dancers resulting in two strands – one for dancers and one for 'people'. Deborah Friedes Galili (2015, p.360), a teacher in this approach, identified Gaga as one solution to the following question: "For those dancers freelancing with multiple choreographers, what training will support the diverse array of styles that they already must grasp?" Gaga is not considered to be a technique nor a method for training novice dancers but an approach to be used "in tandem" with techniques dancers have studied in other contexts as a means of "enhancing" their movement explorations and understanding as well as their "artistic practice" (Friedes Galili 2015, pp.377–378). Therefore, Naharin classifies Gaga as a developing process of movement research. It functions as a means to maintain fitness, extend movement range, address unwanted movement habits and increase creative decision-making in movement. Naharin describes the approach as pushing the dancer beyond their usual limits, to discover new ways to build strength and support and to improve "coordination and efficiency of movement" (Naharin in Friedes Galili 2015, p.384).

> The dancer has to get more explosive, be more stretched, be [quicker], be more developed in [their] multidimensional movement and coordination… and also to be more sensitive,… to find the connection between the dancer's demons and creative force and the power of imagination.
> (Naharin in Friedes Galili 2015, p.384)

Gaga is taught widely on an international basis and can be included in undergraduate or pre-professional training as a regular part of the curriculum or through guest residencies. For example, the Harvard Dance Centre at Harvard University offers courses in Gaga for university credit (Siliezar 2019).

Urban contemporary/Hip Hop

In recent years, urban contemporary, drawing from Hip Hop dance influences, has emerged as a training form in European contexts as well as in the US. In France, for example, Hip Hop dance forms became more prevalent in popular culture in the 1980s and "were taken up first in suburban and immigrant communities, becoming a forum for debate on assimilation and multiculturalism" (McCarren 2013, p.xii). As Hip Hop has developed into "a form of concert dance" and was supported by political and cultural institutions at local and national level, "with master classes given in state-funded dance centers, performances on big 'national stages', and companies touring in France and overseas" (McCarren 2013, p.xv), the dance form has entered the dance training systems in certain contexts as a training technique. It must be noted that the development of this dance form in Europe has differed considerably from its origins in African American culture, in line with the different trajectory and legacies of African immigration in France, for example. The work of Company Käfig, founded by choreographer/dancer Mourad Merzouki, is notable in the French context.

Contemporary urban features as one of the two strands of dancer training at Fontys Dance Academie in The Netherlands alongside contemporary dance. While many of the core training elements are shared, there are differences in approach across the two strands. In the US, Hip Hop dance technique is an important element of many dance programmes, for example Sarah Lawrence College (US), where it sits alongside ballet and West African dance as part of the educational offering. When Hip Hop dance is taught on dance programmes, it is often contextualised through teaching about the history and social impact of the dance form.

Flying Low and Passing Through

As mentioned in Chapter 2, Flying Low is a movement approach developed by Venezuelan choreographer/dancer David Zambrano, which alongside his practice Passing Through has gained popularity as a training approach for contemporary dancers. The origin of Flying Low according to Zambrano was a response to severe injury in the choreographer's twenties when he was required to reassess his relationship to dance training. In this time, he integrated principles from other movement approaches such as Kung Fu to create a system that plays with altered relationships to verticality in dance (Davidzambrano.org n.d.). One of the distinctive aspects of this movement approach is that it develops a more seamless relationship to going in and out of the floor, which is the main focus of the approach, leading to more versatility in developing choreographic movement. Zambrano explains that his class,

> ... utilizes simple movement patterns that involve breathing, speed and the release of energy throughout the body in order to activate the relationship between the center and the joints, moving in and out of the ground more efficiently by maintaining a centered state. ... The body is constantly spiraling, whether running or standing.
>
> (David Zambrano n.d.)

Flying Low classes draw on these spirals to facilitate the movement in and out of the floor through creative and innovative solutions.

Passing Through is another movement approach developed by Zambrano as a means of strengthening awareness of group interaction in improvisation. Sarco-Thomas (2016, p.6) outlines the key principles of this approach which hones "spatial imagination" for the participants to work at "high speeds in limited space to see what creative escape patterns can be generated." This approach is particularly useful in developing group choreography through supporting dancers to become aware of the shapes they are forming in relationship to the space around them. In Passing Through, there is an ongoing focus on adjusting your movement in-the-moment to respond and align with the movement of others in the space. Sarco-Thomas (2016, p.6) explains how the workshop supports the group to navigate around each other in a safe manner,

> Zambrano emphasises a constantly circulating awareness. ... By training to move in spirals, in stillnesses that take their balance from a continual readiness to move, and in running, rolling and jumping in every direction, the dancer can guide

herself creatively through the changing pattern of movement among others.

Countertechnique

Developed by Dutch dancer and choreographer Anouk van Dijk through the Independent dance scene in Holland in the 1980s, Countertechnique is a popular training method for dancers that opens up possibilities for choreographic exploration. The principles of Countertechnique are supported by Alexander Technique, working with the body's skeleton and muscularity to seek functional body movement, it works with the assumption that:

> when dancing, the weight—or the weight of a body part—falls out of the central axis. This weight becomes available for movement. In order to neither collapse nor grip, a counter direction is called upon that will enable freedom and help retain control while moving.
> (Siegmund and Van Dijk 2011, pp.67–68)

With Countertechnique, Van Dijk sought to create a movement system that prepared dancers for creative practice in devising and rehearsing choreography. Rather than a style, it is an approach to training dancing bodies for professional work regardless of the particular aesthetic of the choreography they are dancing (Siegmund and Van Dijk 2011). Relationship to space and to other dancers in the studio are focused upon in Countertechnique, building the dancer's capacity to be responsive to the changing social space of the dance studio (Siegmund and Van Dijk 2011).

These four examples show a move away from the more established Western theatre dance training techniques to augment creativity for dancers in generating movement as part of the dancemaking process. They contrast in many ways with the staple dance training techniques of ballet, Graham or Cunningham techniques, most notably because they do not emphasise a specific form that must be achieved but impart a series of principles that can be applied to the individual's own body. Furthermore, they are becoming more established as training approaches internationally. For example, Flying Low and Passing Through are taught by

Zambrano at the prestigious P.A.R.T.S. dance training institution in Brussels, Belgium (P.A.R.T.S n.d.).

Decolonizing the curriculum

There is another important move in dance training to de-colonize the curriculum by addressing the colonial underpinnings of the notion that ballet and contemporary dance should be the main stalwarts of technical training for dancers, in contrast to recognizing the diverse origins and practices of dance at a global level. While we have outlined a truly diverse dance culture that integrates many traditional forms, dance training has been and continues to be extremely homogenized within institutional contexts worldwide. Therefore, many dance institutions have sought to address this imbalance by including dance forms such as Kathak Dance, Hip Hop, Japanese Butoh, Brazilian Capoeira and West African Dance as part of a more rounded undergraduate dance education.

However, while African dances, for example, have been taught more readily in dance institutions, Alfdaniels Mabingo (2015) explains that many of the core structures of these dance forms can become distorted when taught within Western pedagogical paradigms. He describes these as:

> … Western quantitative assessment methods, theoretical frameworks, archival and digital recording and dissemination of information, formal classroom management strategies, structured feedback provision tools, and technologically driven teaching aids…
>
> (Mabingo 2015, p.133)

These Western approaches can distort the specific pedagogical and cultural ethos underpinning African dance forms. Therefore, in order to ensure that there is an alignment with this original ethos, Mabingo (2015) presents a model that focuses on imparting contextual information about each dance, why it is performed, who performs it and its relationship to the heritage, cultural life and history of the people who usually dance it. Furthermore, he focuses on the interrelation between dancers and how they would interact together, alongside exploration of "polyrhythmic postural and gestural movements" and basic footwork as a foundation of the dances (Mabingo 2015, p.138). Significantly, Mabingo (2015, p.139) emphasises the importance of a culturally responsive engagement with dance for "teachers of non-Western dance forms." Institutional dance training is always in danger of diluting some of the potency of individual dance traditions and styles as they become regulated through the structures of the institution. Additionally, many dance approaches can lose their radical power of innovation, dissent and rebellion when formalised into one part of a larger curriculum. Therefore, Mabingo's attention to culturally responsive teaching is vital across all areas of dance teaching, so that students understand the origins and essential ethos of the material they are encountering.

Entrepreneurial training supports

If you undertake preprofessional dance training within an academic or vocational institution, it is likely that you will learn a range of associated skills to support your development as a dance practitioner. It is understood that dancers and choreographers need to be entrepreneurial in their approach and often are required to construct employment opportunities for themselves. While, arguably, artists have always had to think in these ways, the circulation of information enabled by the internet and social media provides unique pressures for how dance artists can represent themselves, access opportunities, create and maintain working networks and disseminate their work broadly.

What does an entrepreneurial approach mean within a dance context?

While the term 'entrepreneur' originates from the business world and generally refers to an astute business-person who creates a business out of a need they have identified in the marketplace, in this context it is entrepreneurial qualities that dancers and choreographers must cultivate (Duffy 2021). In her publication *Careers in Dance*, Duffy (2021, p.18) outlines some of these qualities, stating that "successful entrepreneurs are most often described as creative, self-confident, knowledge-seeking, purpose-driven, risk-taking, resilient and adaptable." Further qualities that are particular to the creative economy, according to Duffy (2021) include tenacity, openness, perseverance, and the ability to network, collaborate and problem-solve. Finally, success in the dance world requires good time-management and the capacity to manage uncertainty (Duffy 2021). Successful choreographers possess many if not all of these qualities as they navigate an unstructured career path, that is rarely laid out in front of them as a clear series of progressions from one step to the next. In this way, they are required to be lifelong learners (Duffy 2021) as they navigate what can be described as a portfolio career (McWilliam et al. 2006). The portfolio career which evolves over a lifetime and requires a great deal of adaptability impacts on student learning in the following way:

> … they will need to 'unlearn' certain practices and processes at the same time that they learn and embrace others. Getting the mix of learning and unlearning right will be more important for new generations of learners than merely sticking to time-honoured habits that mark a former stable social world.
> (McWilliam et al. 2006, p.25)

This approach to learning is increasingly embedded in dance training programmes, replacing older traditional models of teaching in dance that evolved through ballet academies and the conservatoire or conservatory approach to arts education. As Duffy (2021, p.14) explains, "conservatory settings are different from other institutions in that they prioritize training students specifically for careers in professional performance," often with a focus on technical training rather than the range of other skills that may be needed to navigate a more varied career path outside large performance institutions, such as ballet companies. Students in tertiary education need to have opportunities to foster the kind of entrepreneurial qualities outlined above and to develop their individual creative ideas, approaches and preferences to ensure they are equipped to be successful within a highly competitive field such as choreography.

Networking and producing

A key skill that must be developed in the current employment context is networking. This takes the form of developing professional networks through participating in public classes, attending performances and working on various projects alongside the promotion of your creative work to a wider audience. The elements that go into developing a successful career profile include professional comportment among other things. Being polite, on time and helpful under pressure can significantly enhance the quality and longevity of your professional relationships. Equally, it is important to be a good communicator in person and in other modes, such as via email (Duffy 2021). Additionally, many choreographers will need to communicate with large institutions such as dance and theatre companies, festivals, funding bodies and professional agencies. Therefore, learning to write a well-composed letter or email is important, as well as writing a well-structured and professional funding application. How you interact in these contexts will contribute significantly to your profile in the professional world and can greatly enhance or damage your career opportunities. Finally, the planning for and realisation of dance projects will require some ability to manage finances. This includes designing a realistic and appropriate budget for your project, including payment for all artistic and technical staff as well as any other costs such as dance studio rental, costumes and advertising/marketing budgets. While many freelance choreographers work with producers to manage these aspects of a project, often at the early part of a choreographer's career, they will be required to do some or all of this work.

Dance skills applied to other careers

As outlined earlier on in the chapter, there is a range of ancillary skills cultivated by dancers in training that are very useful when applied across other contexts. Some of the personal attributes underlying these skills are flexibility and openness, resourcefulness, resilience, professionalism, self-motivation, curiosity and willingness to learn. While many students entering dance training hope to be professional dancers and choreographers, during training they may decide not to pursue this career professionally after all and become interested in other dance related areas. One Dance UK (2017), a support organization for dance, has outlined the various potential applications of these skills and attributes developed during a dance degree or after retirement from a professional career. They explain: "Once you have developed key skills such as discipline, motivation, creativity and team work your dance craft can be applied creatively in many ways."

One Dance UK (2017, p.26) identify a broad range of careers in dance that may result from dance training alongside that of professional dancer or choreographer, these could be, "… Community Dance Practitioner, Costume/Set Designer, Dance/Arts/Culture Officer… Dance Movement Therapist, Dance Journalist, Dance Lecturer or Academic Researcher, Dance Photographer… Dance Producer… Dance Teacher, Lighting Designer," among many others involving related fields such as Dance Science or Yoga/Pilates instructor. Dance training imparts a range of transferrable skills that can be directed into other careers, that can develop from or co-exist with a career in dance.

Reflective practice and feedback

As outlined in Chapter 2, students study various tools and techniques for constructing choreography. In addition to in-class training, many dance programmes give students opportunities to create choreography on each other and to perform this in semi-professional environments. Project-based assignments, where students must develop their own choreographic tasks, can become increasingly complex as they cycle through undergraduate training and often culminate in the creation of significant pieces of original choreographic work. Through the practice of making dances, young choreographers must develop many soft skills such as interpersonal dialogue, self-reflection and organisation. Reflective Practice is an area that has been increasingly identified as significant for learning in the arts. This topic is further explored in Chapter 5 in relation to academic study and practice as research. In this section we explore its relevance for self-reflection and in giving and receiving feedback – an important skill to learn in order to develop resilience as a choreographer. Artists are naturally reflective in their approaches. As artist/scholars Brad Haseman and Dan Mafe explain,

> reflexivity is one of those 'artist-like processes' which occurs when a creative practitioner acts upon the requisite research material to generate new material which immediately acts back upon the practitioner who is in turn stimulated to make a subsequent response.
>
> (Haseman and Mafe 2009, p.219)

Reflection

Reflection is extremely important in our cycles of learning and impacts on any projects we engage in. Some key benefits from reflection are: metacognition – the ability to think about our own learning processes; developing criticality – being able to look more objectively at certain activities; making considered decisions; developing ourselves as individuals; developing our own theories from experience and being able to "empower or emancipate ourselves as individuals," or as members of a particular social group (Moon 1999, p.23).

Often university programmes actively engage in reflective process through written and practical assignments. These tools are very important for choreographers in the development of their skills over time. Drawing on Kolb's experiential learning cycle, Graham Gibbs defined reflective practice as a cyclical process, that allows the practitioner to keep building on past experience to hone their skills within their field of operation. Watton, Collings and Moon (2001, p.5) summarise this as a cycle through the following stages: "Description… Feelings… Evaluation… Analysis… Conclusions (general)… (specific)… [and finally] Personal action plans." The first stage encourages you to **describe** the phenomenon you are going to reflect on followed by gathering a sense of your own reaction to this and how it made you **feel**. Next you can start to **evaluate** the positive and negative aspects of the experience, before drawing an **analysis** through a more objective viewpoint about the situation. You are then in a position to draw **general** (more universal) and **specific** (to you) **conclusions** from the experience to create a **personal action plan** which integrates and activates your newfound knowledge when you encounter a similar situation in the future (Watton, Collings and Moon 2001).

The use of blogs and journalling have become more prevalent in undergraduate studies as a means of eliciting reflective practice. These tools support students to develop their own opinions and ideas, track their progress and the process of learning and make connections across different aspects of the learning experience. Particularly in the field of dance where many of the experiences are not articulated through language, reflective practice can be very important in bringing insights on learning experiences to the surface.

Critical thinking is another essential aspect to undergraduate study and is particularly important when addressing the political and social implications of creating dance. Areas that support this enquiry are gender studies, sexual politics, identity politics, racial justice and critical theory (see Chapter 5).

Liz Lerman's Critical Response Process

A popular approach that was developed by Liz Lerman to foster critical and reflective peer response for dance is the *Critical Response Process*. This system is used widely as a means of fostering informed and constructive critique, inspired by Lerman's wish to move beyond what she observed as two ends of a spectrum in the critiquing of dance work. Lerman identified that "critiques coming from those who had the privilege of holding forth – teachers, elders, critics – often felt like attacks, attacks imbued with a passion that seemed intimately connected with the aesthetic values of the beholder" (Lerman and Borstel 2003, Loc 56). At the other end of the spectrum was the feedback delivered by peers, which "often failed to move beyond cheerleading to any kind of useful comment" (Lerman and Borstel 2003, Loc 56). The *Critical Response Process* identifies three roles within the exchange – the artist who is showing the work, the responder(s) giving feedback on the work and the facilitator who mediates this interaction (Lerman and Borstel, 2003). There are four key steps to the process, *Statements of Meaning*, *Artist as Questioner*, *Neutral Questions from Responders*, and *Permissioned Opinions* (Kearns 2017).

The first step, *Statements of Meaning*, acknowledges that all creative works, even in their early stages embody the desire from the artist to communicate something of meaning to the viewer. Therefore, the first questions that the facilitators will ask to the responders will be related to what is meaningful for them and what may have touched them or surprised them (Lerman and Borstel 2003). Different descriptive words are used here and generally the responder is invited to be constructive and positive when considering this question. The second step, *Artist as Questioner*, is where the artist is supported to ask specific questions about the work which may range from broader questions on its overall impact to more particular challenges they are working through in the creative process. Questions that might be asked in this step would relate to particular moments, such as transitions between ideas or whether a particular feeling they are trying to express was experienced by the viewer (Lerman and Borstel 2003). The next step, *Neutral Questions from Responders*, is for the responders to ask the artist "informational or factual questions" (Lerman and Borstel 2003, Loc 259) about the work. In this stage there is an important distinction made between a neutral question and an opinion, so that the question remains open-ended and does not have an underlying value judgement within it. The final step, *Permissioned Opinions*, is when the responders are invited to give opinions by the facilitator while adhering to a particular set protocol. This is presented in the following way, "I have an opinion about the costumes. Do you want to hear it?" (Lerman and Borstel 2003, Loc 292) This gives the artist the opportunity to hear the opinion or not. In the case where they have heard enough about a particular issue or they have not been focusing on costumes, for example, this allows the direction of the discussion to be pointed towards the most useful areas for the artist.

The *Critical Response Process* allows the interaction between artist and responder to move beyond the normal defensiveness that can arise when artists are given feedback on their work. As showing creative work often exposes vulnerabilities, this process can allow the artist to feel somewhat protected from the subjective opinions of the responders, which can often be a matter of personal taste and therefore may not be particularly useful to hear for progressing the work further. The approach requires all participants to think more critically and take ownership of these personal tastes and predilections, so that the critique is truly constructive. According to Kearns (2017, p.273), the significance of Lerman's method to the professional dance world lies in how

> ... it reflects the discipline's emphasis on the individual creative process and empowering the choreographer as a type of author. It further exemplifies the shifting of agency from the external audience member back to the dance artist, an important aspect of the contemporary dance field.

Many undergraduate choreography classes utilise this method or adaptations of it to foster critical thinking, reflection and positive peer exchange between students.

Larry Lavender's ORDER as a feedback method

Another highly useful approach is Larry Lavender's ORDER which stands for *Observation, Reflection, Discussion, Evaluation, and Revision* (Lavender 1996). *Observation* involves developing the students' openness in perceiving dance. This includes remaining open-minded when viewing work, focusing fully on viewing and being willing to watch without making assumptions. *Reflection* utilises reflective writing after viewing as a means of distilling the observations and noticing important elements of the work, such as choreographic patterning and how certain moments relate to the larger arc of ideas. *Discussion* involves sharing reflective descriptions and analysis, which pertain to the aspects of the work that is visible to the viewer (as opposed to making assumptions about the intention or state of mind of the choreographer). Within this mode is the opportunity for the viewer's interpretation and meaning-making about the work. *Evaluation* in this context relies on reasons that are situated in clear observations of what took place in the work. Students through this approach should be supported to understand the source of certain judgements about a piece of work and that a subjective response is more useful when drawn from a critical evaluation that can give substantive reasons for this view. In this approach, the final stage, *Revision*, should take place only after the previous stages have been moved through and the choreographer has a sense of what elements were effective for the viewers and what parts could do with more development. The emphasis here is not on correcting the dance but to apply 'critical evaluations' that might help with improving certain aspects, as Kearns (2017, p.274) explains,

> Recommending revisions is vastly different than trying to fix the dance. Lavender emphasizes the aim of this stage is to guide continued creative exploration and problem solving rather than to dictate choreographic choice. This tactic encourages a deepening of the choreographer's artistic and aesthetic development.

These two methods for critiquing choreography attest to the significant role of reflective practice and critical thinking in the creative process. They are useful in developing more sophisticated and helpful feedback processes within dance peer groups and communities so that choreographers can benefit from feedback and apply it constructively to their creative practice. This builds individual resilience, so that choreographers can learn to take on criticism constructively without becoming disheartened.

SUMMARY

This chapter spans the range of additional skills that choreographers need to navigate an unpredictable working environment. By exploring the current context in which choreographers make work, it highlights the challenges and opportunities that this particular landscape provides. The chapter outlines the prevalent model of choreographic projects that operate in the current arts climate, explaining how the model of dance companies led by a signature choreographer have declined in recent years. Charting the rise of the independent dance scene, supported by dance houses that provide residency opportunities and produce work from independent choreographers, this section explains that this has led to smaller, short-term companies that come together for a particular project.

The chapter describes various structures through which choreographers make work, the skills needed to develop a career path as a choreographer, some of the training approaches that are fostering choreographic innovation and the methods of reflection that are useful for developing a choreographic practice and forging a community of peer engagement. It gives examples of how undergraduate dance programmes address the need for entrepreneurship and help emerging choreographers to become more employable and to build a portfolio career. This is achieved through teaching skills in writing funding applications, project-based learning, business studies, dance in other fields such as health and community practice, teaching dance and managing social media profiles among other subjects. Dance programmes also build resilience through honing reflective practice skills and helping dance artists to create supportive infrastructures and networks in which they can develop and perform their work. A few of these approaches are explored to show how constructive reflection and feedback are essential to build criticality, aesthetic judgement and resilience in this challenging working environment.

FURTHER READING

Bales, M. and Nettl-Fiol, R. eds (2008) *The Body Eclectic: Evolving Practices in Dance Training*, Urbana and Chicago: University of Illinois Press.

Duffy, A. (2021) *Careers in Dance: Practical and Strategic Guidance From the Field*, Champaign: Human Kinetics.

Lerman, L. and Borstel, J. (2003) *Liz Lerman's Critical Response Process: A Method for Getting Useful Feedback on Anything You Make, From Dance to Dessert*, Takoma Park: Dance Exchange, Inc.

REFERENCES

Aerowaves (n.d.) *About*, available: https://aerowaves.org/about-us/ [accessed 16 July 2021].

Bales, M. and Nettl-Fiol, R. eds (2008) *The Body Eclectic: Evolving Practices in Dance Training*, Urbana and Chicago: University of Illinois Press.

Birmingham Dance Network (n.d.) *About*, available: https://birminghamdancenetwork.co.uk/about/ [accessed 16 July 2021].

Claid, E. (2006) *Yes? No! Maybe… Seductive Ambiguity in Dance*, Abingdon and New York: Routledge.

David Zambrano (n.d.) *Teaching*, available: www.davidzambrano.org [accessed 25 June 2020].

Dittman, V. (2008) 'A New York dancer', in Bales, M. and Nettl-Fiol, R., eds, *The Body Eclectic: Evolving Practices in Dance Training*, Urbana and Chicago: University of Illinois Press.

Duffy, A. (2021) *Careers in Dance: Practical and Strategic Guidance From the Field*, Champaign: Human Kinetics.

Foster, S. (1992) 'Dancing bodies', in Crary, J. and Kwinter, S., eds, *Incorporations*, New York: Zone 6, 480–495.

Friedes Galili, D. (2015) 'Gaga: moving beyond technique with Ohad Naharin in the twenty-first century', *Dance Chronicle*, 38(3), 360–392.

Haseman, B. and Mafe, D. (2009) 'Acquiring know-how: research training for practice-led researchers', in Smith, H. and Dean, R., eds, *Practice-led Research, Research-led Practice in the Creative Arts*, Edinburgh: Edinburgh University Press.

Kearns, L. (2017) 'Dance critique as signature pedagogy', *Arts and Humanities in Higher Education*, 16 (3), 266–276.

Kloppenberg, A. (2010) 'Improvisation in process: "post-control" choreography', *Dance Chronicle*, 33 (2), 180–207.

Lavender, L. (1996) *Dancers Talking Dance: Critical Evaluations in the Choreography Class*, Champaign: Human Kinetics.

Lerman, L. and Borstel, J. (2003) *Liz Lerman's Critical Response Process: A Method for Getting Useful Feedback on Anything You Make, From Dance to Dessert*, Takoma Park: Dance Exchange, Inc.

Louppe, L. (1996) 'Hybrid bodies', *Writings on Dance*, 15, 63–67.

Mabingo, A. (2015) 'Decolonizing dance pedagogy: application of pedagogies of Ugandan traditional dances in formal dance education', *Journal of Dance Education*, 15(4), 131–141.

McCarren, F. (2013) *French Moves: The Cultural Politics of Le Hip Hop*, New York: Oxford University Press.

McWilliam, E., Carey, G., Draper, P. and Lebler, D. 2006. 'Learning and unlearning: new challenges for teaching in conservatoires', *Australian Journal of Music Education*, 1, 25–31, available: https://search.informit.org/doi/10.3316/informit.675891806633112 [accessed 10 February 2022].

Moon, J. (1999) *Learning Journals: A Handbook for Academics, Students and Professional Development*, London: Kogan Page.

One Dance UK (2017) 'Guide to careers in dance: championing dance for all young people', available: www.onedanceuk.org/wp-content/uploads/2017/02/Careers-Guide-Digital-version.pdf [accessed 25 June 2020].

Oona Doherty (n.d.) *Hope Hunt and The Ascension in Lazarus*, available: www.oonadohertyweb.com/ [accessed 12 July 2021].

Park Avenue Armory (2015) *Flexn*, available: www.armoryonpark.org/mobile/event_detail/flexn/#Details [accessed 26 June 2020].

P.A.R.T.S. (n.d.) *About*, available: www.parts.be/about [accessed 25 June 2020].

Roche, J. (2018) 'Dancing strategies and moving identities: the contributions independent contemporary dancers make to the choreographic process', in Butterworth, J. and Wildschut, L., eds, *Contemporary Choreography: A Critical Reader* (2nd edn), Abingdon and New York: Routledge.

Sarco-Thomas, M. (2016) 'Spacings: interactive imaginations in dance improvisations', presented at School of Performing Arts Conference: 21st Century Performance and Research, University of Malta.

Siegmund, G. and Van Dijk, A. (2011) 'Introduction: the difficulty of running', in Diehl, I. and Lampert, F., eds, *Dance Techniques 2010: Tanzplan Germany*, Leipzig: Henschel Verlag.

Sierra, G. (2015) 'A Brooklyn dancer flexes his talents and social activism with new show at Park Avenue Armory', *Brooklyn Based*, available: https://brooklynbased.com/2015/03/26/flexn/ [accessed 26 June 2020].

Siliezar, J. (2019) 'With twisting and floating movements, Harvard Gaga dance course teaches students and community members to listen to their bodies', *The Harvard Gazette,* available: https://news.harvard.edu/gazette/story/2019/04/harvard-gaga-dance-course-teaches-students-to-listen-to-their-bodies/ [accessed 25 June 2020].

Watton, P., Collings, J. and Moon, P. (2001) *Reflective Writing: Guidance Notes for Students*, available: https://tinyurl.com/3nnkh39v [accessed 16 July 2021].

CHOREOGRAPHIC (RE)EVOLUTION, DOCUMENTATION AND PRESERVATION

Each choreographer builds on the practices of the choreographers that have come before and most intend to subvert the conventions of their era. Innovation and disruption of previously held ideas in choreography seems to be essential to its existence. While we are standing on the shoulders of giants, we are also always looking for ways to reinvent and reinvigorate our practices. This chapter builds on the overview of Chapter 1 and explores some of the significant innovations in choreography, including developments in teaching approaches to choreographing dances. Choreographic ability cannot be taught *per se*, but develops over many years of trial and error. However, there are recognisable shifts in how choreographers approached their craft at particular moments in time and it is possible to trace some of these influences through methods of teaching. Notating, documenting and archiving choreography is central to our capacity to position ourselves in relation to what has come before. Though it is very challenging to document such an ephemeral art form as dance, there have been exciting advances in how choreographers have pursued this goal. In this way, they leave important legacies behind for coming generations. This chapter maps some of the most significant developments in this area.

ORIGINS OF CHOREOGRAPHY AND THE ROLE OF CHOREOGRAPHER

The term choreography comes from a latinized version of the Greek words *khoreia* (dance) and *graphein* (to write). The writing of dances was intrinsically associated with the emergence of Western theatre dance from the early capture of popular dances such as the Pavane and Courante which were notated in the Orchesographie by Thoinet Arbot as early as 1589 (Monahin 2015) to the more intricate baroque dances notated by Raoul-Auger Fueillet in the 1700s (Franko 2019) through a system that was derived from the choreography of Pierre Beauchamps. Feuillet notation was more complex to understand and decode in comparison to Renaissance notation because it charted how the choreography moved through the space, the step being danced and how it corresponded to the music (Franko 2019). This interlinked the development of baroque dance with its ability to be captured through notation. The relationship to writing, whereby dance might be viewed as a text to be deciphered, gained prominence alongside the contrasting view of dance being somewhat beyond description in words (Franko 2019). The concept of dance as a text gained great traction through the field of dance analysis. Choreography continues to be associated with the notion of writing dances, and the choreographer as an author, despite significant changes (and democratisation) in the process of dance creation.

Vocabulary and language

Ballet, with its highly codified vocabulary lends itself to the notion of composing a dance through the organisation of existing steps that correspond to our experience of sentence construction in spoken or written language, for example, the use of the term *phrase* to denote a series of conjoined movements. However, the ordering of steps in ballet do not in themselves convey the full meaning of a dance and it is often supplementary elements, such as music, costume, sets and more mimetic gestures that add specificity to a narrative through-line when drawing on a fixed vocabulary. So, while different dance forms may be regarded as having a vocabulary and a language, and dance practice draws on many metaphors from writing, it can be over-simplifying to assume that these languages have either a universal meaning or function in the same way that verbal language does. Nonetheless, choreographers are often considered to author dances as 'signature artists'.

Signature artists

However, the idea of the choreographer as a creative (or signature) artist emerged only quite recently in the trajectory of the development of Western theatre dance (Garafola 1989). The role of the choreographer in the late nineteenth and early twentieth centuries was more like a ballet master, who was attached to an opera house and "performed a host of other functions as well – dancing, teaching, coaching, rehearsing and administration" (Garafola 1989, p.195). The Russian impresario, Serge Diaghilev, developed the marketable brand of the choreographer by drawing on the box office success of dancers from the Ballets Russes (1909–1929) who transitioned into choreographers under his mentorship (Garafola 1989). Dancers associated with the Ballets Russes, such as Tamara Karsavina (1885–1978), Vaslav Nijinsky (1889–1950) and Anna Pavlova (1881–1931) had developed great fame and box office power which Diaghilev capitalised on through foregrounding the choreographer as an artist, "on a par with the independent painter, poet, singer or composer" (Garafola 1989, p.196). Michel Fokine (1880–1942) was one of the first choreographers to emerge as 'freelance' in this context, creating world renowned dance works such as *Le Spectre de la Rose* (1911), *Chopiniana/Les Sylphides* (1907) and *The Dying Swan* (1907) that continue to be performed today.

Female innovators

As outlined in Chapter 1, at the beginning of the twentieth century, entirely new dance forms began to emerge out of dissatisfaction with the artistic limitations represented by ballet, which was oftentimes reduced in artistic expression through an overemphasis on virtuosity, spectacle and make-believe (Au 2002). These developments were notable through the work of female American dance pioneers such as Loïe Fuller (1862–1928), Isadora Duncan (1877–1927) and Ruth St. Denis (1879–1968) who "each considered herself an artist rather than a mere entertainer, and each in turn attracted the notice of other artists: writers, musicians, painters and sculptors" (Au 2002, p.87). Fuller developed dance pieces that incorporated innovative visual effects through the combination of stage lighting and elaborate costumes, which extended to the use of mirrors, "coloured gels, slide projections and other aspects of stage technology," while both appearing in and creating her own films (Au 2002, p.88). Fuller experimented with many of the technological advances of her time and made significant innovations in the area of stage lighting, ultimately influencing dance for camera or Screendance (see Chapter 6) which has become its own sub-genre within dance performance.

Doris Humphrey

As introduced in Chapter 2, one of the key choreographic innovators of modern dance was Doris Humphrey, whose book *The Art of Making Dances* (1959) was hugely influential in the development and teaching of choreographic techniques and tools. Humphrey's book addresses how to work with dynamics, rhythm, motivation and gesture, words, music, sets, props and form, in a comprehensive treatise on the craft of creating choreography. This material, taken from the first-person perspective of a choreographer with many years of practical experience, demonstrates the deep value of practitioner knowledge in expanding the knowledge base of their field of study.

Exemplar 1 – Katherine Dunham (1909–2006) and Pearl Primus (1919–1994)

Two pioneering African American female artists of the 1930s and 1940s were Katherine Dunham and Pearl Primus. Each explored their creative practice through the lens of anthropology. Dunham was ground-breaking across the fields of artistic endeavour, activism and ethnographic research. She created the first nationally and internationally recognised black dance company, in the US and according to Das (2017, p.4) "revealed a black feminist political stance" by engaging in:

> a strategy of what I call *aesthetics as politics*. Decisions about thematic content, movement vocabulary, dancers' body types, the arrangement of said dancers in space, and performance venues express a choreographer's commentary on the relations of power governing society.

Dunham's work highlighted the cultural complexity of the African diaspora in America by setting her dances "in Haiti, Martinique, Trinidad, Cuba, Brazil, Northern Africa, and the United States, showcasing the variety and richness of black culture" (Das 2017, p.5). She developed a dance technique and founded the Katherine Dunham School of Dance in 1944. Das (2017, p.5) proposes that Dunham's technique gave coherence to her creative work and "mirrored the creolization she witnessed in the Caribbean. It challenged notions of racial and cultural purity, instead asking dancers to embrace diaspora within their bodies."

Pearl Primus was born in Trinidad and moved to New York at the age of two. Having planned to become a physician, after graduating with a degree in biology and premedical science in 1940, she was unable to find work in her field due to the limitations faced by black women at that time. She started taking dance classes in Manhattan, becoming inspired by the connections between dance and social activism (Schwartz and Schwartz 2011). She was described by renowned dancer Judith Jamison (in Schwartz and Schwartz 2011, p.2) in the following way:

> She created a niche for anyone following her that looked like she looked, that danced like she danced… that lectured the way she lectured, that did anthropology the way she did. She opened a window that had been shut, and that puts her in a spotlight of dance history.

A celebrated dancer, Primus was also an accomplished anthropologist and educator, who did much to raise awareness of racial injustice in America through her creative and educational endeavours. Both of these women informed their choreographies through anthropological research into African and African diasporic dance, making important connections between dance culture and heritage in choreographic practice.

The choreographer's status

Sally Gardner (2007) outlines the contrasting practices of the choreographer in modern dance to classical ballet as this former genre emerged, particularly in the US. She explained that one of the elements that distinguished modern dance was that the choreographer often danced alongside the dancers and that relationships within these networks were less hierarchical and more familial, that is, based on personal relationships (Gardner 2007). The industrialised systems of ballet training and production, that were intrinsically hierarchical, were somewhat challenged within the modern dance movement (Gardner 2007). Gardner proposes that the choreographer dancing alongside the dancers diminished the status of the choreographer, in relation to other art forms, as the choreographer was not seen to take an authority position in relation to the work. This is an interesting idea and one that can be explored in relation to the status of choreographers today and how they are positioned by the arts marketplace. Indeed, many of the choreographer-led enterprises of early modern dance became institutionalised at a later point in time, through the development of established company structures and dance schools that fed the dance ensemble with new generations of dancers.

KEY INFLUENCES ON CHOREOGRAPHIC TEACHING

Practical approaches to teaching choreography have been shaped by pioneering practitioners' concepts, from dance and related fields. These concepts inform our understanding of choreography and are integrated into the ways in which it is taught as a creative practice. Some key influences which are still prevalent in teaching today can be traced from the beginning of the twentieth century.

The birth of Somatics

The modern dance movement was intent on breaking away from the restrictions imposed by Western society to endeavour to free the Western body and spirit, which it was proposed had become diminished through industrialisation. Modernism represented the progress of humankind while returning to the simplicity and naturalness of the human body. At this time there was little recognition of the damage caused by the imperialism and colonialism of previous centuries but there was an opening up to the wisdom of various non-Western cultures in relation to body-mind harmony. Martha Eddy (2009) explains this in relation to the emergence of

Somatics, an important field that has interwoven with dance since the turn of the twentieth century, which described a series of body work approaches and movement education systems that explore body-mind harmony. These changes came out of the Victorian period, which "was ripe for a quantum change in our relationships with our bodies," as Eddy (2009 p.6) explains:

> There was a need to break free of Victorian strictures and also to embody the optimism the Victorian era offered. The possibility of experiencing the body newly came with such diverse movements as 'free love' and 'gymnastik'.

Somatics (a term that was only coined in the 1980s by Thomas Hanna) explores the first person perspective of embodiment, so that rather than viewing the body objectively as mechanical or object-like, you are attuned to the inner sensations that can be experienced through your attention. Émile Jacques Dalcroze (1865–1950) developed musicality (rather than rote learning) in musical training through his Eurythmics method, by incorporating rhythmical movements, and Francois Delsarte (1811–1871) explored the expressivity of movement in voice production and acting. Both of these developments influenced the early modern dancers (Au 2002). In this era, movement became centrally important to the expression of the individual.

Laban principles

In Europe, in the early part of the twentieth century, new attitudes to dance were crystallising through the work of Rudolf Laban (1879–1958) and his most prominent pupils Mary Wigman (1886–1973) and Kurt Jooss (1901–1979). Laban developed a range of new approaches to dance that spanned choreography, performance, pedagogy and analysis. The development of the dance form entitled *Ausdruktanz*, translated as 'expressive dance', is credited to these explorations (Au 2002, p.96), a form that spawned Tanztheater (or Dance Theatre) as exemplified by the work of seminal German choreographer Pina Bausch (1940–2009) (see Chapter 1). According to Au (2002, p.96):

> Many of [Laban's] innovations were sparked by his interest in physical culture, which was then a craze in Germany. Laban's

efforts enlarged the sphere of dance, increasing its importance in recreation, education and therapy.

There are a number of key concepts that Laban identifies as ways of viewing, analysing, recording and developing human movement in time and space. While these terms are not always used in contemporary choreographic teaching, they continue to underscore many of the principles that inform choreographic practices today. They allow us to locate how and where the body is moving and to work from a shared description of the quality and spatial range of movement.

Choreutics and eukinetics

Laban's work significantly impacted on choreographic developments through his relationship to space and expression, concepts for which he created the terms 'choreutics' and 'eukinetics' respectively. Choreutics is described as a kind of harmony of space and spatial direction (Maletić 1987). This categorises the various movements in dance into directions based on how we are oriented in space and corresponding to "the vertical and the horizontals of the three dimensions (height, width, and depth)" (Maletić 1987, p.58). Laban's concepts of eukinetics incorporated exploring qualities of expression, that is, how movement was executed. Laban extended the concept of Eukinetics into Effort Theory which he conceived as "the inner impulse from which movement originates," and categorised this in relation to the interdependent qualities of "space, weight, time and flow" (Maletić 1987, pp.100–101).

Kinesphere and icosahedron

An important concept and term exemplifying Laban's relationship to space is the 'kinesphere', which, "distinguishes the space in general, the infinite space, from the reach space immediately around the body" (Maletić 1987, p.59). This term derived from joining the Greek terms *kinesis* – movement, and *sphaira* – ball, sphere, the latter of which resonates with how the joints rotate in movement (Maletić 1987, p.59). You may hear this term used in many dance contexts today in relation to partnering, for example.

The 'icosahedron' is a template for Laban's structuring of directional movement in space, representing the intersection of the "six directions of high, low, left, right, backwards, and forwards, which form the corners of an octahedron... the eight diagonal directions... [and the] twelve diametral directions," which incorporate the anatomical planes of movement, known as Vertical, Sagittal and Horizontal (Maletić 1987, p.60) (see Chapter 2). Maletić (1987, p.60) explains how Laban found the icosahedron, "the most suitable for practicing harmonious movement sequences," which Laban outlined as:

> nearest to the sphere designed in space when our limbs reach freely around the three dimensional space; it also corresponds to the structure of the body since its three bodily symmetries are contained within the inner structure of the three dimensional planes.

Laban's contribution to the development of choreographic principles and expressivity cannot be overestimated and has impacted on dance training and scholarship internationally. Through this comprehensive mapping of movement, Laban was able to create a system that described movement on its own terms (Maletić 2005). While this has been primarily significant for choreographic development, Laban's system has been used across a broad range of non-dance related contexts such as in theatre, sports and health. Furthermore, Laban Movement Analysis (LMA) was developed by his student Irmgard Bartenieff, to combine Laban's structures with Bartenieff Fundamentals which drew on physical therapies and body related sciences.

The Second World War scattered many European artists across the globe, bringing with them the many new artistic ideas that had been bubbling in Europe in the 1930s. One such dancer, who was greatly influenced by Laban, was Austrian Jewish woman Gertrude Bodenweiser, who fled Vienna after she was removed from her position as professor in choreography at the Vienna State Academy of Music and Dramatic Art (Sassenberg 1999). Bodenweiser finally settled in Australia, becoming foundational to the development of modern dance and ballet in that country.

Black Mountain College and Dartington College

Two schools are credited with spawning important choreographic developments in the US and UK respectively. They were both considered seed beds for innovation and exchange between artists. Black Mountain College was established in North Carolina in 1933, under the principles of John Dewey's educational theories to educate the individual in a holistic way "as a person and as a citizen" (Díaz 2015, p.2) and with a focus on art education. As a refuge for many artists exiled from Nazi Germany, it delivered an experimental education that paved the way for interdisciplinary practice across various artforms (Díaz 2015). The creative ideas of John Cage and Merce Cunningham were developed and disseminated here.

The other was Dartington College, significantly influencing the cross-fertilization of choreographic ideas between Europe and the UK initially and then in the 1960s between the UK and the US. After creating the seminal work *The Green Table* in 1932, which critiqued political machinations, warmongering and the futility of war, Kurt Jooss and his company left Germany for England in 1933 during the rise of National Socialism (Au 2002, p.100). Jooss was invited alongside Sigurd Leeder to direct the dance school at Dartington College, which would become a home for the Ballet Jooss for a period of time. The teaching curriculum at that time was heavily informed by Laban's work. Dartington was a highly influential centre for arts education, coming into further prominence in the 1960s with the influx of US based teachers such as Mary Fulkerson and Steve Paxton bringing developments from the Judson Dance experimentations in New York City. Jooss had co-founded the Folkwang School in 1927 in Essen, which managed to survive his departure overseas during the war and maintain dance teaching throughout that period (Walther 1993). Therefore, Jooss was able to reprise his work on his return to Germany in 1949 and to continue the strands of German modern dance laid down in the pre-war years.

Choreographic teaching and music composition

An important choreographer and performer in her own right, Mary Wigman experimented with music to separate dance from being a subservient art form that solely expresses the intentions of the music. She did this through explorations with percussive accompaniment to her movements (see Chapter 1). Her wish was for dance to become free of music, and an original artform in its own right. In spite of this separation, choreography and the teaching of dance composition have been aligned with musical composition throughout the twentieth century through various collaborations between choreographers and composers. For example, the collaboration between composer Louis Horst and choreographer Martha Graham led to Horst's teaching of solo and group choreography within various colleges in the US (Soares 2005). Horst influenced generations of dancers, teachers and choreographers on the composition of dances. John Cage and Merce Cunningham's creative relationship led to further advances in the development of teaching choreography, particularly through the use of chance operations, explained later in this section. Belgian choreographer, Anne Teresa de Keersmaeker developed choreographic precepts from the music of Steve Reich, which are influential in choreographic teaching today through the use of movement scores, and the ongoing collaboration between choreographer Jonathan Burrows and composer Matteo Fargion has influenced a new generation of choreographers, through pared back choreographies that experiment with complex scores and rhythms. Burrows' ethos can be explored through his book, *A Choreographer's Handbook* (2010).

MODERN DANCE IN THE POST-WAR ERA

Gay Morris (2006) has written about the post-war era in dance, primarily focusing on developments in the US. By the 1940s, modern dance had encountered a range of challenges that undermined its position at the vanguard of the arts (Morris 2006). These issues impacted on choreographic developments and how the second generation of choreographers developed the field. There was a focus on depersonalising movement vocabularies, so that an individual choreographer would not shape a group of dancers through their own movement style. The development of these individual movement languages in the past had served to differentiate the work of various choreographers and promote their uniqueness as creative artists (Morris 2006). Much of the teaching of dance composition had been institutionalized at this stage, in no small way through the influence of Louis Horst and Doris Humphrey, and was primarily based on students creating work on their own bodies, rather than groups of dancers (Morris 2006). Learning particular ways of choreographing through established tools limited the potential for experimentation. According to Morris (2006 pp.18–19) narrative started to intervene, running contrary to the earliest endeavours of modern dance pioneers.

> [M]odern dance's original goals had espoused an autonomous art that placed embodied movement, as dance's essential element, at its center. Communication was crucial, but it was communication through abstract corporeal movement, not through literary, that is, representational means.

While the move towards narrative, even in the later work of earlier pioneers such as Martha Graham, made dance more accessible and commercially successful, it was considered by many critics at the time to undermine the vanguard position of modern dance as an art form (Morris 2006). At stake here was the notion of modern dance being "the only American form of high-art dance" (Morris 2006, p.57). Distancing itself from the structures and concerns of ballet, including narrative, was part of maintaining this distinction.

During the 1940s and 1950s the work of George Balanchine for Ballet Society and then New York City Ballet overlapped with the aesthetics of modern dance. Morris explains how Balanchine's vocabulary was underscored by the *dance d'ecole* or classical ballet roots of his training and early years but incorporated vernacular movements and movement references to 'Africanist' dance, inspired through his work with black artists such as Josephine Baker, Katherine Dunham, Herbie Harper and Buddie Bradley in the 1930s and 1940s "in commercial theatre and film" (Morris 2006, p.51). In ballets such as *The Four Temperaments*, the movements were taken out of their usual logical flow and as in surrealist art at that time, abstracted, dislocated and reorganised into a collage that neutralised their meaning (Morris 2006). While this presented the choreography as experimental, it was still organised within a formal structure that was recognisable as ballet according to its "shape and texture, tempo and dynamics" (Morris 2006, p.53). Furthermore, while it elevated 'low art' dancing from dance halls and commercial contexts into a high-art dance environment, which could be seen to promote American democracy, it did this while upholding an aesthetic that "reinforce[d] the upright, the balanced, the symmetrical and the light" (Morris 2006, p.58).

Merce Cunningham

As evidenced through his prominence across many sections of this book, Merce Cunningham (1919–2009) was a major influence on choreographic developments throughout the twentieth century, influencing future generations of choreographers through his exploration of the dancing body in time and space. Inspired by composer John Cage (1912–1992), who was also his partner in life, Cunningham further separated dance from musical interpretations (as was noted in Wigman's explorations) and removed narrative meanings and representation in his work. This continued the move to depersonalise the dance vocabulary from the individual choreographer's expression, as mentioned earlier, towards creating structures of dancemaking that were impersonal, that is, not based solely on the maker's likes or dislikes. Rather than communicating a specific emotional meaning, which Cage did not believe was possible in dance or music, he saw the role of art as spiritual, that is, to quieten the mind and allow other, perhaps divine, influences to be experienced (Morris 2006, p.81). This liberation from interpreting/aligning with music and narrative expression gave more opportunities to explore diverse choreographic possibilities. In order to achieve these goals, Cunningham utilized chance operations in devising his choreography, through drawing on external decision-making systems, such as the I-Ching, or Book of Changes, an ancient Chinese system of divination which works through throwing three coins and using the corresponding patterns to determine a course of action.

NEW APPROACHES TO CHOREOGRAPHIC TEACHING

Arising out of the collaboration between Cunningham and Cage, musician Robert Dunn (1928–1996) (husband to Cunningham dancer Judith Dunn), was invited to teach composition at the Cunningham studio in 1960. This marked a liberation from what was seen as Louis Horst's somewhat oppressive teachings on dance composition that centred on elements such as beauty, formal design, rhythmic elements and structure and denoted a kind of pre-ordained outcome to what the dance should be (Banes 1993, p.4). Importantly, Dunn's class brought choreographic teaching into line with some of the significant artistic movements of the time and earlier influences from the Dadaists and Marcel Duchamp. Dunn's first group of students included seminal artists in the postmodern dance movement such as Yvonne Rainer, Steve Paxton and Simone Forti (Banes 1993). The freeing of this relationship to choreographing dances evolved into the Judson Dance Theatre (see Chapter 1).

The artists of the Judson Dance Theatre challenged what Steve Paxton (one of the originators of Contact Improvisation and member of the collective) described as "the cults of personality" that grew up through modern dance in the US confronting the hierarchies that operated within choreographer-led dance companies (Banes 1993, p.10). The Judson Dance Theatre's developments are considered to have greatly influenced choreographic approaches worldwide through the proliferation of new pathways to dance creation and performance, and are also referred to as New Dance (Davida 1992). Dena Davida (1992) maps the scope of these influences, highlighting the spread of ideas across Europe through choreographers "sparked... by intensified intercontinental exchange with American choreographers" to form a 'new dance' wave that came into being in "France, Britain, and Holland during the seventies," and

> ... permeated Canada, Belgium, Switzerland, Austria, Spain and Italy and much of Western Europe in the eighties; and currently claims disciples in India, Australia, Scandinavia, Portugal and parts of Central and South America and Eastern Europe; and in the nineties has been carried into parts of Africa and Indonesia.

In London, in the 1970s, the experimental dance project X6 emerged to challenge codified styles, representation of women and prevailing movement practices. Choreographer Rosemary Butcher's (1947–2016) choreography came into prominence from this time and her work in the area of visual art and interdisciplinary practice influenced many generations of British choreographers.

Anti-dance or non-dance

In the late 1990s a new wave of dance performances that were stripped bare of choreography, sets and often costumes emerged in Europe, primarily through a group of young choreographers in France. This approach gained international prominence through the work of Jérôme Bel and included artists such as Xavier Le Roy, Boris Charmatz and the later work of Maguy Marin. These choreographers challenged dance as primarily linked to movement and incorporated performance art and theatrical tools into their work. This wave of choreographic exploration which does not officially have a name but is often referred to as 'non-dance', aligned choreography more closely with critical theory and philosophical concepts about 'the nature of being' rather than representation. This approach continues to influence new generations of choreographers, who have turned to the body itself as a site of exploration.

CONTEMPORARY BALLET

Throughout the twentieth century, ballet developed through the work of key choreographers; often these early innovators emerged out of the creative melting pot of the Ballets Russes. Choreographic innovations in ballet have been generally identified as emerging through male choreographers, such as George Balanchine, Frederick Ashton, Kenneth Macmillan, John Cranko, William Forsythe and more recently, Wayne McGregor (see Chapter 1). However, Twyla Tharp, Crystal Pite, Karole Armitage and in the early twentieth century, Bronislava Nijinska significantly contributed to the development of the ballet vocabulary as an expressive tool, often moving away from direct narrative to the presentation of more abstract configurations and concepts through this dance form. Indeed, the gender power imbalance has been noted by critics Meglin and Matluck Brooks (2012) who observed the low number of female ballet choreographers and artistic directors of ballet companies, questioning whether the corporate culture of large arts institutions reflects the gender imbalance of the corporate sector in general. This is in spite of the fact that many ballet companies were founded by women in the first instance. Equally, they query the capacity for ballet to address more contemporary notions of equality, diversity and gender fluidity, drawing on critic Alistair Macaulay's challenge in 2010 to "contemporary ballet's ability to build narrative ballets that resonate with contemporary gender issues, such as equal rights, same-sex marriage, relaxing of rigidly prescribed gender roles, and fluidity in gender expression" (Meglin and Matluck Brooks 2012, p.4). Meglin and Matluck Brooks (2012) recognise that the codified nature of the ballet repertoire, distinctive and gendered training regimens that prioritise pointe work for women, jumping for men and stereotypical male/female partner work makes it difficult to move outside heteronormative roles. However, Kathrina Farrugia-Kriel and Jill Nunes Jenson (2021) are more optimistic about the potential for contemporary ballet to open up to more current ideas beyond the classics and to address more contemporary societal issues. They explain, that one of the key characteristics of contemporary ballet choreographers is that they

> more often than not, seek to reorient the viewer by celebrating what could be deemed vulnerabilities, reconstructing ideals of perfection, problematizing the marginalized/mainstream dichotomy, bringing viewers closer in to observe, and letting the art become an experience rather than a distant object preciously guarded out of reach.
>
> (Farrugia-Kriel and Nunes Jenson 2021, p.2)

Ballet has developed to a high level of virtuosity that has been exploited by choreographers to push the limits of the body to ever new heights. As Farrugia-Kriel and Nunes Jenson (2021 p.1) explain, this shift means that dancers are now "athletes far removed from noble amateurs." While the ballet classics continue to be performed worldwide, versatility now plays a major role in the repertoire of most ballet companies. Other significant changes are represented by choreographers from the contemporary dance world such as Wayne McGregor and Sidi Larbi Cherkaoui who have taken key artistic positions in major ballet companies, the UK Royal Ballet and Belgian Royal Ballet of Flanders, respectively. Choreographic innovators such as William Forsythe, whose original background was in ballet, have crossed boundaries between ballet and contemporary dance, to extend possibilities for choreographic exploration in both contexts. For example, according to dance writer Ann Nugent (2021, p.16), Forsythe's work is known for

> extending ways of thinking about choreography and questioning not only ballet as a system but also the conventions of dance theatre... [by incorporating] ideas from disciplines such as science, mathematics, and technology, applying them to his interrogation of classical principles.

CHOREOGRAPHIC PRACTICE IN INTERCULTURAL CONTEXTS

As outlined in Chapter 1, the twentieth century witnessed Western dance forms drawing on influences from non-Western cultures to enhance their movement vocabularies, often as a form of appropriation, that is, without an in-depth knowledge of the movement practice and wider culture they were drawing from. The twenty-first century has seen a growth in awareness regarding cultural diversity and inclusiveness, which is beginning to be reflected more fully across the dance spectrum. However, this shift is happening in an ever-increasingly globalised world, where cultural boundaries are particularly porous (Stock 2017). Added to this issue is our easy access to technology, whereby dance videos can easily circle the globe, breaking down barriers of distance and spoken language, to influence dancemaking in immeasurable ways. This makes it challenging, and problematic, to assume that any dance form is 'pure' and untouched by global influences (Stock 2017). In light of these complexities, it is important that choreographers are culturally aware, if and when crossing into other dance traditions. This can work successfully when there are exchanges or collaborations between practitioners from different cultural contexts, with insider knowledge regarding the complexities of each context.

Intercultural exchange

Exploring the nuances of this area of dance practice, dance scholar Cheryl Stock (2017, p.344) organises intercultural exchange into four different categories:

1. In-country cultural immersion
2. Collaborative international exchange/sharing of culturally diverse practices
3. Hybrid practices of diasporic artists
4. Implicit intercultural connections

Stock (2017, p. 345) describes the first category as a possibility to be immersed in another culture and experience the 'positive dislocation' that arises from the new context. This can allow the choreographer to evaluate their ways of working in a new light and to recognise what is taken for granted due to the cultural context in which they usually work. The sharing of culturally diverse practices can generate exciting and dynamic creative dialogue, as exemplified in a pronounced way in the dance collaboration between French choreographer Jérôme Bel and Thai Khon dancer and choreographer, Pichet Klunchun (see Chapter 1). The piece took the form of an on-stage dialogue between both artists, where they explored their respective cultural contexts and the embedded meanings in the dance forms they create and perform within. The verbal dialogue between both artists was interspersed with performed dance vignettes, which highlighted the moments of alignment, confusion and challenge that can arise in the meeting of diverse cultural practices and perspectives (see Chapter 2).

In the third category, Stock (2017, p.348) outlines the rich space produced by experiments in hybrid forms by "diasporic" artists, a term which describes "multiple émigré communities" who may be scattered across different countries, but who identify strongly with the culture of their shared homeland. In the UK, most notable in this category is the work of Akram Khan who merged his initial training in classical South Asian Kathak dance with subsequent training in contemporary dance to create a dance form which he describes as 'Contemporary Kathak' (Khan in Stock 2017, p.349). Other examples of this include the work of Nigerian choreographer, Qudus Onikeku, who trained in dance and acrobatics at the National Higher School of Circus Arts in France and spent a number of years as a diasporic artist in France, creating a hybrid form of dance drawn from Nigerian traditional Yoruba culture and contemporary performance practices. The hybridisation between traditional dance forms and contemporary dance can also unfold within choreographers' countries of origin, as with the work of Irish Traditional dancer Colin Dunne, Flamenco dancer Israel Galvin and within the work of Indigenous Australian choreographer Stephen Page for his dance company Bangarra (see Chapter 1).

Stock's (2017, p.351) final category outlines more subtle exchanges that imprint on choreographic practices, as a kind of trace that transfers unconsciously rather than consciously when artists of different dance cultures and backgrounds interconnect. According to Stock (2017, p.351),

> in the implicit intercultural model, motivations to come together in a collaborative space are more to do with conceptual artistic concerns and content which become 'inflected' by the cultural backgrounds of the collaborations.

Even when unconscious, these kinds of encounters can impact significantly on the movement vocabularies of the artists involved in various unexpected ways (Stock 2017). The possibility for dancers and choreographers to influence each other in these subtle ways attests to how choreography as a practice requires opening to the embodied experience of others through collaboration and how these encounters can subsequently shape future creative processes as they become part of the individual's movement repertoire and moving identity (Roche 2015).

Tradition versus contemporary

It is important not to create a false binary between traditional and contemporary practices within the dance world. Traditions are always evolving and are not always culturally unchanged or uninterrupted by various waves of colonialism, globalisation or shifts in social or political ideologies within various countries. Rather than being constrained by tradition, many artists draw on their traditions to respond to and create within a contemporary context. For example, Onikeku, mentioned above, fuses a range of past and future perspectives in his choreography,

> Personally, I create a movement identity that fuses dance and acrobatics… while I make the guiding philosophies of Yoruba

cultural and science fiction my basis and combining it with several other influences to weave a certain understanding of the human condition.

(Onikeku in McKinley 2019)

Exemplar 2 – Contemporary developments in African dance

African dance forms, contemporary African-based choreographers and diasporic African choreographers have influenced the professional dance culture all over the world. From the work of African American choreographers and dancers in the early generations of modern dance to the diasporic communities in France and the UK, various choreographers and companies such as Dance Theatre of Harlem in New York, Phoenix Dance Theatre in the UK and Germaine Acogny with her company Jant-Bi have presented the experience of artists of colour throughout the dance canon. French and Senegalese choreographer Acogny founded École des Sables in 1998, building a dance centre in 2004 in Senegal as a site for training, research, residencies and exchange "for dancers from Africa and all continents" (École des Sables n.d.). Acogny is considered to be a 'mother figure' to subsequent contemporary African artists who have emerged onto the world stage and are integrating contemporary attitudes and artistic practice with more ancient traditional dance cultures (Noisette 2011, p.114). These include artists such as Salia Sanou and Seydou Boro (who co-founded the Centre de Développement Chorégraphique La Termitière in Ouagadougou, Burkina Faso), Heddy Maalem (Algeria), Kettly Noël (Haiti) and Faustin Linyekula (Democratic Republic of Congo) (Noisette 2011, p.114).

Most recently, École des Sables developed a co-production with Sadlers Wells Theatre, London and the Pina Bausch Foundation to re-stage Bausch's *Rite of Spring* with a company of all African dancers. With a world tour curtailed due to the COVID-19 pandemic, the final rehearsal before lockdown was filmed on a beach as the sun set, a beautifully powerful and life-affirming performance as the world faced into the global pandemic. This film has been shown subsequently at festivals worldwide as *Dancing at Dusk – A Moment with Pina Bausch's The Rite of Spring (2021)*.

Boyzie Cekwana, who highlights social issues circulating through post-Apartheid South Africa, "fuses traditional African forms and the energy of the townships with contemporary methods" (Wex Arts n.d.). His work, which has been performed all over the world confronts the legacies of AIDS, child abuse and violence that continue to afflict citizens in South Africa. In his piece *Influx Controls: I Wanna Be Wanna Be* (2009), Cekwana was exploring the experience of dehumanisation through racism that makes people of colour either "a problematic majority in their own land" or "a problematic minority" in Europe or North America (GVA Dance Training 2010). He explains:

> 'I wanna be' is that asphyxiated cry for total and ultimate assumption of full humanity. 'I wanna be' is I wanna be white, since whiteness is goodness, rightness; whiteness is having, in a world of have-not ness. 'I wanna be' is I wanna have, for to have is to be.
> (Cekwana in KAAI Theatre 2009)

Onikeku, mentioned above, has created a number of choreographies through his Q Dance Company based in Lagos Nigeria. His piece *Yuropa* (2018) explores the migrant experience from the perspective of Africans through an "odyssey of three young travellers who left the shores of their homes, heading to an unknown destination over the sea" (Bitef n.d.). The title is made from an amalgamation of 'Europe' and 'Yoruba', the language and culture that comprises Onikeku's Nigerian heritage, the structures of which underscore his contemporary practice. This work throws important light on the mass migrations which have resulted from humanitarian crises in the twenty-first century. These choreographers draw on their respective dance cultures to address contemporary experiences, bringing vital and resonant voices to the contemporary dance milieu.

PRESERVING CHOREOGRAPHIES

As outlined at the beginning of this chapter, the notation of choreography emerged synergistically with the development of Western theatre dance, through the link between dance and the writing of dances, that is, choreography. Our capacity to notate and document dances has changed over the centuries and shapes how we perceive choreography.

Franko (2011, p.323) outlines how notation or the process of capturing and preserving dance has developed since the late Renaissance, from "geometrical dance, as a choreographic rather than notational phenomenon... [that] emulated the spatial presentation of written characters." He makes a connection between choreography and writing, and the ways in which they have interwoven through different time periods and stages of dance development.

> The history of dance notation always reflects this complex relationship among dance, language, and writing, though the role of notation changes dynamically from the Renaissance through the twenty-first century and thus exerts a powerful influence on what we believe dance to be and on how we experience it.
>
> (Franko 2011, p.322)

Franko (2011, pp.323–324) explains that while notation of baroque dance captured spatial relationships very well, for example, through representing "the concept of floor pattern as the page and the concept of the body as a cipher on the page," this was possible because of the detailed codification of the movements. However, the notational score could not capture the dynamics and expression of movement accurately and so, when the *ballet d'action* underwent reform from 'court ballet' through the influence of ballet masters such as Jean-Georges Noverre over the course of the eighteenth century into 'theatre dance', the Feuillet notation was unable to capture key elements of the dance. In particular, the missing element was *expression* that could not be captured in the notation of this earlier time. Franko (2011) explains that the developments in theatre dance in the nineteenth century led to a focus on technique in technical dance writing. Carlo Blasis (1795–1878), a famous dancer and ballet master/choreographer, noted technical developments rather than preserving choreographies and the most notable change from baroque notation in his writing was how "dance was no longer the figure understood as the path through space, but the figure as the dancer's body itself" (Franko 2011, p.326). This led to a "focus on the body as instrument (to the detriment of any focus on the path through space and on spatial relationships between dancers)" (Franko 2011, p.326). This shift in the positioning of the body arguably impacted significantly on training in ballet which begins the class with a body in place at the barre, mobilising the limbs in different configurations and only really moving through space towards the end of the class.

Notation systems

While many notational systems came into usage throughout the nineteenth and early twentieth century, for example, the notebooks of August Bournonville (1855) and the manuscript score of Nijinsky's *L'Après-midi d'un faune* (1912), no system was widely adopted (Franko 2011). However, one key notation system that emerged in the twentieth century was *Labanotion*, developed by Laban. Franko (2011, p.327) explains that no single notation system has become ubiquitous for dancers and choreographers, even Labanotation,

> However influential it became, though, not even Labanotation became as broadly disseminated among dancers as musical notation is among professional musicians. Dance notation has been specialized and not the subject of a universal professional literacy.

So, in spite of many attempts to develop universal notation systems, "the transmission of dance has remained predominantly a matter of oral tradition" (Franko 2011, p.327).

Documentation of dances

Since the 1970s, dancers and choreographers have used video recording in the creation and documentation of dance. This tool has been prominent as a means of preserving choreographies, however, its limitations lie in the two-dimensional representation of the movement on a screen that cannot give context to the inner workings of the movement or how other dancers might understand the origins of some of the creative ideas. Therefore, while video is often used when restaging existing choreographies on other dancers, this is usually accompanied by a dancer who has danced in the original work or was taught by one of the original cast members.

Preservation of dance has become an important topic in dance research, but also for individual choreographers to manage the legacy of their creative work. Whereas a visual artist or painter can collect and catalogue their artwork over the course of a career, it is infinitely more challenging for choreographers to do this, as they do not produce a written script or score that can fully capture the complexity of the live performance. This has led choreographers and researchers to explore ways of capturing and preserving important information about their works for posterity. For example, eminent British choreographer Siobhan Davies began developing a digital archive in collaboration with researchers from Coventry University in 2006. Entitled *Siobhan Davies RePlay*, the archive is unusual in that it is not based on an existing hard copy archive that was digitised but instead, it was "born digital" (Whatley 2013, p.83). Another distinctive element to this project was that the archive collected the work of a living choreographer while she was still very much active in making dances, and therefore the archive could grow and change alongside Davies' working practices. This resource is highly valuable for professional choreographers, dance students and dance researchers and will continue to be so into the future.

Dancing scores

Another kind of process was undertaken by renowned Belgian choreographer, Anne Teresa de Keersmaeker, in her three-book series *A Choreographer's Score*, co-written with Bojana Cvejić (2016). The impetus for this project was that De Keersmaeker's early dances were being restaged and she was going to dance in them for the last time. So, she proposed that it would be timely to "write these choreographies down" (Cvejić 2016, p.52). This included a process of interviewing to draw out all of De Keersmaeker's thinking, experimentation and creative methods that went into the creation of the four early choreographies such as "the feelings, moods, events, places, people and stories that make up the life-fabric of processes of creation" (Cvejić 2016, p.55). This included Cvejić exploring archival materials such as "numerous notebooks containing sketches, drawings, schemes, and all kinds of notes, program brochures, reviews, technical lists, budget calculations, letters to cultural officials..." (Cvejić 2016, p.54). Through this process of close connection and consultation, the choreography became 'scored', that is, mapped into a diagrammatic and written form. Cvejić (2016, p.55) describes the multi-layered outcome of this project (a book and accompanying DVDs) that is required to capture the choreographies in a transmissible form, which speaks to the complexity of trying to map a dance in its fullness:

> It is comprised of a narrative account about the creation process, a presentation of main choreographic and dramaturgical ideas, compositional principles and dance techniques, linear formal analysis of the entire work abounding in technical detail about the choreographic structure, photography, drawings, documentary materials and video.

Digitising dance – Motion Bank

Extending the question of the challenges of documenting dance further brings us to the use of technology in digitising the moving body to create artistic projects and also to document choreography. Dance and technology as a creative field is explored in Chapter 6, but it is worth noting how it has been used to bring choreographic documentation into virtual spaces.

For example, *Motion Bank* is a research project undertaken by the Forsythe Company, Germany, led by prolific US choreographer William Forsythe (see Chapter 2). The initial focus of this project was to create an online environment for dance research that allowed for critical exchange between peers in the choreographic world, through "the creation of new on-line digital scores in collaboration with selected guest choreographers to be made publicly available via the Motion Bank website" (DeLahunta 2017a, p.131). The first part of this project was the development of an interactive score of Forsythe's choreography, *One Flat Thing, reproduced*. The choreographers whose work is documented through *Motion Bank* are Deborah Hay, Jonathan Burrows and Matteo Fargion, Bebe Miller and Thomas Hauert. DeLahunta (2017a, p.132) explains that "these artists were invited on the basis of their distinctive choreographic work and commitment to ongoing research in relation to their methods of practice." This project extended the concept of a digital archive beyond solely preservation to allow for interaction and exchange between artists, while also giving open access to the materials for educational purposes. In this way, *Motion Bank* paved the way for innovative approaches to capturing and interacting with the creative practices of choreographers through a widely accessible digital platform.

CHOREOGRAPHY IN THE DIGITAL AGE

With the circulation of dance on digital platforms, such as YouTube, it is more difficult for choreographers to protect creative work from appropriation and mimicry. Throughout the twentieth century, dance works were mainly available on hardcopy video tapes or DVDs. This controlled the circulation of ideas and maintained the significance of the live performance as the main means of viewing a dance work. Often dancers did not have access to footage of their own dancing and signature choreographers developed distinctive styles which became attributed to them, somewhat controlling how their work might be referenced by other artists. Recordings of choreographies were less broadly available and not considered as valuable as the live dance experience. Currently, dance performances are publicised through circulating trailers of performance or rehearsal processes on social media. Dancers watch themselves dancing on various platforms from professionally edited recordings to rough studio rehearsal footage, a new development in the experience of being a dancer. With the increased digitisation of dance, students are likely to encounter the legacy of dance history through recordings on YouTube, rather than the live performance which can influence how they experience and understand the significance of a piece of choreography. As dancers and choreographers who are digital natives emerge into the professional dance field, they bring a new approach to creating, presenting, documenting and publicising their choreographies.

Questions of copyright

The wider circulation of dance on digital platforms has instigated new appraisals of what constitutes copyrighted material in choreography. As Francis Yeoh (2013, p.50) outlines, "the digital era has provided greater scope for the choreographer's creativity but concomitant with this development is a loss of control that choreographers had traditionally enjoyed within the dance community." There is an argument that within the 'protective environment' of the dance world, there is a culture of exchange and sharing that allows for some peer to peer borrowing as a mutually beneficial practice (Yeoh 2013, p.49). However, American choreographer Agnes de Mille (1905–1993) observed how vulnerable the choreographer's ideas are through the visibility of the choreographic practice to all members of the cast and creative team, saying:

> the choreographer is glued immobile as a fly in a web and must watch his own pupils and assistants, suborned to steal his ideas and livelihood. Several dancers made paying careers out of doing just this.
>
> (De Mille 1956, p.256)

The question of copyright infringement became relevant, through a high-profile case concerning the use of De Keersmaeker's choreography by famous singer Beyoncé Knowles in her music video *Countdown*. While De Keersmaeker is a very well-established choreographer in contemporary dance, she does not have the international fame and wealth of Beyoncé and in contacting Beyoncé's lawyers, her company was engaging with the might of music producers Sony (Yeoh 2013). Ultimately, De Keersmaeker could be seen to have taken ownership of this experience when she created a website entitled *Re:Rosas!*, whereby anyone could learn her choreography, film it and upload their version to the site (Re:Rosas! n.d.). Indeed, starting in 2020, the COVID-19 global pandemic accelerated dance's move to online distribution and circulation. With severe restrictions on live performance, many choreographers, dance companies and dance festivals sought alternative ways to reach audiences via internet platforms. Dance's relationship to film and technology will be explored further in Chapter 6.

SUMMARY

This chapter outlines the origin of the term choreography (writing dances) and how this emerged through the French court. It gives an overview of some key choreographic innovators who influenced the teaching of choreography, spanning modern dance, postmodern dance and contemporary dance, charting the shifting role of the choreographer from ballet master to signature artist. Some important concepts from Laban's categorisation of movement are covered as well as well as developments in choreography in the post-World-War-II years.

The development of choreographic practice in intercultural contexts is explored as well as the ways in which 'traditional' dance forms interrelate with contemporary hybrid practices through transnational flows of dance ideas. A further topic is the many ways in which choreographies are maintained and transmitted, referencing processes of documentation, restaging existing works, choreographic scoring and archives (both digital and analogue). This touches on questions of copyrighting choreography which have arisen through the increased circulation and access to choreographies on YouTube and other online sources.

FURTHER READING

Bleeker, M. ed. (2016) *Transmission in Motion: The Technologizing of Dance*, Abingdon and New York: Routledge.

Butterworth, J. and Wildschut, L. (2017) *Contemporary Choreography: A Critical Reader*, Abingdon and New York: Routledge.

Keersmaeker, A. T. de et al. (2012) *A Choreographer's Score: Fase, Rosas danst Rosas, Elena's aria, Bartók*, Brussels: Mercatorfonds.

Strauss, M. and Nadel, M. H. (2012) *Looking at Contemporary Dance: A Guide for the Internet Age*, Princeton: Princeton Book Company.

REFERENCES

Au, S. (2002) *Ballet and Modern Dance*, London: Thames & Hudson Ltd.

Banes, Sally (1993) *Democracy's Body: Judson Dance Theatre, 1962–1964*, Durham and London: Duke University Press.

Bitef (n.d.) *Yuropa*, available: https://53.bitef.rs/en/program/yuropa [accessed 21 July 2021].

Cvejić, B. (2016) 'A choreographer's score: Anna Teresa De Keersmaeker', in Bleeker, M., ed., *Transmission in Motion: The Technologizing of Dance*, Abingdon and New York: Routledge, 52–61.

Das, J. D. (2017) *Katherine Dunham: Dance and the African Diaspora*, Oxford: Oxford University Press. ProQuest Ebook Central, available: https://ebookcentral-proquest-com.proxy.lib.ul.ie/lib/univlime-ebooks/detail.action?docID=4854099 [accessed 16 July 2021].

Davida, D. (1992) 'Dancing the body eclectic', *Contact Quarterly: A Vehicle for Moving Ideas* (Summer), available: http://denadavida.ca/articles/dancing-the-body-eclectic/ [accessed 16 July 2021].

DeLahunta, S. (2017a) 'Motion Bank: a broad context for choreographic research', in Bleeker, M., ed., *Transmission in Motion: The Technologizing of Dance*, Abingon and New York: Routledge, 128–137.

De Mille, A. (1956) *And Promenade Home*, Boston and Toronto: Little, Brown and Company.

Díaz, E. (2015) *The Experimenters: Chance and Design at Black Mountain College*, Chicago: The University of Chicago Press.

École des Sables (n.d.) *About*, available: https://ecoledessables.org/about-us [accessed 22 July 2021].

Eddy, M. (2009) 'A brief history of somatic practices and dance: historical development of the field of somatic education and its relationship to dance', *Journal of Dance and Somatic Practices*, 1(1), 5–27.

Farrugia-Kriel, K. and Nunes Jensen, J. eds (2021) *The Oxford Handbook of Contemporary Ballet*, New York: Oxford University Press.

Franko, M. (2011) 'Writing for the body: notation, reconstruction, and reinvention in dance', *Common Knowledge*, 17(2), 321–334, available: https://doi.org/10.1215/0961754X-1188004 [accessed 1 June 2021].

Franko, M. (2019) *Choreographing Discourses: A Mark Franko Reader*, Abingdon and New York: Routledge.

Gardner, S. (2007) 'Dancer, choreographer and modern dance scholarship', *Dance Research*, xxv(1), 35–53.

Garafola, Lynn (1989) *Diaghilev's Ballets Russes*, New York and Oxford: Oxford University Press.

GVA Dance Training (2010) *Boyzie Cekwana on Influx*, available: http://gvadancetraining.ning.com/video/boyzie-cekwana-on-influx [accessed 21 July 2021].

KAAI Theatre (2009) *Influx Controls: I Wanna Be Wanna Be*, available: www.kaaitheater.be/en/agenda/influx-controls-i-wanna-be-wanna-be [accessed 21 July 2021].

Maletić, V. (1987) *Body – Space – Expression: The Development of Rudolf Laban's Movement and Dance Concepts*, Berlin, New York and Amsterdam: Mouton de Gruyter. ProQuest Ebook Central, available: http://ebookcentral.proquest.comlib/univlime-ebooks/detail.action?docID=934658 [accessed 1 June 2021].

Maletić, V. (2005) 'Laban principles of movement analysis', in Cohan, S. J., ed., *The International Encyclopedia of Dance*, Oxford: Oxford University Press, available: www.oxfordreference.com/view/10.1093/acref/9780195173697.001.0001/acref-9780195173697-e-0983 [accessed 13 July 2021].

McKinley, B. (2019) 'First Maker in Residence to lead creative projects on cultural production in diasporic communities', *In the Loop*, Gainesville: University of Florida, available: https://arts.ufl.edu/in-the-loop/news/first-maker-in-residence-to-lead-creative-projects-on-cultural-production-in-diasporic-communities/ [accessed 1 July 2021].

Meglin, J. A., and Matluck Brooks, L. (2012) 'Where are all the women choreographers in ballet?', *Dance Chronicle*, 35(1), 1–7.

Monahin, N. (2015) 'Writing for posterity: a reassessment of Arbeau's Orchésographie (1589)', *Congress on Research in Dance Conference Proceedings*, 125–135.

Morris, G. (2006) *A Game for Dancers: Performing Modernism in the Post-war Years, 1945–1960*, Middletown: Wesleyan University Press.

Noisette, Phillipe (2011) *Talk About Contemporary Dance*, translated by Dusinberre, D., Paris: Flammarion.

Nugent, A. (2021) 'William Forsythe: Stuttgart, Frankfurt and the Forsythescape', in Farrugia-Kriel, K. and Nunes Jensen, J., eds, *The Oxford Handbook of Contemporary Ballet*, New York: Oxford University Press, 13–28.

Re:Rosas! (n.d.) *Home*, available: www.rosasdanstrosas.be/en-home/ [accessed 16 July 2021].

Roche, J. (2015) *Multiplicity, Embodiment and the Contemporary Dancer: Moving Identities*, London: Palgrave Macmillan.

Sassenberg, M. (1999) 'Gertrud Bodenwieser', *Jewish Women: A Comprehensive Historical Encyclopedia*, 31 December, Jewish Women's Archive, available: https://jwa.org/encyclopedia/article/bodenwieser-gertrud [accessed 2 December 2020].

Schwartz, P. and Schwartz, M. (2011) *The Dance Claimed Me: A Biography of Pearl Primus*, New Haven: Yale University Press. ProQuest Ebook Central, available: https://ebookcentral-proquest-com.proxy.lib.ul.ie/lib/univlime-ebooks/detail.action?docID=3420692 [accessed 16 July 2021].

Soares, J. (2005) 'Horst, Louis', in Cohan, S. J., ed., *The International Encyclopedia of Dance*, Oxford: Oxford University Press, available: www.oxfordreference.com/view/10.1093/acref/9780195173697.001.0001/acref-9780195173697-e-0794 [accessed 13 July 2021].

Stock, C. (2017) 'Beyond intercultural to the accented body', in *Contemporary Choreography: A Critical Reader*, in Butterworth, J. and Wildschut, L., eds, Abingdon and New York: Routledge, 342–357. ProQuest Ebook Central, available: https://ebookcentral.proquest.com/lib/univlime-ebooks/detail.action?pq-origsite=primo&docID=5178425 [accessed 16 July 2021].

Walther, S. (1993) 'The dance of death: description and analysis of *The Green Table*', *Choreography and Dance: An International Journal*, 3(2). ProQuest Ebook Central, available: https://ebookcentral-proquest-com.proxy.lib.ul.ie/lib/univlime-ebooks/detail.action?docID=237417 [accessed 16 July 2021].

Wex Arts (n.d.) *Boyzie Cekwana*, available: https://wexarts.org/performing-arts/boyzie-cekwana [accessed 22 July 2021].

Whatley, S. (2013) 'Siobhan Davies RePlay: (re)visiting the digital archive', *International Journal of Performance Arts and Digital Media*, 9(1), 83–98.

Yeoh, F. (2013) 'Choreographers' moral right of integrity', *Journal of Intellectual Property Law & Practice*, 8(1), 43–58, available: https://doi.org/10.1093/jiplp/jps184 [accessed 16 July 2021].

A CHOREOGRAPHIC VOICE

CHOREOGRAPHY FOR SOCIAL CHANGE

Individual artists may freely push boundaries through choreography that addresses themes about gender, politics, sexuality, power relations and environmental concerns. Other dance choreographers create under the radar, working within parameters of conservatism, censorship, societal and political restrictions. While exploring some examples here it is worth noting that controversy, innovation and change-making relate to the time, place and context of both the artist and the audience. Brave and ground-breaking choreography by artists such as Isadora Duncan, Vaslav Nijinsky and Chandralekha, for example, were deemed radical because their point of view was in stark contrast to the prevailing attitudes, morality and gender expectations of their time. What might be termed controversial or provocative is intertwined with the audience's attitudes, experiences and knowledge of what has come before, such that new choreography is also contextualised within the scope of dance history. Some artists may deliberately set out to be provocative or promote a specific point of view; yet all embody the political and social reality of their lived experiences.

Digitalisation has led to a high level of choreographic hybridisation as artists absorb multiple stimuli that can be both invasive and enriching. Increasingly, the process involves filtering and synergising a surfeit of material to emerge with a personal voice. Liminality, or the spaces between these influences, commonly occurs in binaries across generations, between memories and present realities, past processes and current trends, personal space and place.

DOI: 10.4324/9781003020110-6

Artists migrating to another country may work within diaspora communities where re-creations, reiterations, and preservations of cultural material occur alongside new influences and sources of inspiration. These interconnections enable a mesh of embodied pathways to coexist with contemporary relevance – such complex liminality creates active zones of exploration and imagining. The examples that follow exemplify the power of dance as an agency for reflection, transformation and change.

Exemplar 1 – Alvin Ailey, *Cry* for social justice

Alvin Ailey's choreography embraced his family history. A childhood spent in the south of America during the Civil Rights movement of the 1960s and 70s and witnessing the treatment of African Americans, especially his mother, deeply influenced his choreography. Seminal works such as *Revelations* (1960), and in particular the solo *Cry* (1971), were drawn directly from his mother's life and story. What is striking about Ailey's work is his ability to combine the harsh realities of life with joy, and the celebration of humanity. Powerful movement by wonderful dancers, uplifting music sourced from gospel, traditional and jazz sounds work in combination with a thematic sense of overcoming and deep spirituality.

Trained in the Lester Horton technique that incorporates extended lines for the torso through flat backs, lateral tilts and circular connections through the spine, Ailey blends this vernacular with the mobile, percussive body beats and rhythms of African aesthetics. This unites his own cultural identity with Western dance training. Added to the mix are the rhythms of jazz and sheer athleticism that enables virtuosic elegance and grounded, earthy movement to work together – this became the company's signature style. The combination of authentic storytelling, powerful music and eloquent performers has resonated with audiences around the world for decades and has made Ailey's iconic work *Revelations* one of the most watched contemporary dance works of all time.

Cry was created in 1971 as a birthday present for Alvin Ailey's mother. Originally danced by Judith Jamieson, this relatively short (16 minutes) solo moves through three sections recounting the hardships of slavery, the pain of loss for loved ones and family members, and a finale that reverberates with optimism and hope. Each section has a different motivation and pace requiring physical and emotional complexity that is supported by the lyrics and rhythm of the music. A woman appears in white with arms held high, wrapped in a long scarf that later transforms into a cleaning cloth, a flag of defiance and an elegant shawl; however, it is the full white skirt that symbolises the wings of a bird and a metaphor for freedom. Some of the positions, such as the dancer arched backwards and the skirt held behind, echo the shapes in classical ballet's iconic solo *The Dying Swan* created by Marius Petipa for Anna Pavlova. Although it is doubtful that Ailey had this in mind when choreographing *Cry* the legacy of two iconic solos for virtuosic female dancers in white, one classical and the other contemporary, is a compelling story for dance. At the time of its creation in early 1970 a solo danced by an African American woman was almost unheard of – in fact the previously mentioned (Chapter 1) Josephine Baker was probably the only other. The solo is exemplified by dignity and spiritual grace enabling the dancer to soar above the dark, thematic material of slavery and subjugation. *Cry* retains its place as a seminal work in the company repertoire as an anthem to all women around the world, especially women of colour.

Alvin Ailey's choreography came from lived experiences recounted through multi-layered narratives comprising literal situations such as the baptism scene 'Wade in the Water' and the church celebration of 'Rock my Soul' in *Revelations* and the personal expression of anger for injustices in *Cry*. Through his company, he sought to show the beauty of African American dancers to the world at a period in time when there was segregation, with no opportunities for his dancers to join mainstream classical or contemporary companies, or to live the same lives as other young dancers growing up in America. By bringing the company, and the power of storytelling into the theatres of America and around the world he gently expounded the politics of the time through dance. The Alvin Ailey Dance Foundation set up in 1968 continues to support young African American dancers through various programmes that give equal opportunities based on skill and talent while inspiring countless generations of dancers of colour to pursue their dance dreams as professional artists.

Exemplar 2 – Eko Supriyanto, *Cry Jailolo* for climate change

During the political regime of President Sukarno (1945–1967) in Indonesia, there was a rejection of Western values and influences such that artists were encouraged to look inwards towards their local cultures to find inspiration for art-making. This led to a distinctive style that works across all of the arts in Indonesia. In dance, the classical styles of the Javanese court dance, for example, sustained a unique training style until in previous decades Western influences became more pervasive as Indonesian choreographers moved overseas to train and work. Hence the dance ecology was not only diverse but rich in creative platforms and local festivals that encouraged individual expression and the presentation of local issues and concerns (Raditya 2021).

> The emergence of Indonesian contemporary dance evolved through a long process. It was different to the journey of contemporary dance in the West that included modern and postmodern phases. In contrast, contemporary dance in Indonesia was initiated with a spirit of cultural renewal working from existing traditional dance forms.
> (Murgiyanto 2016, p.142)

Eko Supriyanto exemplifies this background. Trained in Javanese court dance and the martial arts form of *penkat silat* from a young age and learning the key attributes of various roles he furthered his dance and choreographic study in the USA completing a Master of Fine Arts in 2001. Artistic Director of Ekos Dance Company and Solo Dance Studio in Surakarta, Indonesia, in 2013 he created the ground-breaking choreography *Cry Jailolo*.

Supriyanto was influenced by his visits to the province of Northern Halmahera, Maluku and wanted to highlight the impact of climate change in the region and the destruction of the island corals. Not only was the habitat affected but also the lives of the local fishermen were impacted. In response, Supriyanto assembled a group of local young fishermen with no dance experiences and worked to create a powerful piece based on their lived experiences – it has since toured and touched audiences in many countries.

Their context is remarkable: daytime farmers and fishermen unfurling their nets in Jailolo, a remote seaside village in Indonesia. Yet the intensity of their simple actions, the pride of their stamps, and the depth of a rich cultural heritage demand attention. The endless passing of lines back and forth with military precision might wear thin as it constitutes the substance of the choreography; but just as it lulls us into a certainty, suddenly a new template emerges... Over time, the dance becomes a riveting exposé about survival as the context of the dancers/fishermen merge to those at the front line of global warming facing drought and ghost nets of dying fish. The poignancy intensifies as the region is blanketed in the haze from Indonesian forest fires and farmers, such as these, are caught in one of the biggest catastrophes of our time.

(*Critical Dance*, UK, Burridge 2015)

Exemplar 3 – Lin Hwai-Min, *Portrait Of The Families* (家族合唱): voices for freedom

Although the content of Cloud Gate Dance Theatre of Taiwan's decades-spanning repertoire is diverse, the context is always about home, belonging and identity. The company style is distinctive and contemporary, yet deeply rooted in Chinese traditions; the superb dancers have embraced stringent training to develop an innovative, East/West organic dance language as introduced in Chapter 1. Dancers move in a liquid vertical plane, rising and falling through strong use of the legs and circular motions of the arms and torso channelling spirituality and the somatic connection between body and mind.

Coming from a literary background and being a published author has impacted the choreographer's emphasis on training well-rounded articulate artists. This holistic concern extends to incorporating traditions like calligraphy into their training and underpins an understanding of works like *Cursive* (行草 《稻禾) and *Pine Smoke* (松烟). These choreographies not only extol the elegance of line as the dancers echo the movement of delicate brushstrokes and marks on paper; they juxtapose this within the metaphoric emptiness of the spaces in between. Space becomes an equal catalyst for what is added and what is left behind in a rich transposition from paper to movement. Expressing balance and harmony with profound humanity, Lin Hwai-min's choreography reaches into the hearts and minds of the audience and engages them in a special way that is intangible and unique. It is realised through a complexity of storytelling, movement, creativity in conjunction with a personal investigation into the context of his beloved country and his ability to connect past, present and future. An example is the 1997 *Portrait of the Families* (家族合唱).

Here a sense of urgency permeates as the dancers frantically leap, roll, yell and climb over each other in defiance of the prevailing politics of the day, retelling the 1947 massacres in their country after an anti-government uprising. Using multiple projectors with old family photos and images, it parallels the realities of people's lives confronted with the harrowing challenges they faced through civil war and of living with fear. Told through five female protagonists, the language of the soundtrack includes local dialects, western music together with Beijing opera, to paint a picture of past and present, East and West. As in all of Lin's choreography, there are many atmospheres and episodes. Layers include a hypnotic stepping dance of rice planting accompanied by a local song – this inclusion of an age-old folk dance immediately juxtaposes a simple life of maintaining daily necessities against the frantic call to action of the moment. It is bold and raw – an immediate rally to fight injustices and policies of exile and control. Taipei Post reporter Diane Baker (2011) writes that "Lin has repeatedly said that *Portrait* is not political." She continues to observe that he does want to draw attention to photos such as the one from 1947 that shows a burned-out car on Taipei's Dihua Street (迪化街). She states:

> The area was 'ground zero' for the 228 Incident, when the Taiwan Provincial Monopoly Bureau personnel beat and arrested a cigarette vendor on Feb. 27, 1947, for selling illegal cigarettes, triggering riots and protests against the KMT administration.

Exemplar 4 – Candoco and Claire Cunningham: dance and diversity

Candoco was introduced in Chapter 1 as part of a discussion on versatile choreographers like Arlene Phillips and is further explored in Chapter 6 in relation to diverse voices in dance. Candoco is an inclusive repertory dance company based in the United Kingdom, working with disabled and non-disabled performing artists. Founded in 1991 by Celeste Dandeker-Arnold OBE and Adam Benjamin, the company honours "different ways of seeing, of being and of making art" and positions itself "at the forefront of the conversation around dance and disability" (Candoco Dance Company n.d.). The company collaborates with notable local and international guest choreographers, staging Hofesh Shechter's *The Perfect Human* (2008), Jérôme Bel's *The Show Must Go On* (2014, 2017), and *Unspoken Spoken* (2018), a dance film by Fin Walker and recipient of the One Dance UK Dance On Screen – Impact Award 2018. The company has inspired diverse-ability dancers across the world with inclusive companies being established and a strong independent artist sector.

Scottish multidisciplinary performer and choreographer Claire Cunningham also creates with diversity making innovative and provocative work. Sculptures and imagery synergise to make evocative narratives while her crutches are sometimes an extension of her body, a point of balance, an external character, or a prop – usually all of these. As an acclaimed artist, Cunningham's practice is "rooted in the study and use/misuse of her crutches and the exploration of the potential of her specific physicality with a conscious rejection of traditional dance techniques (developed for non-disabled bodies)" (Claire Cunningham n.d.). Her choreographies range from intimate solos to group ensembles, with notable works *Give Me a Reason to Live* (2014) inspired by the works of Medieval painter Hieronymus Bosch and duet/co-choreography of *The Way You Look (at me) Tonight* (2016) with Jess Curtis. An eloquent speaker, teacher, and mentor, she works towards promoting inclusive dance in her workshops and collaborations.

While these examples present established artists, there are numerous initiatives for the disability sector across schools, communities, dance companies, and independent projects. Spaces for performances extend beyond traditional theatres into public arenas, art galleries and museums with activity only limited by accessibility. While performances by diverse bodies have progressed into the mainstream consciousness of dance audiences, there are substantial gaps to be addressed before dance education programmes offered in schools, training institutes and professional companies are truly diverse. Structures in place for dance training (including access and studio design), embedded aesthetics, access opportunities, trained teachers and mentors, choreographers alongside fellow dancers who can create and collaborate across diversity continue to limit opportunities. For many contemporary choreographers, unique creative opportunities arise through working in integrated dance projects.

Exemplar 5 – Lloyd Newson: social issues explored through physical theatre, verbatim and film

Australian born Lloyd Newson trained initially in psychology before attending the London School of Contemporary Dance in the 1980s. A talented dancer, he worked with many renowned choreographers and companies before founding the physical theatre company DV8. His creative works have helped shape physical theatre and confronted social issues through arresting pieces such as *Dead Dreams of Monochrome Men* (1988), exploring male sexuality and homoeroticism through the lens of the serial killer Dennis Nielson; *Enter Achilles* (1995) which explores masculine identity; and *The Cost of Living* (see Chapter 6), which was commissioned as a film by the UK's Channel 4 in 2004. Newson's recent works have used verbatim interpretations of interview texts from accounts of homosexual encounters, abuse and racism to challenge current social issues. For example, *Can We Talk About This?* (2011) explored "the interrelated issues of freedom of speech, multiculturalism and Islam as manifest in Western democracies" drawing on interviews from a range of public figures and ordinary citizens discussing topics such as censorship, religious fundamentalism and multiculturalism (DV8 n.d.).

CHOREOGRAPHY AS A FIELD OF INQUIRY

Making a dance always involves research and inquiry. In the creative process (Chapter 2) it can be shown that from the early stages of 'preparation' to the 'incubation' this aspect is particularly highlighted, although it continues throughout the entire process. Practical consideration and creative building of the work are foregrounded – these could be termed the 'representational' aspects. 'Non-representational' aspects occur in parallel and offer rich fields of exploration that connect choreography with wider philosophical questions; for example, on identity, embodiment and the notion of 'being'. Articulating and identifying these foundations in a project focuses the work for the artists by offering a contextual lens and theoretical underpinning that situates the choreography in a wider field of artistic practice. For dance makers working towards practice-based degrees in universities and institutes of higher learning (IHL), incorporating some of these 'markers' throughout the creation process is crucial. This section gives a brief overview of some of these intersections.

Choreographic practice as research

Each stage of the creative process can be unpacked, investigated, interrogated in conjunction with theoretical framing. This dialogical approach between practice, research and articulation underlies the concept of 'practice as research'. Choreographers can implement strategies that structure tasks for themselves and their dancers – some are suggested earlier in this volume. This conscious, reflective and critical aspect of dance practice as research that is undertaken at choreographic laboratories, dance-house residencies or through performative practice as higher degree study centralises inquiry as an objective.

Choreographic laboratories and dance houses

Organisations such as Critical Path (Australia), Dance Nucleus (Singapore) and The Choreographic Lab (UK) for example, are set up as dance research laboratories for artists to experiment, investigate, present and host conversations about developing work. They aim to share practice and, importantly, act as networking spaces for independent artists who create outside of either a company framework or tertiary institutions. An essential aim is process-focused research. Performance outcomes are often in a hybrid format including dialogues, showing of excerpts of dance material, works-in-progress, film, interdisciplinary collaborations, exhibitions, and 'sharings'. Allied dance practices like curatorship, heritage, photography, film and archival research are important aspects of these centres with many taking up a role of cultural preservation through combining interview material from artists, with exhibitions, written material and performances.

These platforms, the participating artists along with their audiences, remain a niche sector of the dance community and enrich the space by enabling the exploration of alternative performance modes, the presentation of current issues and themes that are often at the edge of the mainstream. They also offer independents essential studio time in tandem with resources and support.

Performative practice

The concept of this term relates to the notion that performance involves action that is transformative for the choreographer, dancer and viewer. The dancer/choreographer embodies their history, race, identity, education and knowledge (Bourdieu 1977; Foucault 1972) with a sense of self in relation to the 'other' (the viewer) who finds points of connection, nodes of disparity and difference. The performative space between is alive and a temporal zone for exchange. Many artists undertake periods of deep personal research of their practice that are reflective and reflexive; realigning choreography in new ways that encompass a deeper understanding of past and present work while predicting new directions. The difference relates to an initial process of personal review of thoughts and feelings about the process and a second that invites insights in a wider contextual frame.

Creativity emerges from the embodiment of memories that reflect both literal and abstract narratives either overtly or subliminally. American dance philosopher Maxine Sheets-Johnstone states, "As one might wonder about the world in words, I am wondering the world directly, in movement" (Sheets-Johnstone 2011, p.422). The writer's intensive research into phenomenology enables a fluid dialogue between mind/body connections, bodily texts and language texts. The notion is that a dancer improvising is communicating with the 'now' and exists beyond drawing from their past experiences.

International dance artist and educator Susan Sentler, for instance, has had a career spanning making, creating and performing dance along with academic teaching and writing. Sentler's work is multidisciplinary underpinned by an interest in somatics and the relationship to digital imagery. Together with Glenna Batson, the duo has developed a practice-based research method titled *Human Origami*, an improvisation on the biological archive of bodily folding. Performances occur in gallery/museum contexts creating 'responses' or 'activations' within exhibitions as well as durational installations orchestrating objects, sound, moving/still images highlighting absence and presence in the performing body.

> *Human Origami* is an improvisational exploration of body folding that addresses multiple levels of embodiment – biological, meta-physical, creative and performative. This process-based, somatic movement approach to expanding the corporeal, took its point of departure from phenomenologist Gilles Deleuze, explicitly from his writings on the *fold*.
>
> (Sentler and Batson 2020, pp.35–61)

The performative here is defined through a multidisciplinary, embodied approach with reflection on and in action (Schön 2011). This theory was first developed to understand how practitioners in fields like health and education develop professionally, but also seems relevant to understand the practise of choreography. Donald Schön (1990) speaks of these two types of reflection: reflection-on-action and reflection-in-action. This duality is applicable to choreography 'as' research and 'in' research; that is the reflection occurs on both the creative process and the decisions made, combined with reflection on the action/performativity in a somatic equation that connects extrinsic and intrinsic experiences. Reflection within the 'on-action' concept is a three-pronged process: to *recall* specific instances that warrant further exploration, to *reflect* critically on the whole choreography and parts, then to *react* to these reflections. The connections and disruptions are in constant dialogue enabling shifts, growth and change (see Chapter 3).

WRITING AND CHOREOGRAPHY

Over the past decades, opportunities for formal study in dance at the higher degree level have presented many possibilities. Worldwide, universities offer dance at the degree level through Diploma courses, BA programmes and electives, BA Honours, Master's (MA) and Doctoral (PhD) degrees. The basis for all of these is inquiry: research, investigation and practice that is underpinned by critical articulation. Practice-based degrees include these components in different configurations and points of emphasis moving between written text and the text of the body. Such degrees validate choreography and other dance-based practise on par with a traditional thesis as outcomes, with universities assigning different assessment weightings for practical portfolio work and a written exegesis.

Postgraduate degrees at MA and PhD level based specifically on choreography exist and some are listed at the end of this chapter. All require a structured approach comprising a workable research question, research design with aims and objectives, theoretical framing, anticipated literature topics, methodologies incorporating quantitative and qualitative components, data collection and analysis strategies, summary findings with recommendations and outcomes. These elements interweave throughout the study and are interdependent. Most research studies will encompass several methods and approaches. Intersecting, and cross-relating material is useful to not only check findings but also view them in multiple ways through varying lenses. The model shown in Figure 5.1 indicates these spheres of action and inquiry. Some research areas of interest to dance researchers follow and are presented by way of a general introduction with key contributors and directions.

Philosophical framing

Dance research and criticism, insights and some comprehension of philosophical strands and schools of thought enable points of reference, ideas for consideration, and ways to frame the choreographic

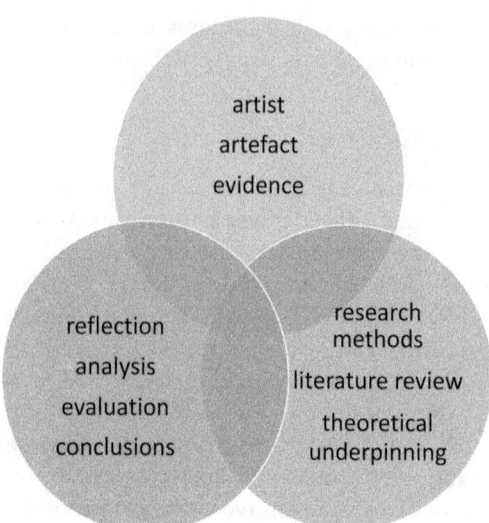

Figure 5.1 Frame or lens of research – a convergence of interdependent dialogues

process. Some of these fields are presented in a general discussion below.

Notions of aesthetics

Chapter 2 ended with some points for reviewing dance in the immediate sense through responding to a performance or reflecting on your own choreography and that of peers. Chapter 3 elaborated on this further through articulating the approaches developed by Liz Lerman and Larry Lavender. Criticism at a deeper level is a complex field of inquiry that relates to the philosophical position the viewer might take to validate their judgements and arguments.

The study of aesthetics goes back to Ancient Greece and the time of Aristotle and Plato. The concepts are revisited and recalibrated throughout history; essentially the two underlying principles are the balance between the representation/object (the dance performance) and the interpretation of it (response to it). The interplay between these two, the 'weight' given, and how judgments are made to articulate them are aligned to evolving schools of thought. In the critical review model in Chapter 2 the components of describing, analysing, contextualising and evaluating appear in a continuous cycle that interweaves and overlaps. Of these elements, the most personal or subjective perspective is evaluation. Here an opinion of 'like' or 'dislike' should be supported by a deeper evaluation that seeks to support personal preferences; the essence is to differentiate between a subjective approach to critiquing and an objective one based on knowledge and contextualisation.

To continue this debate, philosophers such as Immanuel Kant (1724–1804) believed that personal 'taste' (subjectivity) could be included in the debate about 'good' and 'bad' art. Surmising that this idea was based on personal, sensory perception it can be concluded that it is a purely subjective judgment; however, if a wider notion that something is 'beautiful' be based on wider consensus, for instance, that other observers would also agree with this point of view it would be considered true. This thesis, however, becomes outdated within the parameters of cultural choice and preference where there are divergent views. Kant's contemporary Scottish philosopher David Hume (1711–1776) somewhat agreed with this idea about taste but conceded cultural difference as an influence. He elaborates in his Essay on Taste:

> You will never convince a man, who is not accustomed to Italian music, and has not an ear to follow its intricacies, that a Scotch tune is not preferable ... So the good critic must overcome the challenge of cultural prejudice.
>
> (Gracyk 2020, n.d)

In concluding these examples from Kant and Hume, the relevance is in noting that subjectivity, personal opinion and taste, is limited to our sphere of experience – by stepping back and extending knowledge through a wider frame the work (choreography) reflection can occur in both a subjective and objective context. This tenet is repositioned and validated in further work by twentieth-century phenomenologists.

Intentionalism

Other developments that are relevant to dance research, and in particular the assessment of conceptual art, are judgments made about 'intention'. Philosopher Monroe Beardsley and literary theorist William K. Wimsatt (1987) were unequivocally opposed to the idea that the artist's intentions were relevant to judging an artefact (the choreography) believing that the artwork stands alone irrespective of what the intention is or how the viewer reacts to the concept. A major issue with this approach is that it is tied to a product (the performance) that is deemed finished and final rather than as a living site for interaction and transformation as a shared experience between the artist and the viewer.

Some resonance to this notion exists today in the context of social media where often the pre-publicity phase outlining the intention and predicting the choreography through online postings, sharing of rehearsal clips and comments is extensive. The audience can become so well versed in the intention that it is embedded in their consciousness and approaching a performance with fresh eyes and an objective perspective is not easy.

Phenomenology, embodiment and 'becoming'

In a practice-based degree, the choreographer is always oscillating between subjectivity and objectivity in framing their inquiry. For dance researchers, the field of phenomenology supports such investigations. In essence, the acceptance of the subjective including empathy, personal sensations and 'felt' experiences in conjunction with intellectual assessments are considered authentic. Being free to be intuitive, expressive and create without constant reference to outside perspectives and reference points through maintaining a personal voice has revitalised and authenticated performative practice.

> Phenomenology is the study of structures of consciousness as experienced from the first-person point of view… issues of intentionality, consciousness, qualia, and first-person perspective have been prominent in recent philosophy of mind.
>
> (Smith 2018, para 1 and 2)

French phenomenologists Maurice Merleau-Ponty and post-structuralist Gilles Deleuze are widely cited as sources in choreographic practice-based higher degrees. The reasons being that Merleau-Ponty united the essential notions of embodiment with phenomenology while Deleuze iterated the idea of transformation and 'becoming'.

Deleuze worked with compatriot Felix Guattari (1987) to contribute the notion of a 'rhizomatic' approach to research validating multiple, non-hierarchical entry and exit points to break down a linear way of reflection – this is particularly relevant to analysing dance in both the choreographic process and in critiquing dance in general. In contrast to the systematic accumulation of information and patterns akin to a philosophical structuralist approach to arrive at a conclusion, Deleuze and Guattari acknowledge tangents, unrelated episodes and non-linear processes of data collection that are more aligned to making art.

Multiple intelligences and proprioception

Martha Graham famously said "Movement never lies" (Graham 1991, p.8). Graham intrinsically knew that the body is a site for memories, experiences with ways of moving that are intertwined with learned behaviours, accumulated knowledge, perception and intuition. It encapsulates ways of knowing and seeing the world that is embodied and accumulates layering traces of historiography (Foucault 1997) over time.

Studies in Multiple Intelligences and Multiliteracies concede such multiple ways of knowing. Howard Gardner's work became popular in the 1980s and 1990s; however, in later years these theories were superseded by embracing interdisciplinary practices. In relation to bodily intelligence he observes:

> To see these other competencies (musical, linguistic, bodily intellects) at work, we need to look at the kind... of ballet a Martha Graham might choreograph (perhaps about a set of equations or a proof!).
>
> (Gardner 1983, p.169)

Dancers intrinsically understand the meaning of the term 'muscle memory'. It enables them to recall a dance they have not performed for a long time, execute the essentials of a classical ballet class or a traditional dance step with unnatural postures as second nature. This is possible by the neurological mechanism whereby the body recalls pathways of movement termed 'proprioception' – the ability to sense, locate and feel body parts. The concept of embodiment relates to a holistic understanding of somatic mind/body connections and the iteration of creative dialogues across multiple memory zones.

Critical lens

A critical lens can focus inquiry and cross-correlate practice around a larger context. Scaffolding the research within, for example, feminist theory, post-colonialism, the gendered body, Queer theory, hermeneutics, proxemics and others adds a deeply researched field that can work in parallel with your own investigation. This duality not only ensures the creative research project is grounded in an established canon with supportive literature but importantly, stimulates choreographic directions that are reflective and responsive. Developing choreographic task-building activities around a thematic lens, delving into previous writing and examples of past work with a similar focus, can inform and inspire new directions. Examples of choreographers working in theory and practice with a 'gendered' lens follow.

The gendered body

Choreographers such as Matthew Bourne in his previously mentioned choreography *Swan Lake* (see Chapter 1) have made clear statements about gender roles and stereotypical expectations by including male swans. In Indonesia, Rianto's work *Medium* (2016) questions expectations of traditional role-playing in Javanese dance by breaking cultural boundaries and social class. In this performative work, he interrogates the issue of gender migration in the cross-gender dance form Lengger Lanang.

> Although Rianto learnt and danced *lengger* for so many years, it was not until 2007 that he found out about Dariah (1920–2018), the last living *lengger lanang* (male *lengger* who does female impersonation) ... In *Medium* Rianto departs from questioning a trance-dancing body to chart his personal artistic journey.
> (Minarti 2018)

Rianto also performed with Akram Khan in *Until the Lions* (2016), inspired by an excerpt from the Mahabharata.

Female classical dancers have historically been objectified and defined variously across cultures as little more than prostitutes to low-paid workers (Burt 1998; Manning 1997; Thomas 1993). The repressive role of women in dance, coupled with a hierarchical system of pedagogy and company structures, leaves them prey to abuse and exploitation. In relation to Indian classical dance Hanna wrote…

> Dance not only reflects what is but also suggests what might be. In this process dance generally both mirrors and prefigures shifts in sexual mores and gender roles. Changing dance styles and dramatic themes are cultural constructions that respond to an altered environment, encompassing the views and behaviour of women.
>
> (Hanna in Thomas 1993, p.132)

In 1965 postmodern dancer Yvonne Rainer penned her 'No Manifesto' that became an affirmation for empowerment of contemporary women in dance:

> No to spectacle, no to virtuosity, no to transformations and magic and make believe… no to seduction of spectator by the wiles of the performer…
>
> (quoted by Copeland in Thomas 1993, p.142)

A gendered lens for research in dance offers many points of investigation offering acute insights into dance as a mirror of society. Bourne, Khan and Rianto all completed choreographic-based dance degrees and their deeply layered works exemplify research as practice and current directions in which many leading choreographers are teaching artists and have attachments with academic institutions as artists or companies in residence.

Methods of inquiry

All research involves methods of investigation to gather information, test a hypothesis, track an intervention and experiment with options and possibilities. Immersive experiences, autoethnographic documentation and the incorporation of 'lived experiences' are part of current research practices in dance. Some examples are listed below although connectivity, mixed methods of research and fluid approaches are commonly incorporated and valued in research projects.

Performative practice

Performative practice is both a research practice and a method. As was demonstrated in the previous section, choreographers explore areas of interest both specifically and generally. Concepts from theoretical framing can be trialled and the dancers' response logged, filmed, journaled, and performed – often a storyboard of short tasks is generated, each addressing a component of the larger objectives for the research. Performative practice is an umbrella term that involves many layers of process and investigation.

Qualitative and quantitative data collection

Quantitative research involves data collection through surveys, multiple-choice questions and other means that require rapid responses and little extra information. Researchers use this method to lay the groundwork for deeper investigation as it is useful to illustrate preferences, trends, profiles and demographics of the respondents through numbers presented in graphs, tables and charts. Other quantitative data may be incorporated when the researcher implements a coding system to accurately note observations according to a pre-designed framework and inquiry methods. In the arts, researchers are questioning the value of this sort of information favouring qualitative methods.

Qualitative research data is gleaned from interview and observation material. It usually incorporates a mix of one-to-one interviews (including those sourced via email or facetime), small or focus group interviews and observations.

Both methods allow the researcher to gauge the option to incorporate 'interventions' into a study whereby something new is introduced and trialled with responses analysed in contrast to a control group where nothing is changed. In medical science, this is common practice with a placebo administered to a control group.

Narrative research

A subset of the qualitative method is narrative research that is gaining validity in academic degree programmes. Accurately observing, recording and transcribing the work and stories of artists has taken on added importance, particularly when working with senior artists practitioners who pre-date the digital age. There is an urgency to ensure their essential place in the history of dance is documented, critiqued and included in contextual discussions about dance. This method involves taking a position as an interpreter and analyst – synergising what the researcher might consider as key points of someone's life, with evidence-based documentation such as media reviews, photographs and anecdotal material from other respondents who can confirm and augment the story.

The process should be clearly defined through developing key research questions and include some acknowledgement of personal interest and bias in terms of the researcher's lens and point of view. The literature has several models to assist the research in design and interpretation (Denzin and Lincoln 2017).

Action research

This methodology is widely adopted in education settings to encourage teachers, and whole schools, to reflect on their practice. It encompasses research in action and reflection in action. The basic principles revolve around a set of spirals (Kemmis and McTaggart 2000, p.595) that begin with the tenet of plan, act and observe, reflect – moving on progressively to act and observe, reflect; thus, moving through continual stages of reassessment. For choreographers, this might be considered a normal process as each rehearsal involves these components then moving forward, at the next set of rehearsals will be further reflection, assessment, and a new plan of action is trialled with the dancers. Action research and reflective practice (Schön 1987) are also fundamental tenets to such learning experiences.

Mapping

Often an overview of the current scene in a topic to be investigated benefits from a process known as 'mapping'. This is a survey method to systematically find out what studies have preceded your research and current work in the topic area such that the data can be located within a wider context. Mapping is useful for localised or smaller regional studies to ascertain the key players in the field and discover the work done so far. This approach will also assist in identifying possible interviewees and give an 'emotive' sense of the terrain as investigating people, places and histories underpin this process.

A/r/tography

The term a/r/tography was created to signify the multiple roles played in arts-based research: artist-researcher-teacher. Practice-based underpinnings focus on how "theorizing through inquiry seeks understanding by way of an evolution of questions within the living-inquiry processes of the practitioner." The practices of artists and educators are considered to be forms of research and the "intellectual, imaginative, and insightful work" they create is "grounded in ongoing forms of recursive and reflexive inquiry engaged in theorizing for understanding" (Irwin and Springgay 2008, p.xxii).

Through this research method, artist/researcher/teacher are represented in one individual. This approach recognises that these three roles are often united, particularly in the tertiary arts sector where the term 'teaching artists' is applied to staff who may be equally active in all areas. These three strands enable a research design incorporating the duality of objectivity and subjectivity across them, crystalizing experience from multiple perspectives. Recordings of inner/personal reflections might be journaled, filmed and archived then sampled against tasks that require an objective/outside view. In a sense, there would be six strands of research within the same project as it moves between the crystalized roles and intrinsic and extrinsic viewpoints.

Case study approach

Generally, the length of time (three years) devoted to a postgraduate degree cannot include longitudinal studies. This is common practice in research institutions that often follows a sample group for five to ten years or more. Hence a case study approach is adopted that moves from a larger understanding of a topic through literature research, to an application-based approach involving small case samples. This method can suggest, or make inferences about themes, trends, patterns and outcomes within the context of the cases studied. There may be wider implications that emerge from the case study, however it is contextualised within a small frame involving the participants included as case examples.

Autoethnographic inquiry

Autoethnography occurs when the researcher incorporates their personal experience as an access point to develop an understanding of the experience (Ellis and Bochner 2000). Many dancers embarking on postgraduate university degrees come from backgrounds that include years of professional performing, choreographing and participation in the dance community. This method not only recognises the embodied self as a valid site for research but supports the incorporation of invaluable historiography, wisdom and traces of lived participation that can contextualise and support further investigations. Stranding self-actualisation in conjunction with wider contexts gleaned from literature sources and the practice of other artists enables transference from past experience to present directions via a structured, articulated approach defined by a clear methodology.

Immersive and experiential practice

Various dance companies work with this principle of 'felt' experiences (see Cloud Gate Dance Theatre and Butoh dance, Chapter 1) to enable an authenticity of expression and understanding of what the choreography is about. Performance artists often undergo extreme physical and emotional discomfort that is hyperreal such that their pain is viscerally transmitted to the viewer, which in turn confronts the audience with their own fears. This could include components such as isolation, sleep deprivation, starvation or physical harm such as puncturing the skin. Serbian artist Marina Abramović, for example, is known for endurance pieces that involve the audience directly such as her 2010 *The Artist is Present* at the MoMA, New York. Spanning 75 days she sat opposite an audience member who decided to come forward and stare into each other's eyes. Inevitably, it was the viewer who took the inward journey to confront their uncertainties as described by novelist Heather Rose (Rose 2016). The artist was a catalyst and the facilitator of this experience that became transformative for the hundreds of participants.

As a research method, the researcher can instigate tasks that can be logged, observed, coded and recorded then analysed. The aims and objectives of immersive research should be clearly defined and shared with participants who should formally confirm their participation through signing an agreement and ethics form.

Interdisciplinary practice

Modelling interdisciplinary creative practice enables choreographers to extend artistic boundaries through collaboration and inquiry with other fields. Theoretical framing, methodologies, common creative practices, along with performative descriptors, can flow and align within a broader scope gleaned from multiple perspectives across different art practices. In recent times, many dance artists work with digital technology; however, interdisciplinary work can extend into fields such as film, fashion, architecture, science and literature to name a few. For choreographers, the unifying element is the body in space, place and time.

A plurality of meanings can reach beyond the physical, culturally contextualized body, to synergise explorations of mind/body connections, somatic and visceral experiences (Burridge, 2020). Although research from each art form in an interdisciplinary study might be conducted as a discrete component with specific case examples to share, an underlying intention is to find core commonalities and linkages between them. Such approaches offer insights across art-making perspectives through actively engaging myriad entry points to creativity while acknowledging juxtapositions and directional tangents. While undertaking interdisciplinary research is enriching, in the twenty-first century, such skills are invaluable across multiple fields including the arts, science, education and business where curiosity, the ability to collaborate, move across fields of knowledge and extend boundaries are essential.

UNIVERSITY DANCE COURSES

As a full-time training option at the university level, dance may be offered through a humanities or social science faculty school or an academy of performing arts. Underpinning most such courses is a technical requirement with dancers typically needing to audition to enter the course. Internationally, prior training in a classical form (Western classical ballet, Indian Bharatanatyam, Thai Khon, Cambodian Khmer for example) is expected and other genres encouraged such as contemporary, jazz or street dance. Dancers are required to participate in technique classes as part of the audition process, participate in improvisation or composition class, or perform a short solo. Potential students are usually interviewed to ascertain their background and reasons for wanting to pursue dance as a career and candidates may also have to submit a written paper.

While being accepted into a tertiary dance programme is exciting, many dance students do not always fully comprehend the nature of their commitment. The linking of theory and practice is fundamental in conjunction with a large amount of reading, analysis and written work such as journaling and assignments. Developing articulate and reflective dancers is on par with training in technical proficiency and skills in performance and choreography. Appreciating the correlation between these components is vital to completing a dance degree with success.

In recent years many universities have further clarified and stranded options for the undertaking of postgraduate degrees. This is a rapidly evolving terrain as universities grapple with the economics of funding specific courses, such as dance studies, coupled with a wider industry need for graduates who can work in diverse areas, apply knowledge creatively and independently, thrive across disciplines plus work with new technologies. For some institutions, dance may be included as part of the ethos of a liberal arts approach where participation in modules and electives in the humanities enhance critical thinking, aesthetic appreciation cooperation, and collaboration capabilities to learning in other subjects via a holistic approach.

Diploma in Dance

A diploma degree is usually of shorter duration than a BA and is often recommended for talented dancers and choreographers who want to take a conservatoire approach foregrounding an intense focus on developing technique and choreographic skills. Students move rapidly through the programme with the aim to audition for professional work as soon as possible. Typically, these courses require less academic theory and writing components and include industry attachments and internships with companies. Because of this, dancers that are less proficient in written subjects might also be attracted to a diploma course along with students who want to 'test the ground' of dance studies before committing to further academic-based study. The time range can be three years to a one-year foundation course that allows a student to transition to a BA course. There are also diploma courses offered in dance teaching by organisations such as the Royal Academy of Dance (RAD). Currently, in many countries, university-based diploma courses are being phased out and BA and BA (Hons) offered as the first undergraduate course.

Bachelor of Performing Arts (Dance)

Students cover the components of the diploma course in terms of technique, choreography and reflection but align practice with dance theory, aesthetics, history, intercultural studies, interdisciplinary practice, dance pedagogy and elective modules. Electives might include dance therapy, dance for special needs, film, community dance, pedagogy, arts management, and curatorship among many others.

Urban cities include large diasporas of immigrant populations and dancers from diverse cultural backgrounds work together under the same BA Dance programme creating a rich opportunity for shared learning. Some universities offer double degrees so that dance students can take, for example, dance and law, economics, psychology or philosophy. The purpose of undertaking a BA dance degree is to broaden options for dance-based careers and enable the progression towards Honours, Master's and Doctoral studies.

BA Hons degree

An Honours (BA Hons) degree typically involves all of the BA components with an added requirement of writing a dissertation. Based on research into an area of the candidate's choice, the structure for the study usually includes modules such as research methods, academic writing and referencing, plus the submission of a well-defined proposal. Crafting a research question, aims and objectives, suggested literature to support the study, methodology for data collection, and proposed analyses should be clearly articulated. Many courses offer practice-based degrees allowing submission of performance and written work with percentage allocations for each component. The candidate will have a supervisor to guide and mentor the process. After completing such a degree many dance graduates move into the industry as performers, choreographers, teachers, community dance artists, independent practitioners, or a combination of all of these where they come under the umbrella term of 'freelancers'. While many want to immediately experience working in the industry, a proportion return after some years to continue in postgraduate dance programmes.

Master's degree

A dance-based Master's degree (MA) can include strands of study from a wide scope. For many institutions, this course is favoured by established dance professionals who want to make a career move into teaching at an arts institution, education department school, college or similar places that require the completion of a higher degree. For others, it is the chance to spend time on self-learning, exploration and extending skills and knowledge. Pedagogy, performance studies, interdisciplinary arts, therapy, somatic practice, dance science and medicine, dance research, ethnology and anthropology are among the many fields that dancers might move into. Dance can be the core of research in cultural studies, curatorial practices, women's studies, theology, psychology, philosophy, literature and film to name a few. Robotics, AI and interactive technologies also open up new ways of thinking about dance.

Courses specifically geared for specialising in choreography enable the best opportunities for self-learning within a mix of structured modules and personal growth. Practitioners that have worked in the industry benefit from time out for exploration with critical support and facilities that not only include studios, but also a variety of performance spaces and the latest digital technologies.

Doctorate by research, practice-based or portfolio

Although pathways and options vary, the outcome of obtaining a PhD can be life-changing for many dancers who want to move into areas of research, academic teaching and learning through working as teaching artists. While a PhD (Dance) or (Dance Studies) are specific courses, there are many alternative pathways via other faculties where candidates can make dance the core study. As university budgets are tightened, specialised courses like dance are in danger of being cut, forcing universities to constantly adapt and find new ways to work across faculty. Shared modules such as research methodologies, cultural studies, philosophy of art, criticism and aesthetics, might be shared across arts practices enriching the experience and networks of candidates through such interaction. There are positives in this approach but also negatives in that the position of dance as a valid field of inquiry is being diminished and eroding hard-fought battles over generations to have parity with all course options.

PhD degrees either occur through coursework modules or as a portfolio study process where the candidate is largely free to carry out a research project with supervision from the university and experts related to the investigation. Many institutions combine both of these streams and engage the students in interactive sessions such as performance showcases, seminars and sharing sessions where candidates can dialogue about their work-in-progress. In the later stages, they might also be encouraged to present aspects of their project at conferences, perform and publish some of their findings. It is common for full or part-time staff members in a tertiary dance programme to be engaged in completing a PhD with institutions committed to giving staff the opportunity to upgrade skills and take time out for professional development.

SUMMARY

In this chapter inspiring examples of choreography have demonstrated that dance is transformative and can be a powerful agent for reflection, inspiration, and a call to action. The scope of dance is rapidly moving as it responds to developments across the world. Social, political and cultural changes challenge many young people's possibilities and options, yet dance, as a non-verbal universal language, is often at the forefront. Whether dancer teacher volunteers are conducting programmes for traumatised young people in refugee camps, auditioning professional dancers fleeing war zones and arriving in a new country as refugees (Svendler Neilsen and Burridge 2020) or rediscovering and appreciating indigenous dance practices within their own country, the artform prevails and empowers.

Take the opportunity to find out about tertiary dance options in your own country and internationally. Many dance scholars decide to take up a dance programme in another country to experience a different culture, enrol in a specialised programme not available at home, or open up to a wider network of peers. Dance courses at the postgraduate level typically attract older candidates, many of whom have had exciting careers and want to open up to research and new ways of moving and thinking about dance. Others are interested in a multidisciplinary approach at an art institution or university that enables them to work across disciplines seeking points of connection and inspiration. To conclude, a list of sample university courses that specialise in dance and choreography are presented – there are many more throughout the world that celebrate the joys and challenges of dancing and choreographing.

Australia

Victorian College of the Arts, Melbourne University
https://finearts-music.unimelb.edu.au/study-with-us/discipline-areas/dance
Queensland University of Technology
www.qut.edu.au/courses/bachelor-of-fine-arts-dance
Western Australian Academy of Performing Arts
www.waapa.ecu.edu.au/courses-and-admissions/our-courses/postgraduate-studies-and-research

Finland

Uniarts Helsinki
www.uniarts.fi/en/study-programmes/dance-bachelors-programme/

Germany

HZT – Inter-University Centre for Dance
www.hzt-berlin.de/en/courses/study-courses/ba-dance-context-choreography/

Hong Kong

Hong Kong Academy of Performing Arts
www.hkapa.edu/dance/study-programmes/master-of-fine-arts-in-dance

Ireland

University of Limerick
www.ul.ie/gps/course/dance-performance-ma

Malta

University of Malta
www.um.edu.mt/performingarts/dance

New Zealand

The University of Auckland
www.auckland.ac.nz/en/study/study-options/find-a-study-option/master-of-dance-studies-mdancest.html

South Africa

University of Cape Town
www.ctdps.uct.ac.za/CTDPS/Programmes/Postgraduate Programmes

Sweden

Stockholm University of the Arts
www.uniarts.se/english/about-uniarts/department-of-dance

Taiwan

Taipei National University of the Arts
http://1www.tnua.edu.tw/~TNUA_DANCE/main.php

The Netherlands

Amsterdam University of the Arts – School for New Dance Development
www.atd.ahk.nl/en/dance-programmes/sndo/
Fontys Dance Academy
https://fontys.edu/Bachelors-masters/Bachelors/Dance.htm

UK

London Contemporary Dance School in association with University of the Arts London

www.lcds.ac.uk/postgraduate
Trinity Laban Conservatoire of Music and Dance: Choreography
www.postgrad.com/trinity-laban-conservatoire-of-music-and-dance-dance-choreography/course/
University of Roehampton
www.postgrad.com/university-of-roehampton-dance-choreography/course/
Central School of Ballet: MA Choreography
www.centralschoolofballet.co.uk/training/degree-courses/ma-choreography/

USA

State University of New York Purchase College
www.purchase.edu/academics/dance/
New York University Tisch School of the Arts
https://tisch.nyu.edu/dance

FURTHER READING

Alexandre, J. M. (2017) *Dance Leadership: Theory Into Practice*, London: Palgrave Macmillan.

Bunker, J. et al. (2013) *Thinking Through Dance: The Philosophy of Dance Through Performance and Practices*, Binsted: Dance Books.

Dodds, S. ed. (2019) *The Bloomsbury Companion to Dance Studies*, London: Bloomsbury Academic.

Fraleigh, S. H. and Hanstein, P. (1999) *Researching Dance: Evolving Modes of Inquiry*, Pittsburgh: University of Pittsburgh Press.

Jackson, N. M. and Phim, T. S. (2008) *Dance, Human Rights, and Social Justice Dignity in Motion*, Lanham: Scarecrow Press.

REFERENCES

Baker, D. (2011) 'Looking through a nation's family album', *Taipei Times*, 9 December, available: www.taipeitimes.com/News/feat/archives/2011/12/09/2003520280 [accessed 20 June 2021].

Burridge, S. (2015) 'Scene in Singapore: October 2015', *Critical Dance*, 31 October, available: https://criticaldance.org/scene-in-singapore-october-2015/ [accessed 30 June 2021].

Burridge, S. ed. (2020) *Embodied Performativity in Southeast Asia: Multidisciplinary Corporealities*, Abingdon: Routledge.

Burt, R. (1998) *Alien Bodies: Representations of Modernity, 'Race', and Nation in Early Modern Dance*, London: Routledge.

Candoco Dance Company (n.d.) *Home*, available: https://candoco.co.uk/ [accessed 25 June 2021].

Claire Cunningham (n.d.) *About*, available: www.clairecunningham.co.uk/about/ [accessed 23 June 2021].

Copeland, R. (1993) 'Dance, gender and culture', in Thomas, E., ed., *Dance, Gender and Culture*, London: Macmillan, 119–127.

Denzin, N. K. and Lincoln, Y. S. eds (1998) *Collecting and Interpreting Qualitative Materials*, Thousand Oaks: SAGE Publications.

DV8 (n.d.) *Can We Talk About This?*, available: www.dv8.co.uk/projects/can-we-talk-about-this/foreword-by-lloyd-newson [accessed 15 July 2021].

Gardner, H. (1983) *Frames of Mind: The Theory of Multiple Intelligences*, New York: Basic Books.

Gracyk, T. (2020) 'Hume's aesthetics', in Zalta, N. E., ed., *The Stanford Encyclopedia of Philosophy*, available: https://plato.stanford.edu/archives/sum2020/entries/hume-aesthetics/. [accessed 20 June 2021].

Graham, M. (1991) *Blood Memory: An Autobiography*, London: Macmillan

Hanna, J. L. (1993) 'Classical Indian dance and women's status', in Thomas, H., ed., *Dance, Gender and Culture*, London: Macmillan, 119–127.

Kemmis, S. and McTaggart, R. (2000) 'Participatory action research', in Denzin, N. K. and Lincoln, Y. S., eds, *Handbook of Qualitative Research* (2nd edn), Thousand Oaks: SAGE Publications, 567–607.

Minarti, H. (2018) *Rianto – A Transgressive Body*, Off Stage, available: www.esplanade.com/offstage/arts/rianto-a-transgressive-body [accessed 12 June 2021].

Murgiyanto, S. (2016) *Pertunjukan Budaya dan Akal Sehat*, Jakarta: Fakultas Seni Pertunjukan IKJ and Komunitas Senrepita.

Raditya, H. B. (2021) 'Revealing cultural representation in Indonesian contemporary dance', in Burridge, S., ed., *The Routledge Companion to Dance in Asia and the Pacific: Platforms for Change*, New Delhi: Routledge India.

Schön, D. A. (2011) *The Reflective Practitioner: How Professionals Think in Action* (Reprinted), Farnham: Ashgate.

Sheets-Johnstone, M. (2011). *The Primacy of Movement* (Expanded 2nd edn), Amsterdam: John Benjamins Pub. Co.

Smith, D. W. (2018) 'Phenomenology', in Zalta, E. N., ed., *The Stanford Encyclopedia of Philosophy*, 16 November, available: https://plato.stanford.edu/archives/sum2018/entries/phenomenology [accessed 25 June 2021].

Springgay, S., Irwin, R. L. and Kind, S. W. (2005). 'A/r/tography as living inquiry through art and text', in *Qualitative Inquiry*, SAGE Publications.

CHOREOGRAPHY FOR SITES, SCREENS AND COMMUNITY PRACTICE

Choreography has evolved over the course of the twentieth and early twenty-first century in response to a range of different factors. Societal mores have shifted over time, influencing our relationship to bodies on stage, including more inclusivity in representing differently abled and minoritized performers. Technology has allowed us to push the boundaries of dance performance into site-specific, screen-based and virtual spaces. Increased access to new media technologies has extended the versatility of choreographers and given many options for how they can develop and present new ideas. As a choreographer, you may find yourself working across many different contexts and spaces, with professional and/or non-professional dancers – sometimes with a particular focus on the process of making and other times prioritising the finished production. You might collaborate with a software designer to create a new choreographic tool or develop a choreography for younger audiences. This chapter explores the various possibilities that choreographic skills afford dance artists and the many ways that their creative ideas find expression.

SITE-SPECIFIC CHOREOGRAPHIES

Traditionally, Western theatre dance has been viewed within specifically constructed theatre spaces and has developed accordingly. In the 1800s, classical ballet reached its pinnacle, positioned within the proscenium arch of the theatre. This created a picture-book experience as the corps de ballet framed the principal dancers at the centre of the stage. In the early twentieth century, Isadora Duncan is credited with shifting the priorities in experiencing dance from visual to kinaesthetic, influencing how and where dance might be encountered by an audience (Cooper Albright 1997). Indeed, modern dancers have explored various possibilities to take dance into other spaces to break the separation between audience and performer. As US choreographer Meredith Monk explains,

> [s]ite work gave me the ability to create an immersive experience. A proscenium implies a separation between the performance and the audience. Taking people out of the theater and including them in the same space as the performers blurs boundaries and transforms experience, expanding notions of time and space.
> (Monk in Barbour et al. 2019, p.28)

Dance has always occurred in various spaces outside of a theatre context, this can include "folk, religious and indigenous dance practices" that occur in places with specific spiritual importance or more secular sites where particular festivals or rituals take place (Hunter 2015, p.4). These longstanding practices have deeply influenced the development of site-specific dance through utilising "promenade performance, folk dance informed group dance patterns and formations, audience interaction and performer-audience proximity" (Hunter 2015, p.4).

Location

Site-specific choreography can be a means to reveal the qualities of a space in a new way by making the background qualities come to the foreground to enhance, challenge or alter the function that the site would normally fulfil (Hunter 2015). In this way the choreography can bring out qualities of a space that might otherwise go unnoticed, or challenge the usual uses of the site. Engaging with a particular site in the twenty-first century will no doubt require a site-specific artist to encounter issues regarding ownership of the space, current or past usage, legacies and histories, cultural meaning and even contested stories which could include "questions about land ownership, traditions, access, sovereignty, policy and planning" (Barbour et al. 2019, p.9). With this awareness in mind, space and place become complex topics:

A work performed on a contested site where indigenous peoples are re-claiming guardianship or ownership, for example, will be quite different than a work sited in a corporate-owned food court, but both have been and will be impacted by power, privilege and political systems.

(Barbour et al. 2019, p.9)

Site activism

With the growing global ecological crisis, site-specific work has taken on new themes, as artists explore the implications of the 'Anthropocene', a term given to the current geological period whereby the impact of human activity can be seen to be dominating and altering natural ecological systems (Barbour et al. 2019, p.11). This creates the potential for site-specific dance to engage with climate justice and activism. Due to the fixed nature of a site, there is the possibility for artists to highlight significant local events, histories, traditions and stories in a site-specific performance, thereby creating an alternative to the model of touring dance performances to various festivals and venues around the world. Indeed, with the concerns about air travel linked to climate change, some artists such as Jérôme Bel have decided they will no longer travel by plane (Jérôme Bel n.d.).

Urban sites

Dance artists have often used site-specific performances to explore bodies in the urban environment, from the works of postmodern choreographer Trisha Brown in New York such as *Man Walking Down the Side of Building* (1970) (see Chapter 1) to the New Dance experimentations of X6 in London in the 1970s and 1980s with choreographers such as Rosemary Butcher (see Chapter 4) presenting work in non-theatrical spaces, for example *Landings* (1976), *Dances for Different Spaces* (1978) and *Imprints* (1983) (Barbour et al. 2019, p.91). These choreographies have positioned dancing bodies in dialogue with industrialised environments and explored the resonances between movement and architecture. A more recent example of this kind of work is Austrian choreographer Willi Dorner's project *Bodies in Urban Spaces*, which is a site-adaptive project that brings the audience through an urban landscape to encounter brightly clothed performers stacked on top of or crammed into spaces between buildings. These figures, who wear hooded track suit tops, do not show their faces and so bring attention to the dissonances and harmonies between their bodies and the urban architecture. This site-specific work resonates with the phenomenon of Parkour or 'free-running', a form of urban athleticism and gymnastics that uses the city as a series of obstacles to move through and around, which gained prominence in the suburbs of French cities in the 1990s.

Dance and architecture

Site-specific theory and performance is informed by architectural theory and so there are some key concepts that are important to be aware of in this field. Some theorists who address how humans "experience, perceive and interact with space" are Henri Lefebvre (1991), Michel de Certeau (1988), Brian Lawson (2001) and Gaston Bachelard (1994) among others (Hunter 2015, p.25). Lefebvre (1991) outlines the relationship between socially constructed space and personally constructed space as real versus mental spaces. He maps the internal (mental) space and external (physical) space that comprises human experience – accordingly, "we produce ourselves in the world while also physically constructing spaces and environments" (Hunter 2015, p.30). Another key element as outlined by Brian Lawson (2001) is scale as a means of emphasising social hierarchy and reflecting the importance of activities taking place within a particular building. In this way power is demonstrated and enacted upon individuals who enter or move around the built environment. We are moved through public spaces by external means, from traffic signals and road construction to the design of corridors and doorways in buildings – all these devices direct us through a space (Lawson 2001). Equally, we transition from experiences of individuality to institutionalisation as we enter certain spaces such as schools or hospitals (Lawson 2001). Bachelard (1994) explores the poetic qualities of space, making connections between the house and the human soul and psyche, by linking the structure of the buildings we inhabit with our mental architecture. Another layer to understanding site is that concerning the practices that are undertaken in a space which can demonstrate how a space does not always have a fixed purpose or that purpose can be altered by how people use it from day to day (De Certeau 1988). As Lefebvre (1991, p.143) explains, we produce outside and inside spaces through first building towns and cities (outside/real space) and then journeying through these spaces (inside/mental space) and this encounter is ultimately a transaction between self and environment: "Space commands bodies, prescribing or proscribing gestures, routes and distances to be covered." Imagine for a moment how the everyday spaces you occupy shape and direct your movement.

Creating a site-specific performance

These considerations mentioned above can inform the kind of dance movement developed for a site-specific piece. Many choreographers use the site to shape the movement language, rather than bringing a ready-made choreography into a particular space. The particular contours of the space, the textures of the different surfaces and the history of the site are just some of the elements that influence the choreography. Stephan Koplowitz (in Hunter 2015, p.33), an influential US choreographer in the field of site-specific dance, describes his multi-layered approach to the creation of a site-specific performance:

> I'm interested in becoming a part of the design and rhythm of the site and amplifying that. This kind of work is not necessarily about big extensions and triple turns, but what is most appropriate for the site. The most virtuosic movements might simply be everyone raising their arms together.

Indeed, there are some useful ideas to consider when approaching this kind of dance project, which might include spending time exploring the history of the site by looking at archival documents if they are available, local stories and/or legends about the building or area alongside more detailed physical exploration of the contours, atmosphere and 'feel' of the environment. As mentioned earlier, these explorations could include noticing how the site influences you to move within it and letting that emerge organically, rather than ordering your movements according to other choreographic themes or structures. It is useful to maintain a balance between being influenced by the site and retaining your main ideas so that the site does not end up being the choreographer and overpowering the intention for the piece (Hunter 2015). Another consideration is how the audience receive the site in your performance as the audience do not experience the site alone, but a heightened environment through performance which is enhanced and augmented through the performers and sets, lights, costumes and design elements that are introduced to the space (Hunter 2015). Therefore, the audience rather than experiencing the "true site" are encountering the "*place* of performance" (Hunter 2015, p.109).

Exemplar 1 – Noémie Lafrance, Stephan Koplowitz and Carol Brown

New York based, French Canadian choreographer Noémi Lafrance creates large-scale site-specific works, from the film noir inspired piece *Noir* (2004), which took place in a car park and was viewed by audience members in parked cars, to her ambitious choreography *Rapture* (2008). This latter piece was danced on the roof of the Fisher Centre, New York, a building designed by renowned architect, Frank Gehry. Six dancers connected to the structure via complex harnesses danced across its undulating roof surfaces, embodying a sense of freedom and fluidity. Stephan Koplowitz created a 'site-adaptive' piece entitled *Red Line Time* (2013) which took place across 14 stations of the Los Angeles Metro's Red Line. The piece comprises a five-minute choreography that is adapted to each new performance space by eight performers. "The entire event is designed to match the ebb and flow of the commuting public, and to take place within the strict schedule of the trains" (Stephan Koplowitz n.d.). New Zealand born choreographer Carol Brown created *Tongues of Stone* (2011) a series of urban site performances commencing in Perth, Australia and adapted into further performances in Auckland, New Zealand, drawing inspiration from the network of stories that inhabit the sites of each city. These performances reframe urban (often corporate) spaces into performative and poetic sites that enliven and reactivate the hidden histories of our lived cityscapes (Brown 2015).

Dance in gallery spaces

Numerous cross overs between dance, visual arts and performance art have placed choreography in gallery spaces, such as through the work of Tino Sehgal (see Chapter 1) and French choreographer, Boris Charmatz. Charmatz's *If Tate Modern was Musée de la Danse* (2015) presented live dance performance over two days in London's Tate Modern asking audiences to imagine what a museum of dance might look like. Included in this programme was the piece *20 Dancers for the XX Century*, whereby 20 prominent dancers performed moments from their repertory of movement. They interacted with the audience and discussed the history of these movements in relation to their life stories (Finbow 2016), connecting to the notion that the dancing body itself is an archive, albeit a fleshy and impermanent one. Congolese choreographer Faustin Linyekula presented a performance *My Body, My Archive* (2020) which collated a series of his works *Sur les traces de Dinozord* (2006), *Statue of Loss* (2014), *Batanaba* (2017) and *Congo* (2019), originally designed as an exhibition but filmed as a one-off performance in Tate Modern and distributed online during the COVID-19 pandemic (Tate n.d.). Gallery performances allow audiences to encounter dance outside the frame of a conventional theatre. Moving the dancing body away from association with the narrative logics of live theatre and towards the more experiential space of visual arts, shifts how it may be perceived in significant ways. For this reason, many choreographers continue to seek out opportunities to present work in these environments.

CHOREOGRAPHY AND THE CAMERA

While live dance performance has its own particular power, dance has had a long and fruitful relationship with film. Choreographers explore this relationship through the genre of Screendance as well as through hybrid performances, such as in the works of Rosemary Butcher (see Chapter 4), that often juxtaposed live dance performers with filmed footage on stage.

Early influencers

Early experimentations in modern dance developed in tandem with the growth of cinema. Indeed, one of the early innovators of modern dance, Loïe Fuller, is considered to have even anticipated the innovations of cinema through utilising continuous movement alongside "popular entertainment technologies" to produce a "moving image" with a new "kinetic range" that was unlike the movement that had been presented in ballet or music hall dancing previously (Brannigan 2011, p.22). Erin Brannigan (2011, p.23) describes the spectacle that Fuller created through the use of fabric on panels that extended the reach of her arms into a butterfly shape, adding "… different coloured lighting effects to create what would have been a remarkable theatrical display."

> As indicated in various artistic representations of Fuller, the material extends and surrounds the dancer, creating a motile, fluid figure that obscures and dissolves the dancing body. The resulting spectacle is a figure in constant transformation.
> (Brannigan 2011, p.23)

Another important influence on the development of cinematic dance is Maya Deren, whose work with film was highly innovative in the 1940s and 1950s, for which she utilised "cinematic techniques and effects" such as "multiple exposures, jump cuts, slow-motion, negative film sequences, superimposition, matches-on-action, freeze-frame, and acute camera angles" (Brannigan 2011, p.100).

The exchange and influence between dance and film continued throughout the twentieth century, for example with Ballets Russes choreographer Leonide Massine who collaborated with Giacomo Balla, one of the artists identified with the Italian Futurists, a movement of artists who created several films around this time. The work they created, *Feu d'artifice*, used a light show to produce film-like effects (Brannigan 2011, p.4). Reciprocally, cinema could be regarded to have influenced many choreographic devices from those developed by Ballets Russes choreographers Bronislava Nijinska, such as "slow-motion action, freezes, and silent film characters" and Michel Fokine who drew on silent film action to incorporate a full body "mimetic" rather than using solely hand gestures in his ballets (Brannigan 2011, p.4). This influence extends to contemporary dance (Brannigan 2011) and is identified by Anna Sanchez Colberg (1993, p.220) as "montage, cross-fades, fade-outs, and foreground/background contrast," for example, in the work of German choreographer, Pina Bausch. These devices, translated from a filmic context into real time on stage have become widely used as choreographic tools (Sanchez Colberg 1993).

Screendance

The term Screendance has been adopted widely to denote the genre of dancemaking that is modified and mediated by the screen as the 'point of reception', that is, how and where the work is viewed by an audience (Rosenberg 2012). While there are other terms such as 'dance for camera' and 'cine dance', the term Screendance has gained traction perhaps because it speaks strongly to the specific approach required to create a piece of work in this genre (Rosenberg 2012). For the purposes of this publication, we refer to the genre as Screendance to recognise the prominence of this field, which is further demonstrated by the development of the MA in Screendance at London Contemporary Dance School and focus on Screendance in Dance Masters' programmes such as at University of Utah in the US and University of Limerick, Ireland. There are now a range of Screendance Festivals worldwide including the Screendance Festival in Stockholm; Lightmoves Festival of Screendance in Limerick, Ireland; London International Screendance Festival; Cinedanse, Montréal; Reel Dance, Australia; and International Screendance Festival at American Dance Festival.

Processes of making Screendance

The processes of making a Screendance diverge from the logic of choreographing for a live performance, as the choreographer is not bound by the limitations of the time and space of the performance. Indeed, this process can unfold very differently to making a piece of choreography as Doug Rosenberg (2012, p.2) explains,

> Composition may come in isolated bits; kinesthetic transitions may become virtual or nonexistent, slated to be inserted later in the editing process. Movements and gestures, released from the physical boundaries of weight, time and space, are digitally archived to be retrieved and reconstructed at a later date.

Scottish filmmaker Katrina McPherson's (2019) excellent book *Making Video Dance* describes in detail the steps to creating a piece of Screendance. The book traverses the various stages from the origin of the idea, through working with the camera, situating the work through location and costume to managing the roles of the individuals involved (McPherson 2019). This progresses through how to work with light and sound, choreographing the edit, postproduction stages and finally, the presentation and promotion of your work (McPherson 2019). The next section will summarise some key concepts that are useful tools for starting to work in this genre.

Framing through the camera

As it creates the frame through which the viewer can see into the world depicted on screen, the camera is key in forming the emotional environment and atmosphere of your film, therefore "the camera is a lead performer in your video dance" (McPherson 2019, p.26). The frame refers to the rectangular shape formed by the lens of the camera and corresponds to the screen where the film will be viewed. The camera has the potential to allow the viewer into closer proximity to the dancer than would usually be available, creating an increased sense of intimacy as the camera can move into the dancer's 'kinesphere' (see Chapter 4) (McPherson 2019, p.26). This kind of closeness is not generally available in live dance performance. Playing with the positioning of the frame, where the subject is not always in the middle, invites the viewer to imagine what is not seen, creating more interest in watching the action (McPherson 2019). Exploring how the focus of your eye is drawn when looking at the frame is important as well as tracking how that might shift as the action develops. Other considerations are the interplay of depth, light, movement of bodies or objects (traversing the frame or changing proximity to the camera lens), as well as how the camera's movement is impacting on the overall effect (McPherson 2019).

In filming dance, the figure is likely to be moving as is the camera, so the frame may be changing all the time. An important term to note is the 'shot' which unfolds in time as a series of 'individual frames' (McPherson 2019, p.30). The shot can be described in relation to how the subject is positioned for the viewer, such as via a wide shot which seems as if the viewer is further away from the subject and the close-up which positions the viewer near the subject, so that the subject fills the frame. Another essential element to consider is the movement of the camera, which for dance can create more sense of movement and kinaesthetic resonance for the viewer. This can be achieved by a hand-held camera being moved through space or tracking on a trolley, or through zooming in or out.

Editing as a choreographic process

The editing stage of a Screendance project is where the choreographic process is most prominent, as the director is organising the footage into a linear structure to be viewed on screen. Whereas in a live choreography, the logistics of moving dancers around the stage, creating transitions between sections of movement or managing entrances and exits must be solved, these considerations are not as restrictive with film as shots can fade in or out, be superimposed or be cut to move to another shot. The timeline is the baseline for editing when working with digital software and on this are placed various clips of film footage and audio tracks. Editing has become much more accessible to artists who can now work individually on their personal computers, rather than being required to pay for an expensive editing suite and trained specialist technicians. McPherson (2019) explains that how you structure the edit can depend on the kind of piece you are making, for example, if your film is narrative based then the key scenes for the story might be put in place first. If a project is focused on an existing piece of choreography or music score, this will determine the structure of how you order the footage or you can just allow yourself to be led by the material, to see what feels right instinctively, as McPherson (2019, p.200) outlines, "it feels very sculptural as you respond to the shape of the work as it emerges from the material itself." Some of the elements to be aware of in the editing process are 'creating flow', 'creating pace' and 'creating story' (McPherson 2019, pp.206–209). 'Creating flow' involves how you choose to cut from one shot to the other, for example, cutting on the movement so that you cut away from one shot before the movement is fully completed and introduce the new shot just after the movement has begun, this means that the audience can complete the missing movements in their imagination and it can create a dynamic tension that keeps the viewer engaged (McPherson 2019, p.207). 'Creating pace' is concerned with whether the edit is fast or slow, that is, the speed that the edit moves between different clips of footage, and 'creating story' is focused on how the editing may be communicating a meaning and relationship between the subjects on screen, whether there is an intended narrative or not (McPherson 2019, p.208).

Presenting and viewing Screendance

The key avenues to presenting Screendance works are through online platforms, in festivals (with a Screendance focus or not), screening on television or cinema or through other events that take place in the artistic community. There are many international festivals with a focus on Screendance and often prizes associated that can build the profile of your work if you win. Usually, there is an entrance fee to submit your work to a festival and though you do not need to attend the festival, there are often post-screening talks that the filmmakers are invited to attend (McPherson 2019). Many Screendance artists show their work on online platforms such as YouTube and Vimeo as this has a broad audience reach. However, making your work public and free may not be advisable if you also want to submit it to festivals, so many Screendance artists show a shorter trailer of the work to build interest (McPherson 2019). Screenings on television and in cinemas are more challenging to achieve but opportunities occasionally arise through specific commissions for dance on television or for cinema screenings as part of a dance festival, for example. Many arts organisations include Screendance showings as part of their regular programming and these can lead to presentation opportunities outside of a festival circuit.

> ### Exemplar 2 – Maya Deren, Merce Cunningham and Lloyd Newson
>
> Watch Maya Deren's short film *A Study in Choreography for Camera* (1945) to see early experiments with the dancing form positioned in different locations (Deren 1945). Also, see *Channels/Inserts* (1982), with choreography by Merce Cunningham and direction by Charles Atlas. In this latter work, you can view the shifting spaces and perspectives of the dancers composed through using

chance operations to decide the order of the action, the number of dancers in various sections and how the rooms would be used (Cunningham 1982). Finally, explore Lloyd Newson's choreography in *Dead Dreams of Monochrome Men* (1990) directed by David Hinton. In this film you can observe how the structure of the edit builds the intense physicality, sense of proximity and growing claustrophobia over time (Newson 1990).

DANCE AND TECHNOLOGY

The collaborations between dance and technology have led to exciting new developments in digital performance. As mentioned earlier in this chapter, Loïe Fuller was a trailblazer in her experimentation with electricity from the late 1880s, when it was still an innovative technology (Dixon 2007). Fuller was the first modern dancer to use new technologies such as electrically powered lights in her choreography alongside more basic tools, such as wooden poles that were hidden under fabric to increase the span of her movement, as Steve Dixon (2007, pp.40–41) explains:

> billowing robes became a kind of 'screen' on which were projected multidirectional, multicolored lights, including those emanating from a glass panel in the floor that lit her from below. The complex plays of light on the vast folds of material ... transformed (or, in computer parlance, 'morphed') the dancer's body.

Since Fuller's time, choreographers have explored ways of enhancing their performances through technology and are often at the forefront of applying innovative technological tools to generate new choreographic possibilities in their work.

Exemplar 3 – Merce Cunningham and Wayne McGregor

Digital software can be used to generate choreography as well as to enhance the performance experience. Two examples are the use of *Life Forms* by Merce Cunningham and the *Choreographic Language Agent* (CLA) by Wayne McGregor. The *Life Forms*

> software used by Cunningham allowed him to create choreography with animated figures, using a computer as if it were a drawing board, that could then be learned by his company dancers, or projected as part of a live dance performance (Dixon 2007). To enhance his choreographic process, McGregor instigated the development of the CLA as "an extended interactive digital notebook" (DeLahunta 2017b, p.108). The CLA is an interactive system that uses "artificial intelligence algorithms to generate unique solutions to choreographic problems and augment McGregor's creative decision-making processes in the studio" (DeLahunta 2017b, p.108). The tool collates choreographic movement phrases into a format that can be made more complex through arrangement in various combinations, producing a sketch-like image that inspires the dancers to generate different movement responses in the development stages of a choreography (DeLahunta 2017b).

Virtual dancers

Motion capture is a tool to digitally map body movement in 3D. It works through an array of cameras which pick up information from markers positioned on various points of the body. This information is then relayed to computers which process the data in relation to a humanoid figure or other animated form and position it within a 3D digital space. A seminal work that explored this technology in dance is Cunningham's *BIPED* (1999) (see Chapter 2) in which, during the live performance, projected figures that were created from motion-captured Cunningham dancers were:

> cast onto a front scrim, allowing the live dancers to appear to interrelate with the virtual dancers in various abstractions and spatial configurations. These projected figures, handdrawn abstractions but capable of unerringly lifelike movement, also changed in scale, from giant thirty-foot dancers to smaller, life-sized ones.
>
> (Dixon 2007, p.190)

In 1999, choreographer Bill T. Jones developed *Ghostcatching*, a video installation and animated film, using motion capture technology. The material was produced through reflector sensors taped to his naked body as he danced, which were captured by a series of cameras that were positioned throughout the studio. The resulting avatars of Jones, that resembled sketched figures but were computer modelled animations, were duplicated so he could dance with multiple figures of himself in the film. Questions about how motion capture apparently subtracts the movement from the dancing figure arose in this project by seemingly reducing a flesh and blood figure to a dancing trace (Dixon 2007). This issue of how motion capture seems to separate dancers from their movement continues to be pertinent. Furthermore, this has implications for ownership of the data that is produced as it can be circulated without the body of the dancer and far removed from the original site where it was danced (Whatley 2015). This concern was articulated by Jones when watching his avatar in *Ghostcatching*, as he asked himself "who is that really?" (Paul Kaiser in Dixon 2007, p.193).

Despite these concerns, motion capture continues to have great value as a creative, archiving and teaching tool in dance. For example, the WhoLoDancE project funded by EU Horizon 2020 uses motion capture and virtual reality environments to enhance learning in dance. Among other tools, this uses:

> the choreomorphy tool [which] provides an interactive experience for the dancer who, when wearing a motion capture suit and improvising, can see the movement visualised on screen in real-time, rendered through a variety of different avatars and settings, so as to enhance the user's self-reflection and experimentation.
>
> (Cisneros et al. 2019, p.61)

Virtual reality performances

Digital dancing avatars can inhabit virtual reality environments that are then accessed by viewers through an appropriate VR headset, such as an Oculus Rift. An example of one such choreography is *DAZZLE* (2020) by Ruth Gibson and Bruno Martelli who create work under the moniker Gibson/Martelli. *DAZZLE* was made in collaboration with the costume and set design company Peut-Porter and is inspired by the 1919 Dazzle Ball at the Chelsea Arts Club following World War I, in which attendees dressed in black and white to mimic the dazzle camouflage used on British naval ships during the war. Dance critic Sanjoy Roy (2020 n.p.) describes how in this virtual reality space,

> you can jump between different scenes, each with their own giddying perspectives, algorithmic choreography and psychedelic dancing figures – humanoid, geometric or entirely abstract – that can pass right through you like digital ectoplasm.

As motion capture equipment has become relatively more affordable and user-friendly, more university dance departments and dance companies have access to this technology, expanding the creative and pedagogical range for dance in the virtual world.

Interactive dance and technology

Another important development for digital dance since the late 1980s is the *Isadora* software, developed by Mark Coniglio, artistic director of dance company Troika Ranch. This software was developed to work with *Midi Dancer*, a movement-sensing system that is worn by the dancer. Triggered through flexing of the joints, it sends wireless signals to a computer that then activates and manipulates media outputs such as sound and visuals. While this process has been described as the dancer playing a musical instrument, by activating the various media through movement, it diverges somewhat from this idea as the dancer is more than just operating the system but is also creating meaning through their movement (Dixon 2007). This issue adds a layer of complexity to the choreographic process, as the choreography equally has a functional and aesthetic purpose, that is to activate the outputs and to express meaning (Dixon 2007). Other non-wearable tools have been developed with this same principle in mind, such as floor sensors or lasers that cross the performance space, so that dancers activate media outputs by moving through the environment (Dixon 2007). An example of this technology is *Mortal Engine* (2008), a visually arresting piece by Australian choreographer Gideon Obarzanek for his company Chunky Move, in collaboration with computer engineer Frieder

Weiss. Obarzanek explains that *Mortal Engine* is completely interactive and happening in real time:

> [it] has no pre-rendered video, light or laser images ... the music mix is open allowing various sounds to be completely generated from movement data. In addition, pre-composed phrases are triggered by the dancers' motion or by the operator in relation to where the performers are in any given sequence.
> (Chunky Move n.d.)

While this connection is demonstrated seamlessly in *Mortal Engine*, one of the challenging elements of this interactive loop in performance is making the exchange between the performers and the technology perceivable without breaking the flow of the performance. It can be difficult for example for an audience member to experience how the performers may be triggering certain visual or sonic effects. This can mean that a very complex system operating 'behind the scenes' in a performance can appear very simple, looking just like a performance that uses pre-recorded and pre-sequenced media. While choreographers continue to experiment with technology, it is therefore very important to balance this with how the technology enhances the performance experience, so that it does not compromise the quality or innovative nature of the choreographic movement.

Accessing technological tools

Connecting with some of these technological tools can be challenging for an emerging choreographer, as the technology is difficult to access and requires specialist skills to operate. Rather than becoming expert at using technology, it is usual that choreographers collaborate with technical experts such as computer programmers and coders. In order to foster these kinds of interactions in the artistic sphere, initiatives such as Choreographic Coding Lab (CCL), which resulted from the Motion Bank project by the Forsythe Company, have been established (Choreographic Coding Labs n.d.). The CCL is an open format project that can be adopted freely by organisers who wish to foster dialogue between choreographers working with technology and experts in the fields of digital media and coding.

DANCE IN COMMUNITY SETTINGS

Choreographic skills can be applied to a range of different contexts outside of the field of professional performance. Many professional dancers and choreographers supplement their professional work through teaching dance across a variety of settings from conservatory training environments to local dance schools. Importantly, many professional dance companies have outreach programmes that connect them to their community. This can involve anything from creating projects with schoolchildren to Dance for Parkinsons, a model that teaches dance to people with Parkinson's disease and that has been adopted by many companies around the world. This teaching method, first developed by the Mark Morris Dance Company in New York has gained prominence in many countries, leading to the study of the benefits of dance for addressing some of the physical and psychological symptoms of the disease.

What is community dance?

It can be problematic to make distinctions between community and professional dance, as this assumes a hierarchy of value and quality, also falsely aligning work in the community with solely amateur practice. Community dance as a term in the UK defines a field of practice that is usually led by trained facilitators with the goal of creating opportunities for diverse groups of participants to engage in dance (Amans 2017). While the background of community dance practitioners may vary widely, some key values of the field are identified as:

- A focus on participants.
- Collaborative relationships.
- Inclusive practice.
- Opportunities for positive experiences.
- Celebration of diversity.

(Amans 2017, p.9)

This means that the work undertaken through community dance activities is often 'process-oriented' rather than focused on the end performance product (Amans 2017, p.9). The priority in this context is that participants experience the many benefits bestowed by engaging with dance. These could be pure enjoyment, self-expression, connection to community, understanding of own and other cultures, learning new dance skills and knowledge about dance, and overall increased confidence in moving (Amans 2017). These attributes are additional to the health benefits of being more mobile and physically active, which have been widely reported in scientific studies.

Untrained or trained performers

Many choreographers are interested in working with 'untrained' dancers as part of the dance aesthetic they want to present. This shows a more diverse range of performers on stage with different shaped bodies, that do not conform to pre-conditioned ideas of what a dancer 'should' look like. Rosemary Lee (2017) works with performers of different ages and levels of training, making choreographies that demonstrate the power of intergenerational creativity. Her interest for undertaking this work lies in her appreciation of the benefits to all group members when diverse groups of participants embark on a shared creative endeavour, whether they are trained dancers or not. Lee (2017, p.77) explains that she enjoys observing people of all ages and skill levels dancing, because "their movement often speaks to me and inspires me more deeply than their words can" and this enables her work "to reflect and communicate our common humanity."

Exemplar 4 – Rosemary Lee, Fevered Sleep, Jérôme Bel and Lucy Guerin

Lee's site-specific piece *Square Dances* (2011) worked with a cast of 200 professional and community dancers of all ages travelling between four squares in the Camden Borough of London. Moving through the garden squares, the performance created a serene and vibrant space of contemplation for audiences. *Men and Girls Dance* (2015) by London-based company Fevered Sleep is an example of an intergenerational dance piece that explores in a joyful way the potential for shared creativity and expression between a group of young girls and adult professional male dancers. While the piece supports a playful and light-hearted interaction between the two groups of performers, it points to many important issues regarding how touch and connection have become taboo between adults and children (Fevered Sleep n.d.). Two pieces which have showcased untrained performers are Jérôme Bel's *The Show Must Go On* (2004) and Australian choreographer Lucy Guerin's piece *Untrained* (2009). Both choreographies show a fascination, not with displaying virtuosic dancing, but seeing human movement in a more spontaneous and raw form. These works allow the performers to be more immediately expressive, without creating a distance between the audience and performers through displaying heightened technical skills. This could be seen to be continuing the questioning of the expertise of the dancer, emphasised by the Judson Dance Theatre choreographers.

Considerations for community dance choreography

At various stages of their careers, choreographers may be commissioned by an organisation to make a piece of dance with a community group. When choreographing work for a community dance project, there are some elements that should be taken into consideration even before the project begins. In this context, advance preparation is important for understanding who your participants are. For example, do they know each other? Is participation voluntary or part of a wider programme they are involved in? How many participants are there? What are their "interests/expectations/needs"? And importantly, who is representing them to you? (Amans 2017, p.175). Furthermore, understanding important issues such as the mobility and general health of the participants, ensures that you plan for safe dance practices in your creative work. It is essential to establish clear roles within the studio environment, particularly if you are working with vulnerable adults, children or young people where there may be issues regarding 'duty of care', in which case the following questions should be asked:

> What are the duty of care issues? ... Who is the carer? Who else will be in the session? If you are working with other artists,

co-leaders or support workers, are your respective roles clear? Will there be teachers/parents/carers in the room? Do you want them to join in or watch?

(Amans 2017, p.176)

Other considerations are where the activities will take place, the time you have with the participants for each session, the content that you will be developing and how that will be decided (collaboratively with the group or part of a larger festival context, for example) and the expected outcome from the stakeholders involved (Amans 2017). For example, are there funders who will require you to make a report, or will there be external evaluation of the project?

Community dance practitioner, Diane Amans (2017) describes some essential interpersonal considerations when setting the scene that help to make participants feel at ease in the space. While seemingly obvious, they can be forgotten due to distractions that arise in setting up the space. For example, it is important to make eye contact and to take time to greet each person, arrive in time to assess any mobility issues or injuries that need consideration, take time to learn everyone's name and find ways to break the ice and ensure participants learn each other's names if needed (Amans 2017). As the facilitator it is important to take notice and give support if members have difficulty taking part or fitting into the group, this may add more pressure to your role as a choreographer but can make the difference in bringing the group together to work creatively. Indeed, sensitivity to the interpersonal dimension is useful in establishing a healthy teaching and working environment across all areas of choreographic practice but is particularly so with performers who have little or no experience in dance.

Dance and disability

An important growth in diversity of representation is through choreography that is by and features disabled dancers. In the field of community dance practice, this is hugely significant in creating access for all members of society to engage in dance. This area of practice has crossed from community-based work to wider 'industry based' contexts, as in the case of Candoco Dance Company (UK) (see Chapter 5). The company continues to be instrumental in highlighting disabled performers and their work has directly inspired the development of other dance companies who feature disabled dancers. As co-founder Adam Benjamin (2017, p.101) explains, "In an incredibly fertile period between 1994 and 1997 the education work helped launch (amongst others) Blue-Eyed Soul, Velcro, StopGap, Independance, Tardis and HandiCapace Tanz Kompanie (Germany)."

Other companies working with disabled dancers are Dancing Wheels, Axis, Joint Forces, Bill T Jones (USA), Amici, Common Ground, DV8 (UK) and Touch Compass (New Zealand) (Cheesman 2014). In Australian choreographer Lloyd Newson's dance film, *The Cost of Living* (2004), renowned disabled dancer David Toole, a double-amputee, is featured alongside Eddie Kay as a lead character in the story. While the film was made several years ago, it continues to be a relevant example of boundary breaking within choreography for the way that it critiques the conventional concept of the dancing body. According to Ann Cooper Albright (2013 p.298) "Western theatrical dance has traditionally been structured by an exclusionary mindset that projects a very narrow vision of a dancer as white, female, thin, long-limbed, flexible, heterosexual and able-bodied." These companies have challenged this assumption and showcased the skills, athleticism and expressivity of disabled dancers.

Youth dance and dance for younger audiences

Ludus Dance Company was founded in 1975, as the first company in the UK to focus on Dance in Education. The company makes work for and by young people. Youth dance initiatives are highly significant means of exposing young people to the possibilities of a career in dance or a life of appreciation of dance. You may have come to studying dance through this avenue, via a youth dance project or youth dance company. Choreography in this context allows young people to be part of a creative and performance experience that usually explores issues of relevance to the participants.

Exemplar 5 – Alessandro Sciarroni, Barrowland Ballet, Wang Ramirez and Philip Saire

Home Alone (2015) is a piece by choreographer Alessandro Sciarroni for Balletto di Roma. The focus of this choreography is to introduce young children to contemporary dance and technology, giving them a sense of the potential for technology to be a creative and fun tool. This work has an interactive section whereby the young spectators have an opportunity to play with the technological device that is at the heart of the production (Balletto di Roma n.d.). Created by Natasha Gilmore and Robert Alan Evans, Barrowland Ballet's *Tiger Tale* (2014) explores a family story that becomes uprooted by the invasion of a 'tiger'. With an elaborate set made of criss-crossing strings and hanging buckets, the piece is aimed at audiences of seven years and older (Barrowland Ballet n.d.). *We Are Monchichi (W.A.M.)* (2018) is a choreography by Honji Wang and Sébastien Ramirez that explores the challenges of engaging with others in the face of cultural stereotypes and embodying multiple cultural identities. The two choreographers have Korean and Spanish heritage respectively and the performers, one from Taiwan but living in Paris and one from Italy living in Berlin, find a common language to connect despite the complexities of their personal stories (Company Wang Ramirez n.d.). Finally, a work for seven to 11-year-olds by Swiss choreographer Philip Saire, *Hocus Pocus* (2017), explores "the power of images, their magic and the sensations they provoke. The very unique set design allows for a playful and magical exploration into a game of appearances and disappearances of both bodies and accessories" (Philip Saire n.d.). All these choreographies are developed with younger audiences in mind and address issues that are relevant for young children in ways that are accessible, engaging and stimulate the imagination.

There are many festivals worldwide that showcase dance for young people as the main programme or part of a programme such as Edinburgh International Children's Festival; Baboro International Children's Festival, Ireland; AWESOME Festival, Perth, Australia; International Theatre Festival Okinawa for Young Audiences, Japan; and Festival De Betovering/The Enchantment, The

Netherlands. While some choreographers only make work for younger audiences, all choreographers mentioned above mainly make pieces for adult audiences.

Anna Halprin life/art

Making a distinction between work as an artist and our lives in general can separate dance from some of its most valuable attributes, such as community engagement, personal wellbeing and expression of life events. Seminal choreographer, Anna Halprin (1920–2021) inspired generations of artists through her integration of life with artmaking. Halprin advocated for life feeding art as a creative interchange, so that the process of creativity allows participants to access their life story and equally, this life story is nourished by the creative process (Worth and Poynor 2004). Halprin put this philosophy into action in countless ways, for example, when working with an all-male group with HIV/AIDS in the piece *Carry Me Home* (1990). Inspired by the lived experience of the group members, this piece dealt with some of the issues the group faced in confronting this illness.

Halprin's own brush with cancer at the age of 51 led to a deeper exploration into the value of her life and what she might contribute through her dance practice (Worth and Poynor 2004). She said, "before I had cancer, I lived my life in service of dance, and after I had cancer, I danced in the service of life" (Halprin in Worth and Poynor 2004, p.34). Halprin created large scale projects for up to 100 community performers, focusing on ritualistic enactments that addressed environmental and social issues. One such project was *In the Mountain, On the Mountain* (1981), which took place on Mount Tamalpais, near to where Halprin lived with her husband, the architect Lawrence Halprin. The mountain had been the site of a series of murders of local women, leading to a closure of many of the walking paths. This ritual performance, which involved 80 community members over two days, was a process of reclaiming the mountain for the community and soon afterwards the killer was apprehended. This creative process demonstrates the potency of community focused dancemaking and how it can impact on the social and environmental context of participants and makers.

SUMMARY

This chapter has given an overview of the extensive field of site-specific dance, including a range of exemplars and tools used in this context. These show ways to enter into a choreographic process with consideration and focus on the performance site. It has introduced the developments in the field of Screendance and how choreography develops through a different logic to the creative process for a live performance. It explores the development of this genre throughout the twentieth century, highlighting how choreographic tools and cinematic structures have influenced each other. The chapter demonstrates how Screendance has gained prominence as a creative outlet and new platform for disseminating choreography and outlined some basic tools for consideration when developing choreography in this context.

By mapping significant developments in Dance and Technology, the chapter profiles how choreographers use technology to develop choreography and to enhance performance experiences. This includes software developments for interactive performances, motion capture and artificial intelligence agents.

The section ends with an overview of dance and community practice, charting key considerations when working across community contexts and different age groups. Prominent developments in dance with disabled performers and the power these projects have to challenge limiting stereotypes about dancing bodies is also explored. Finally, the relationship between life and art through the work of inspirational choreographer, Anna Halprin brings the chapter to a close.

FURTHER READING

Amans, Diane (2017) *An Introduction to Community Dance Practice* (2nd edn), London: Macmillan Education UK.

Barbour, K., Hunter, V. and Kloetzel, M. eds (2019) *(Re)positioning Site Dance: Local Acts, Global Perspectives*, Bristol: Intellect Books Ltd.

Burridge, S. and Svendler Nielsen, C. eds (2017) *Dance, Access and Inclusion*, Abingdon and New York: Routledge.

Dixon, Steve (2007) *Digital Performance: A History of New Media in Theater, Dance, Performance Art, and Installation*, Cambridge, MA: MIT Press.

McPherson, Katrina (2019) *Making Video Dance: A Step-by-Step Guide to Creating Dance for the Screen* (2nd edn), Abingdon and New York: Routledge.

Rosenberg, D. (2012) *Screendance: Inscribing the Ephemeral Image*, New York: Oxford University Press.

REFERENCES

Amans, D. (2017) *An Introduction to Community Dance Practice* (2nd edn), London: Macmillan Education UK.

Bachelard, G. (1994) *The Poetics of Space*, translated by Jolas, M., Boston: Beacon Press.

Balletto di Roma (n.d.) *Home Alone*, available: www.ballettodiroma.com/en/company-productions/home-alone-en/ [accessed 17 July 2021].

Barbour, K., Hunter, V. and Kloetzel, M. eds (2019) *(Re)positioning Site Dance: Local Acts, Global Perspectives*, Bristol: Intellect Books Ltd.

Barrowland Ballet (n.d.) *Tiger Tale*, available: https://barrowlandballet.co.uk/production/tiger-tale/ [accessed 17 July 2021].

Benjamin, A. (2017) 'Second time open', in Amans, D., ed., *An Introduction to Community Dance Practice* (2nd edn), London: Macmillan Education UK.

Brannigan, E. (2011) *Dancefilm: Choreography and the Moving Image*, New York: Oxford University Press.

Brown, C. (2015) 'City of lovers', in Hunter, V., ed., *Moving Sites: Investigating Site-specific Dance Performance*, Abingdon and New York: Routledge.

Cheesman, S. (2014) 'Dance and disability: embracing difference, tensions and complexities', *Dance Research Aotearoa*, 2, 20–30, available: https://doi.org/10.15663/dra.v2i1.26 [accessed 16 July 2021].

Choreographic Coding Labs (n.d.) *About*, available: http://choreographiccoding.org [accessed 29 July 2021].

Chunky Move (n.d.) Mortal Engine, available: https://cmarchive.net/list-of-works/mortal-engine [accessed 17 July 2021].

Cisneros, R. E., Stamp, K. Whatley, S. and Wood, K. (2019) 'WhoLoDancE: digital tools and the dance learning environment', *Research in Dance Education*, 20(1), 54–72.

Company Wang Ramirez (n.d.) *We Are Monchichi*, available: www.wangramirez.com/en/work/we-are-monchichi [accessed 17 July 2021].

Cooper Albright, A. (1997) *Choreographing Difference: The Body and Identity in Contemporary Dance*, Hanover: Wesleyan University Press.

Cooper Albright, A. (2013) *Engaging Bodies: The Politics and Poetics of Corporeality*, Middletown: Wesleyan University Press.

Cunningham, M. (1982) *ChannelsInserts*, available: www.youtube.com/watch?v=_C0z6eHboss [accessed 27 July 2021].

De Certeau, M. (1988) *The Practice of Everyday Life*, Berkeley: University of California Press.

DeLahunta, S. (2017b) 'Wayne McGregor's choreographic language agent', in Bleeker, M., ed., *Transmission in Motion: The Technologizing of Dance*, Abingdon and New York: Routledge.

Deren, M. (1945) *A Study in Choreography for Camera*, available: www.youtube.com/watch?v=3A3caYPlnk8 [accessed 27 July 2021].

Dixon, S. (2007) *Digital Performance: A History of New Media in Theater, Dance, Performance Art, and Installation*, Cambridge, MA: MIT Press.

Fevered Sleep (n.d.) *Men and Girls Dance*, available: www.feveredsleep.co.uk/project/men-and-girls-dance [accessed 16 July 2021].

Finbow, A. (2016) *If Tate Modern was Musée de la Danse 2015*, available: www.tate.org.uk/research/publications/performance-at-tate/case-studies/musee-de-la-danse [accessed 16 July 2021].

Hunter, V. ed. (2015) *Moving Sites: Investigating Site-specific Dance Performance*, Abingdon and New York: Routledge.

Jérôme Bel (n.d) *Performances*, available: www.jeromebel.fr/index.php?p=2 [accessed 16 July 2021].

Lawson, B. (2001) *The Language of Space*, Oxford: Architectural Press.

Lee, R. (2017) 'Aiming for stewardship not ownership', in Amans, D., ed., *An Introduction to Community Dance Practice* (2nd edn), London: Macmillan Education UK.

Lefebvre, H. (1991) *The Production of Space*, translated by Nicholson-Smith, D., Oxford: Blackwell.

McPherson, K. (2019) *Making Video Dance: A Step-by-Step Guide to Creating Dance for the Screen* (2nd edn), Abingdon and New York: Routledge.

Newson, L. (1990) *Dead Dreams of Monochrome Men*, available: www.youtube.com/watch?v=aNGpDfAQ4QI/ [accessed 27 July 2021].

Philip Saire (n.d.) *Hocus Pocus*, available: www.philippesaire.ch/en/projets/hocus-pocus [accessed 17 July 2021].

Rosenberg, D. (2012) *Screendance: Inscribing the Ephemeral Image*, New York: Oxford University Press.

Roy, S. (2020) 'Virtual voguing and digital razzle-dazzle: London film festival takes the arts into a new dimension', *The Guardian*, 13 October, available: www.theguardian.com/stage/2020/oct/13/london-film-festival-arts-lff-expanded [accessed 19 June 2021].

Sanchez Colberg, A. (1993) 'You can see it like this or like that: Pina Bausch's *Die Klage Der Kaiserin*', in Jordan, S. and Allen, D., eds, *Parallel Lines: Media Representations of Dance*, London: John Libbey Publishing, Ltd. 217–235.

Stephan Koplowitz (n.d.) *Red Line Time*, available www.stephankoplowitz.com/redlinetime [accessed 29 July 2021].

Tate (n.d.) *What's On*, available: www.tate.org.uk/whats-on/tate-modern/exhibition/bmw-tate-live-exhibition-2020 [accessed 29 July 2021].

Whatley, S. (2015) 'Motion capture and the dancer: visuality, temporality and the dancing image', Whatley, S., Garrett Brown, N. and Alexander, K., eds, *Attending to Movement: Somatic Perspectives on Living in This World*, Axminster: Triarchy Press, 193–204.

Worth, L. and Poynor, H. (2004) *Anna Halprin*, Abingdon and New York: Routledge.

CONCLUSION
Next steps on your choreographic journey

In this book we have introduced you to some of the key considerations when thinking about choreography as a career, as well as giving you an overview of choreography as a field of study. We are writing this book in the wake of the COVID-19 pandemic, where live dance performance has been greatly reduced alongside face-to-face teaching, and opportunities to connect with others through dance have been curtailed. Despite this, dance continues to be an area of growth and vitality – a necessary human expression – demonstrated by the myriad online classes, workshops, performances and festivals which took place during various lockdowns all over the world. So, while a career as a choreographer is not guaranteed to be a secure one, the adaptability of dance artists to apply their skills across many different settings ensures that this area will continue to grow into the future. Furthermore, it is vitally important that the skills we hold as dancers and choreographers are part of the development of our societies as we enter even closer relationships to technology and the virtual world.

On your next steps toward developing your career as a choreographer, you are likely to start with an undergraduate or conservatoire training in dance. Choreographers normally enter the professional dance field after having gained experience through dancing for other choreographers. Experience as a dancer gives you the chance to develop your individual interests and aesthetics, also providing opportunities to study various ways that choreography is constructed from the inside. Often, this kind of apprenticeship builds up over the years following your graduation, however some choreographers identify a strong interest and capacity to organise

DOI: 10.4324/9781003020110-8

movement and synthesise ideas at an early stage in their career. In either case, the development of artistic individuality is key.

There are several courses that address the need for developing individuality in choreographic practice and embedding critical thinking about choreography from the beginning of your undergraduate training. Many of these are listed at the end of Chapter 5. These courses recognise that learning to dance *per se*, does not necessarily teach you how to choreograph and with the growing sophistication of the professional choreographic field, it is important to be exposed to contemporary ideas from many different art forms and disciplines. When you begin to create choreography, you will enter an artistic conversation that has been flowing for many years and will continue to flow into the future. Understanding how different choreographic ideas originated and how they may be referenced in various choreographic pieces, also helps to position your ideas in a broader context.

When choosing a course, it is important to research the teaching focus and ethos of the institution, its location and perhaps even the community of practice that surrounds it. For example, if you are interested in the European dance scene, you might look to studying on a course based there or the same for the UK or US contexts. Deciding to move to another country to study is an exciting and challenging step and preparation to make sure you are adequately resourced, emotionally and materially is an important consideration. Training in any of the performing or creative arts requires resilience and self-belief, as the nature of this kind of career involves displaying your inner thoughts and ideas in a public arena and dealing with any subsequent critique. Remaining open to learning from your mistakes while cultivating an inner strength is vital to carry you through the challenging landscape of the arts industry. However, following your desires for creative expression is its own reward and if right for you, can give you lots of inner resolve to support you on your journey. As with most aspects of dance, you learn by doing. Choreography requires lots of practice, trial and error and plenty of failure before you build the vision and confidence needed to navigate the professional scene.

Alongside third-level study, there are many opportunities to develop choreographic skills outside of a formal training programme. Most capital cities have dance organisations that create programmes for choreographic development through bursaries and/or residencies. There are many short-term informal training programmes such as at the ImpulseTanz annual festival in Vienna, which offers myriad classes, workshops and research projects through which you can encounter the creative approach of professional choreographers. Independent Dance in London also offers a range of training and research opportunities for emerging choreographers. In the pre-professional training space, youth dance companies offer wonderful opportunities to be part of a choreographic process, or even to lead one. It is worth researching the dance activity in your area to see what is available to you.

As we have outlined in this book, there are many contexts in which you can practice choreography, across various cultural locations and for various kinds of outputs, be they in a theatre performance, street dance, commercial musical theatre dance, Screendance, site-specific work or through new technologies on various online platforms. As outlined through the various chapters, choreography can be applied in various educational, community and disability contexts to enhance inclusion and representation in dance. Ultimately, being a choreographer requires taking a leadership role, where you may be required to oversee dancers, collaborators, technicians, funders and the relationship to your public. While not for the faint-hearted, it is exhilarating to put your vision out into the world and to communicate with others through your dance work. As you do this, you will be aligning with the ancient human impulse to express the stories of our lives through movement – joining a vibrant creative conversation that extends into the past, present and future of the human experience.

GLOSSARY

Abstract work A work in absence of a narrative, plot and/or character(s).
Abstractionism Using and working only with parts of an overall concept or movement phrase.
Aesthetic Specific appearance, effect or style.
Alignment Consideration of the skeletal structure in the dancer's posture.
Amateur dance Dancing as a pastime rather than as a profession.
Appreciation (dance) Understanding the whole construction of steps, phrases, sections, the nexus of patterns, repeated movements, variation and canon concerning the relationships of the dancers; the progression and the high points or climaxes of the dance.
Ausdruckstanz A German term for 'free dance' or 'expressive dance' movements that moved away from the constraints of classical ballet form in the 1900s.
Autoethnography A form of qualitative research that involves introspective, anecdotal and self-reflective perspectives in academic writing and data collection.
Barre A stationary handrail that is used during ballet warm-up exercises. The term also refers to the exercises that are performed at the barre, as well as that part of a ballet class that incorporates barre exercises.
Choreography The art of creating dances.
Classical dance A classical dance form characterized by grace and precision of movement and by elaborate formal gestures, steps and poses.

Classicism Aesthetic attitudes and principles based on the culture, art and literature of ancient Greece and Rome, and characterized by emphasis on form, simplicity, proportion and restrained emotion.

Clog dancing A type of folk dance with roots in traditional European dancing, early African American dance, and traditional Cherokee dance in which the dancer's footwear is used musically by striking the heel, the toe, or both in unison against a floor or each other to create audible percussive rhythms.

Codified techniques Formal, pre-established dance techniques.

Collaborator (choreographer) Interactive method of choreography between two or more collaborators.

Community dance A field promoting dance practices with groups and communities to express diverse local identities and to raise awareness about social, political and environmental issues.

Composition (dance) Learning the skills, devices and approaches to making dances.

Conceptual choreography An area of contemporary dance appointed to the critique of various practices and conventions.

Conservatoire An educational institution or college in higher learning, specialising in performing arts.

Contact improvisation A form of improvised movement involving body awareness, weight sharing and physical contact.

Contemporary dance A style and philosophy of dance developed during the twentieth century, following modern dance developments in the USA.

Contraction and Release A modern dance concept devised by Martha Graham that emphasizes the opposing forces of relaxation and tension, characterised by sharp dynamic movements, breathing cycles and manipulation of the pelvis and torso.

Cultural exchange Where people of diverse backgrounds partake in the experiences and ideas of each other's culture.

Dance Theatre A combination of stylistic dance movements treated with theatrical stage elements and movement devices.

Deconstruct To reduce something in order to reinterpret.

Diaspora The movement or migration of displaced people away from an established homeland; a community of those who maintain strong cultural ties with their homeland.

Didactic (choreographer) Instructional method of choreography.

Dramaturg An individual with extensive knowledge and research in theatrical works, who acts as a mentor, moderator and advisor to the creative process.

Embodiment A tangible expression of a feeling, quality or idea that is visible in form.

Embody Represent in bodily form.

Emic Denoting an 'insider' perspective of a specific culture.

Enchaînements Long complex movement phrases.

Facilitator (choreographer) Nurturing and mentoring choreographic method.

Fall and Recovery A modern dance concept devised by Doris Humphrey emphasising the cycle of relaxation and tension through the use of suspension in the body.

Feminism A range of principles and social movements that advocate for equality of the sexes..

Flexibility Capable of being bent or flexed.

Folklore The traditional beliefs, myths, tales and practices of a people, transmitted orally.

Freestyle dancing Can be defined as any style of dance where the moves are not thought out ahead and where no choreography of the moves occurs before the dance begins.

Gender studies An interdisciplinary study that analyses race, ethnicity, sexuality and location. In Gender Studies, the term 'gender' is used to refer to the social and cultural constructions of masculinities and femininities, not to the state of being male or female.

Genre A category of artistic composition.

Group dynamic Processes that develop through interaction among members of a given group and could include norms, roles, relations, development, need to belong, social influence and effects on behaviour.

Historical dancing A collective term covering a wide variety of dance types from the past as they are danced in the present.

Hybrid Of mixed origin or composition.

Icosahedron (Laban) A physical structure designed to integrate the dimensions of a movement performer.

Improvisation To create, perform and build something spontaneously with little to no preparation.

Interdisciplinary The merging or synthesis of two or more academic disciplines or styles normally considered distinct.

Isolation Movement made by one body part, separate from other parts of the body.

Kinaesthetics The sense by which motion, weight and the position of various body parts is perceived.

Kinesiology The study of the anatomy, physiology and mechanics of body movement, especially in humans.

Kinetic energy The capacity for work or vigorous activity; vigour; power.

Liminality A term used in Anthropology to describe the process of transitioning or being 'in-between' periods, boundaries and states.

Matriarchal society A social system where positions of power and leadership are held by women.

Metaphor A figure of speech used to refer to one thing to mean another.

Modern dance A serious theatrical dance developed in the USA in the 1930s, outside the classical ballet tradition.

Morris dancing A form of English folk dance usually accompanied by music. It is based on rhythmic stepping and the execution of choreographed figures by a group of dancers.

Motifs Short movement phrases capable of being developed.

Motion capture A technological tool used to digitise movement.

Movement (vocabulary) Rhythmic articulations and gestures of the body to express meaning and tell stories.

Natya shastra An ancient Indian treatise on the performing arts, encompassing theatre, dance and music.

Patriarchal society A social system where positions of power and leadership are held by men.

Penkat Silat A term used to describe a wide range of styles in Indonesian martial arts.

Ramayana A key text in Hinduism that is one of two major Sanskrits of ancient India narrating the story of King Rama and his wife Sita.

Release technique A technique developed to enhance movement and energy efficiency, minimise tension, heighten clarity and use of breath.

Representational dance vocabulary Movements that show a relationship between world/art and copy/model.

Ritual A ceremonial form of physical expression derived from religious, spiritual and/or cultural beliefs.

Romanticism An international artistic and philosophical movement that redefined the fundamental ways in which people in Western cultures thought about themselves and about their world.

Rote learning A learning technique that focuses on memorization.

Screendance (see also Videodance) A dance work that is created for and viewed on screen.

Site-specific work Work that is created for a specific site or place.

Social dancing Social dance is a major category or classification of dance forms or dance styles, where sociability and socializing are the primary focuses of the dancing. Social dances can be danced with a variety of partners and still be led and followed in a relaxed, easy atmosphere.

Solar plexus Complex of radiating nerves at the pit of the stomach.

Somatic Of the body (Greek), corporeal, physical, sensate.

Somatics Refers to a mind-body connection that is incorporated in one's practice or discipline.

Spiraling A characteristic of Graham technique that involves the rotation of the spine on its vertical axis at a 45-degree angle.

Sprung floor A shock-absorbent floor that protects dancers' bodies.

Stamina Endurance or strength.

Street dancing An umbrella term used to describe dance styles that evolved outside dance studios in any available open space such as streets, parks, school yards or nightclubs.

Tanztheater A performance form that combines dance, speaking, singing and chanting, conventional theatre and the use of props, set and costumes in one amalgam. It is performed by trained dancers. Usually, there is no narrative plot; instead, specific situations, fears and human conflicts are presented.

Time-signature A sign that indicates the metre of a piece of music e.g. 2/4, 5/8.

Turn out (movement) Outward rotation of the hips and feet.

Versatility Adaptivity, having multiple capabilities.

Videodance (see Screendance) Genre of film making specific to dance and choreography, using stylized or pedestrian movements, though protagonists could be human, animal or inanimate objects, using visual rhythm and perhaps special effects. Other terminology could include: Screendance, dancefilm, choreography for the camera, cinedance, and dance for the camera.

Visceral A deep, inward sensation, emotion or feeling in the body.

ACKNOWLEDGEMENT

This Glossary is reproduced and augmented with the kind permission of Jo Butterworth, from Butterworth, J. (2012) *Dance Studies: The Basics*, Abingdon and New York: Routledge.

REFERENCES

Aerowaves (n.d.) *About*, available: https://aerowaves.org/about-us/ [accessed 16 July 2021].
Akram Khan Company (2015) *Home*, available: www.akramkhancompany.net/ [accessed 26 April 2021].
Amans, D. (2017) *An Introduction to Community Dance Practice* (2nd edn), London: Macmillan Education UK.
Au, S. (2002) *Ballet and Modern Dance*, London: Thames & Hudson Ltd.
Bachelard, G. (1994) *The Poetics of Space*, translated by Jolas, M., Boston, MA: Beacon Press.
Baer, N. (1999) 'Design and Choreography', in Hall, S., ed., *From Russia with Love: Costumes from the Ballets Russes 1909–1933*, Canberra: National Gallery of Australia Publications Department, 40–55.
Baker, D. (2011) 'Looking through a Nation's Family Album', *Taipei Times*, 9 December, available: www.taipeitimes.com/News/feat/archives/2011/12/09/2003520280 [accessed 20 June 2021].
Bales, M. and Nettl-Fiol, R. eds (2008) *The Body Eclectic: Evolving Practices in Dance Training*, Urbana and Chicago, IL: University of Illinois Press.
Ballet Theatre Foundation (2020) *Home*, available: www.abt.org/ [accessed 1 June 2021].
Balletto di Roma (n.d.) *Home Alone*, available: www.ballettodiroma.com/en/company-productions/home-alone-en/ [accessed 17 July 2021].
Banes, Sally (1993) *Democracy's Body: Judson Dance Theatre, 1962–1964*, Durham, NC and London: Duke University Press
Bangarra Dance Theatre Australia (2021) *Home*, available: www.bangarra.com.au/ [accessed 20 April 2021].
Bangarra Dance Theatre Australia, Knowledge Ground (n.d.) *Home*, available: https://bangarra-knowledgeground.com.au/ [accessed 23 May 2021].
Barbour, K., Hunter, V. and Kloetzel, M. eds (2019) *(Re)positioning Site Dance: Local Acts, Global Perspectives*, Bristol: Intellect Books Ltd.

Barrowland Ballet (n.d.) *Tiger Tale*, available: https://barrowlandballet.co.uk/production/tiger-tale/ [accessed 17 July 2021].

Benjamin, A. (2017) 'Second Time Open', in Amans, D., ed., *An Introduction to Community Dance Practice* (2nd edn), London: Macmillan Education UK.

Birmingham Dance Network (n.d.) *About*, available: https://birminghamdancenetwork.co.uk/about/ [accessed 16 July 2021].

Bitef (n.d.) *Yuropa*, available: https://53.bitef.rs/en/program/yuropa [accessed 21 July 2021].

Brannigan, E. (2011) *Dancefilm: Choreography and the Moving Image*, New York: Oxford University Press.

Brown, C. (2015) 'City of Lovers', in Hunter, V., ed., *Moving Sites: Investigating Site-specific Dance Performance*, Abingdon and New York: Routledge.

Burridge, S. (2015) 'Scene in Singapore: October 2015', *Critical Dance*, 31 October, available: https://criticaldance.org/scene-in-singapore-october-2015/ [accessed 30 June 2021].

Burridge, S. ed. (2020) *Embodied Performativity in Southeast Asia: Multidisciplinary Corporealities*, Abingdon: Routledge.

Burt, R. (1998) *Alien Bodies: Representations of Modernity, 'Race', and Nation in Early Modern Dance*, London: Routledge.

Butterworth, J. (2012) *Dance Studies: The Basics*, Abingdon and New York: Routledge.

Candoco Dance Company (n.d.) *Home*, available: https://candoco.co.uk/ [accessed 25 June 2021].

Cheesman, S. (2014) 'Dance and Disability: Embracing Difference, Tensions and Complexities', *Dance Research Aotearoa*, 2, 20–30, available: https://doi.org/10.15663/dra.v2i1.26 [accessed 16 July 2021].

Choreographic Coding Labs (n.d.) *About*, available: http://choreographiccoding.org [accessed 29 July 2021].

Chunky Move (n.d.) *Mortal Engine*, available: https://cmarchive.net/list-of-works/mortal-engine [accessed 17 July 2021].

Cisneros, R. E., Stamp, K. Whatley, S. and Wood, K. (2019) 'WhoLoDancE: Digital Tools and the Dance Learning Environment', *Research in Dance Education*, 20(1), 54–72.

Claid, E. (2006) *Yes? No! Maybe… Seductive Ambiguity in Dance*, Abingdon and New York: Routledge.

Claire Cunningham (n.d.) *About*, available: www.clairecunningham.co.uk/about/ [accessed 23 June 2021].

Clarke, G. and Bramley, I. eds (1997) *Supporting, Stimulating, Sustaining: Independent Dance*, London: Arts Council England, available: www.independentdance.co.uk/wp-content/uploads/2010/11/SupportingStimulatingSustaining.pdf [accessed 19 June 2021].

Company Wang Ramirez (n.d.) *We Are Monchichi*, available: www.wangramirez.com/en/work/we-are-monchichi [accessed 17 July 2021].

Cooper Albright, A. (1997) *Choreographing Difference: The Body and Identity in Contemporary Dance*, Hanover: Wesleyan University Press.

Cooper Albright, A. (2013) *Engaging Bodies: The Politics and Poetics of Corporeality*, Middletown, CT: Wesleyan University Press.

Copeland, R (1993) 'Dance, Gender and Culture', in Thomas, E., ed., *Dance, Gender and Culture*, London: Macmillan, 119–127.

Cuncic, A. (2020) 'What is Cultural Appropriation?', *verywell mind*, available: www.verywellmind.com/what-is-cultural-appropriation-5070458 [accessed 4 June 2021].

Cunningham, M. (1982) *ChannelsInserts*, available: www.youtube.com/watch?v=_C0z6eHboss [accessed 27 July 2021].

Cvejić, B. (2016) 'A Choreographer's Score: Anna Teresa De Keersmaeker', in Bleeker, M., ed., *Transmission in Motion: The Technologizing of Dance*, Abingdon and New York: Routledge, 52–61.

Das, J. D. (2017) *Katherine Dunham: Dance and the African Diaspora*, Oxford: Oxford University Press. ProQuest Ebook Central, available: https://ebookcentral-proquest-com.proxy.lib.ul.ie/lib/univlime-ebooks/detail.action?docID=4854099 [accessed 16 July 2021].

David Zambrano (n.d.) *Teaching*, available: www.davidzambrano.org [accessed 25 June 2020].

Davida, D. (1992) 'Dancing the Body Eclectic', *Contact Quarterly: A Vehicle for Moving Ideas* (Summer), available: http://denadavida.ca/articles/dancing-the-body-eclectic/ [accessed 16 July 2021].

De Certeau, M. (1988) *The Practice of Everyday Life*, Berkeley, CA: University of California Press.

DeLahunta, S. (2017a) 'Motion Bank: A Broad Context for Choreographic Research', in Bleeker, M., ed., *Transmission in Motion: The Technologizing of Dance*, Abingdon and New York: Routledge, 128–137.

DeLahunta, S. (2017b) 'Wayne McGregor's Choreographic Language Agent', in Bleeker, M., ed., *Transmission in Motion: The Technologizing of Dance*, Abingdon and New York: Routledge.

Denzin, N. K. and Lincoln, Y. S. eds (1998) *Collecting and Interpreting Qualitative Materials*, Thousand Oaks, CA: SAGE Publications.

De Mille, A. (1956) *And Promenade Home*, Boston, MA and Toronto: Little, Brown and Company.

Deren, M. (1945) *A Study in Choreography for Camera*, available: www.youtube.com/watch?v=3A3caYPlnk8 [accessed 27 July 2021].

Díaz, E. (2015) *The Experimenters: Chance and Design at Black Mountain College*, Chicago, IL: The University of Chicago Press.

Dittman, V. (2008) 'A New York Dancer', in Bales, M. and Nettl-Fiol, R., eds, *The Body Eclectic: Evolving Practices in Dance Training*, Urbana and Chicago, IL: University of Illinois Press.

Dixon, S. (2007) *Digital Performance: A History of New Media in Theater, Dance, Performance Art, and Installation*, Cambridge, MA: MIT Press.

Duffy, A. (2021) *Careers in Dance: Practical and Strategic Guidance From the Field*, Champaign, IL: Human Kinetics.

DV8 (n.d.) *Can We Talk About This?*, available: www.dv8.co.uk/projects/can-we-talk-about-this/foreword-by-lloyd-newson [accessed 15 July 2021].

École des Sables (n.d.) *About*, available: https://ecoledessables.org/about-us [accessed 22 July 2021].

Eddy, M. (2009) 'A Brief History of Somatic Practices and Dance: Historical Development of the Field of Somatic Education and its Relationship to Dance', *Journal of Dance and Somatic Practices*, 1(1), 5–27.

Farrugia-Kriel, K. and Nunes Jensen, J. eds (2021) *The Oxford Handbook of Contemporary Ballet*, New York: Oxford University Press.

Fevered Sleep (n.d.) *Men and Girls Dance*, available: www.feveredsleep.co.uk/project/men-and-girls-dance [accessed 16 July 2021].

Finbow, A. (2016) *If Tate Modern was Musée de la Danse 2015*, available: www.tate.org.uk/research/publications/performance-at-tate/case-studies/musee-de-la-danse [accessed 16 July 2021].

Forsythe, W. (2011) 'Choreographic Objects', in Spier, S., ed., *William Forsythe and the Practice of Choreography*, New York and Abingdon: Routledge.

Foster, S. (1992) 'Dancing Bodies', in Crary, J. and Kwinter, S., eds, *Incorporations*, New York: Zone 6, 480–495.

Foster, S. (2010) *Choreographing Empathy*, Abingdon and New York: Routledge.

Franko, M. (2011) 'Writing for the Body: Notation, Reconstruction, and Reinvention in Dance', *Common Knowledge*, 17(2), 321–334, available: https://doi.org/10.1215/0961754X-1188004 [accessed 1 June 2021].

Franko, M. (2019) *Choreographing Discourses: A Mark Franko Reader*, Abingdon and New York: Routledge.

Friedes Galili, D. (2015) 'Gaga: Moving beyond Technique with Ohad Naharin in the Twenty-first Century', *Dance Chronicle*, 38(3), 360–392.

Gardner, H. (1983) *Frames of Mind: The Theory of Multiple Intelligences*, New York: Basic Books.

Gardner, S. (2007) 'Dancer, Choreographer and Modern Dance Scholarship', *Dance Research*, xxv(1), 35–53.

Garafola, L. (1989) *Diaghilev's Ballets Russes*, New York and Oxford: Oxford University Press.

Gracyk, T. (2020) 'Hume's Aesthetics', in Zalta, N. E., ed., *The Stanford Encyclopedia of Philosophy*, available: https://plato.stanford.edu/archives/sum2020/entries/hume-aesthetics/ [accessed 20 June 2021].

Graham, M. (1991) *Blood Memory: An Autobiography*, London: Macmillan

GVA Dance Training (2010) *Boyzie Cekwana on Influx*, available: http://gvadancetraining.ning.com/video/boyzie-cekwana-on-influx [accessed 21 July 2021].

Hanna, J. L. (1993) 'Classical Indian Dance and Women's Status', in Thomas, H., ed., *Dance, Gender and Culture*, London: Macmillan, 119–127.

Haseman, B. and Mafe, D. (2009) 'Acquiring Know-How: Research Training for Practice-Led Researchers', in Smith, H. and Dean, R., eds, *Practice-led Research, Research-led Practice in the Creative Arts*, Edinburgh: Edinburgh University Press.

Hunter, V. ed. (2015) *Moving Sites: Investigating Site-specific Dance Performance*, Abingdon and New York: Routledge.

Jérôme Bel (n.d) *Performances*, available: www.jeromebel.fr/index.php?p=2 [accessed 16 July 2021].

KAAI Theatre (2009) *Influx Controls: I Wanna Be Wanna Be*, available: www.kaaitheater.be/en/agenda/influx-controls-i-wanna-be-wanna-be [accessed 21 July 2021].

Kate Lawrence (2013) *Home*, available: www.verticaldancekatelawrence.com [accessed 5 June 2021].

Kearns, L. (2017) 'Dance Critique as Signature Pedagogy', *Arts and Humanities in Higher Education*, 16 (3), 266–276.

Kemmis, S. and McTaggart, R. (2000) 'Participatory Action Research', in Denzin, N. K. and Lincoln, Y. S., eds, *Handbook of Qualitative Research* (2nd edn), Thousand Oaks, CA: SAGE Publications, 567–607.

Kloppenberg, A. (2010) 'Improvisation in Process: "Post-Control" Choreography', *Dance Chronicle*, 33 (2), 180–207.

Kolesnikov-Jessop, S. (2010) 'Walking in Nijinsky's Footsteps', *New York Times*, 23 June, available: www.nytimes.com/2010/06/24/arts/24iht-jessop.html [accessed 19 June 2021].

Lakes, R. (2005) 'The Messages behind the Methods: The Authoritarian Pedagogical Legacy in Western Concert Dance Technique Training and Rehearsals', *Arts Education Policy Review*, 106(5), available: www.tandfonline.com/doi/abs/10.3200/AEPR.106.5.3-20 [accessed 19 June 2021].

Lavender, L. (1996) *Dancers Talking Dance: Critical Evaluations in the Choreography Class*, Champaign, IL: Human Kinetics.

Lawson, B. (2001) *The Language of Space*, Oxford: Architectural Press.

Lee, R. (2017) 'Aiming for Stewardship Not Ownership', in Amans, D., ed., *An Introduction to Community Dance Practice* (2nd edn), London: Macmillan Education UK.

Lefebvre, H. (1991) *The Production of Space*, translated by Nicholson-Smith, D., Oxford: Blackwell.

Lerman, L. and Borstel, J. (2003) *Liz Lerman's Critical Response Process: A Method for Getting Useful Feedback on Anything You Make, From Dance to Dessert*, Takoma Park, MD: Dance Exchange, Inc.

Lin, H. M. (2012) 'Foreword', in Wang, Y. and Burridge, S., eds, *Identity and Diversity: Celebrating Dance in Taiwan*, New Delhi: Routledge India, xi–xiii.

Louppe, L. (1996) 'Hybrid Bodies', *Writings on Dance*, 15, 63–67.

Lucinda Childs (2021) *History*, available: www.lucindachilds.com/history.php [accessed 4 June 2021].

Mabingo, A. (2015) 'Decolonizing Dance Pedagogy: Application of Pedagogies of Ugandan Traditional Dances in Formal Dance Education', *Journal of Dance Education*, 15(4), 131–141.

Maletić, V. (1987) *Body – Space – Expression: The Development of Rudolf Laban's Movement and Dance Concepts*, Berlin, New York and Amsterdam: Mouton de Gruyter. ProQuest Ebook Central, available: http://ebookcentral.proquest.com/lib/univlime-ebooks/detail.action?docID=934658 [accessed 1 June 2021].

Maletić, V. (2005) 'Laban Principles of Movement Analysis', in Cohan, S. J., ed., *The International Encyclopedia of Dance*, Oxford: Oxford University Press, available: www.oxfordreference.com/view/10.1093/acref/9780195173697.001.0001/acref-9780195173697-e-0983 [accessed 13 July 2021].

Marian Goodman Gallery (2021) *Tino Sehgal*, available: www.mariangoodman.com/artists/62-tino-sehgal/ [accessed 25 June 2021].

Massey, R. (2007) 'Chandralekha, Controversial Indian Dancer Whose Ideas Challenged Convention', *The Guardian*, 9 February, available: www.theguardian.com/news/2007/feb/09/guardianobituaries.india [accessed 30 April 2021].

Mazo, J. H. (1977) *Prime Movers, The Makers of Modern Dance in America*, Princeton, NJ: Princeton Book Company.

McCarren, F. (2013) *French Moves: The Cultural Politics of Le Hip Hop*, New York: Oxford University Press.

McKinley, B. (2019) 'First Maker in Residence to Lead Creative Projects on Cultural Production in Diasporic Communities', *In the Loop*, Gainesville: University of Florida, available: https://arts.ufl.edu/in-the-loop/news/first-maker-in-residence-to-lead-creative-projects-on-cultural-production-in-diasporic-communities/ [accessed 1 July 2021].

McPherson, K. (2019) *Making Video Dance: A Step-by-Step Guide to Creating Dance for the Screen* (2nd edn), Abingdon and New York: Routledge.

McWilliam, E., Carey, G., Draper, P. and Lebler, D. 2006. 'Learning and Unlearning: New Challenges for Teaching in Conservatoires', *Australian Journal of Music Education*, 1, 25–31, available: https://search.informit.org/doi/10.3316/informit.675891806633112 [accessed 10 February 2022].

Meglin, J. A. and Matluck Brooks, L. (2012) 'Where are All the Women Choreographers in Ballet?', *Dance Chronicle*, 35(1), 1–7.

Millennium Dance Complex (n.d.) *Home*, available: https://millenniumdancecomplex.com/ [accessed 2 June 2021].

Minarti, H. (2018) *Rianto – A Transgressive Body*, Off Stage, available: www.esplanade.com/offstage/arts/rianto-a-transgressive-body [accessed 12 June 2021].

Monahin, N. (2015) 'Writing for Posterity: A Reassessment of Arbeau's Orchésographie (1589)', *Congress on Research in Dance Conference Proceedings*, 125–135.

Moon, J. (1999) *Learning Journals: A Handbook for Academics, Students and Professional Development*, London: Kogan Page.

Morris, G. (2006) *A Game for Dancers: Performing Modernism in the Post-war Years*, 1945–1960, Middletown, CT: Wesleyan University Press.

Murgiyanto, S. (2016) *Pertunjukan Budaya dan Akal Sehat*, Jakarta: Fakultas Seni Pertunjukan IKJ and Komunitas Senrepita.

Newson, L. (1990) *Dead Dreams of Monochrome Men*, available: www.youtube.com/watch?v=aNGpDfAQ4QI/ [accessed 27 July 2021].

Noisette, P. (2011) *Talk About Contemporary Dance*, translated by Dusinberre, D., Paris: Flammarion.

Nugent, A. (2021) 'William Forsythe: Stuttgart, Frankfurt and the Forsythescape', in Farrugia-Kriel, K. and Nunes Jensen, J., eds, *The Oxford Handbook of Contemporary Ballet*, New York: Oxford University Press, 13–28.

One Dance UK (2017) 'Guide to Careers in Dance: Championing Dance for All Young People', *One Dance UK*, available: www.onedanceuk.org/wp-content/uploads/2017/02/Careers-Guide-Digital-version.pdf [accessed 25 June 2020].

Oona Doherty (n.d.) *Hope Hunt and The Ascension in Lazarus*, available: www.oonadohertyweb.com/ [accessed 12 July 2021].

Park Avenue Armory (2015) *Flexn*. available: www.armoryonpark.org/mobile/event_detail/flexn/#Details [accessed 26 June 2020].

P.A.R.T.S. (n.d.) *About*, available: www.parts.be/about [accessed 25 June 2020].

Philip Saire (n.d.) *Hocus Pocus*, available: www.philippesaire.ch/en/projets/hocus-pocus [accessed 17 July 2021].

PKLifeWork (2012) 'Black and White' (Khon), *Pichet Klunchun Dance Company* [video], available: https://youtu.be/KlRfkTLSICM [accessed 3 May 2021].

PKLifeWork (2012) 'Nijinsky Siam', *Pichet Klunchun Dance Company* [video], available: www.youtube.com/watch?v=t2vgbYpo8Yc [accessed 29 July 2021].

PSBT-India (2014) *Sharira – Chandralekha's Explorations in Dance* [video], available: www.youtube.com/watch?v=vyXh_5dT0zw [accessed 5 April 2019].

QL2 Dance (n.d.) *Our Vision*, available: www.ql2.org.au/ourvision [accessed 4 June 2021].

Raditya, H. B. (2021) 'Revealing Cultural Representation in Indonesian Contemporary Dance', in Burridge, S., ed., *The Routledge Companion to Dance in Asia and the Pacific: Platforms for Change*, New Delhi: Routledge India.

Re:Rosas! (n.d.) *Home*, available: www.rosasdanstrosas.be/en-home/ [accessed 16 July 2021].

Robinson, K. and Aronica, L. (2018) 'Why Dance is Just as Important as Math in School', *TED Conferences*, 21 March, available: https://ideas.ted.com/why-dance-is-just-as-important-as-math-in-school/ [accessed 3 June 2021].

Roche, J. (2015) *Multiplicity, Embodiment and the Contemporary Dancer: Moving Identities*, London: Palgrave Macmillan.

Roche, J. (2018) 'Dancing Strategies and Moving Identities: The Contributions Independent Contemporary Dancers Make to the Choreographic Process', in Butterworth, J. and Wildschut, L., eds, *Contemporary Choreography: A Critical Reader* (2nd edn), Abingdon and New York: Routledge.

Rosenberg, D. (2012) *Screendance: Inscribing the Ephemeral Image*. New York: Oxford University Press.

Roy, S. (2020) 'Virtual Voguing and Digital Razzle-Dazzle: London Film Festival Takes the Arts into a New Dimension', *The Guardian*, 13 October, available: www.theguardian.com/stage/2020/oct/13/london-film-festival-arts-lff-expanded [accessed 19 June 2021].

Royal Academy of Dance (2021) *Home*, available: www.royalacademyofdance.org/ [accessed 28 May 2021].

Sanchez Colberg, A. (1993) 'You Can See it Like This or Like That: Pina Bausch's *Die Klage Der Kaiserin*', in Jordan, S. and Allen, D., eds, *Parallel Lines: Media Representations of Dance*, London: John Libbey Publishing, Ltd. 217–235.

Sarco-Thomas, M. (2016) 'Spacings: Interactive Imaginations in Dance Improvisations', presented at School of Performing Arts Conference: *21st Century Performance and Research*, University of Malta.

Sassenberg, M. (1999) 'Gertrud Bodenwieser', *Jewish Women: A Comprehensive Historical Encyclopedia*, 31 December, Jewish Women's Archive, available: https://jwa.org/encyclopedia/article/bodenwieser-gertrud [accessed 2 December 2020].

Schön, D. A. (2011) *The Reflective Practitioner: How Professionals Think in Action* (Reprinted), Farnham: Ashgate.

Schwartz, P. and Schwartz, M. (2011) *The Dance Claimed Me: A Biography of Pearl Primus*, New Haven, CT: Yale University Press. ProQuest Ebook Central, available: https://ebookcentral-proquest-com.proxy.lib.ul.ie/lib/univlime-ebooks/detail.action?docID=3420692 [accessed 16 July 2021].

Sheets-Johnstone, M. (2011). *The Primacy of Movement* (Expanded 2nd edn), Amsterdam: John Benjamins Pub. Co.

Siegmund, G. and Van Dijk, A. (2011) 'Introduction: The Difficulty of Running', in Diehl, I. and Lampert, F., eds, *Dance Techniques 2010: Tanzplan Germany*, Leipzig: Henschel Verlag.

Sierra, G. (2015) 'A Brooklyn Dancer Flexes His Talents and Social Activism with New Show at Park Avenue Armory', *Brooklyn Based*, available: https://brooklynbased.com/2015/03/26/flexn/ [accessed 26 June 2020].

Siliezar, J. (2019) 'With Twisting and Floating Movements, Harvard Gaga Dance Course Teaches Students and Community Members to Listen to Their Bodies', *The Harvard Gazette*, available: https://news.harvard.edu/gazette/story/2019/04/harvard-gaga-dance-course-teaches-students-to-listen-to-their-bodies/ [accessed 25 June 2020].

Smith, D. W. (2018) 'Phenomenology', in Zalta, E. N., ed., *The Stanford Encyclopedia of Philosophy*, 16 November, available: https://plato.stanford.edu/archives/sum2018/entries/phenomenology [accessed 25 June 2021].

Soares, J. (2005) 'Horst, Louis', in Cohan, S. J., ed., *The International Encyclopedia of Dance*, Oxford: Oxford University Press, available: www.oxfordreference.com/view/10.1093/acref/9780195173697.001.0001/acref-9780195173697-e-0794 [accessed 13 July 2021].

Springgay, S., Irwin, R. L. and Kind, S. W. (2005). 'A/r/tography as Living Inquiry through Art and Text', in *Qualitative Inquiry*. SAGE Publications.

Stephan Koplowitz (n.d.) *Red Line Time*, available: www.stephankoplowitz.com/redlinetime [accessed 29 July 2021].

Stock, C. (2017) 'Beyond Intercultural to the Accented Body', in Butterworth, J. and Wildschut, L., eds, *Contemporary Choreography: A Critical Reader*, Abingdon and New York: Routledge, 342–357.

Studio Wayne McGregor (n.d.) *Studio Wayne McGregor*, available: https://waynemcgregor.com/about/studio-wayne-mcgregor/ [accessed 4 June 2021].

Tate (n.d.) *What's On*, available: www.tate.org.uk/whats-on/tate-modern/exhibition/bmw-tate-live-exhibition-2020 [accessed 29 July 2021].

Trisha Brown Company (n.d.) *Home*, available: https://trishabrowncompany.org/ [accessed 23 May 2021].

Twyla Tharpe (2021) *Home*, available: www.twylatharp.org/ [accessed 5 May 2021].

Walther, S. (1993) 'The Dance of Death: Description and Analysis of *The Green Table*', *Choreography and Dance: An International Journal*, 3(2). ProQuest Ebook Central, available: https://ebookcentral-proquest-com.proxy.lib.ul.ie/lib/univlime-ebooks/detail.action?docID=237417 [accessed 16 July 2021].

Wang, Y. and Burridge, S. eds (2012) *Identity and Diversity: Celebrating Dance in Taiwan*, New Delhi: Routledge India.

Watton, P., Collings, J. and Moon, P. (2001) *Reflective Writing: Guidance Notes for Students*, available: https://tinyurl.com/3nnkh39v [accessed 16 July 2021].

Wex Arts (n.d.) *Boyzie Cekwana*, available: https://wexarts.org/performing-arts/boyzie-cekwana [accessed 22 July 2021].

Whatley, S. (2013) 'Siobhan Davies RePlay: (Re)visiting the Digital Archive', *International Journal of Performance Arts and Digital Media*, 9(1), 83–98.

Whatley, S. (2015) 'Motion Capture and the Dancer: Visuality, Temporality and the Dancing Image', in Whatley, S., Garrett Brown, N. and Alexander, K., eds, *Attending to Movement: Somatic Perspectives on Living in This World*, Axminster: Triarchy Press, 193–204.

Worth, L. and Poynor, H. (2004) *Anna Halprin*, Abingdon and New York: Routledge.

Yeoh, F. (2013) 'Choreographers' Moral Right of Integrity', *Journal of Intellectual Property Law & Practice*, 8(1), 43–58, available: https://doi.org/10.1093/jiplp/jps184 [accessed 16 July 2021].

INDEX

Aboriginal and Torres Strait Islanders 30
Abramović, Marina 147
abstraction 43, 47, 48
accredited dance courses 8, 9, 11–12
Acogny, Germaine 115
action research 145
Aerowaves platform 76
aesthetics 138–139
Africa/African artists 115–116
Africa/African dances 49, 83–84
African American dancers 128
Ailey, Alvin 127–128
Alexander Technique 82
Amans, Diane 177
American Ballet Theatre 17, 25
appraising 11–12
appropriation 15, 121
Arbot, Thoinet 97
architectural theory 160–161
archives 119
art galleries 20
a/r/tography 146
arts councils 74
Asian classical dance 14–15, 24
Asian traditions 28–35, 44
asymmetry 40
audience: children 179; and site-specific performance 162
Ausdruckstanz movement 23, 46, 102
Australia 14, 30–31, 49, 65
Australian Ballet 16

autoethnography 147
avant-garde 21
avatars 171

BA and BA Hons (Dance) 150–151
Bachelard, Gaston 160
Baker, Josephine 21–22, 107
Balanchine, George 25–26, 51–52, 107, 110
Bales, Melanie 72, 79
Balla, Giacomo 164
ballet: classical. *See* classical ballet contemporary 110–112; limitations of 98; vocabulary 97, 110
ballet barre 41
Ballet Frankfurt 41
Ballet Jooss 105
Ballet Nationale de Marseille 76
Ballets Russes 24, 25, 33, 49, 98, 164
Bangarra Dance Theatre 30–31, 65, 114
barefoot dancing 22, 49
baroque dances 97, 117
Barrowland Ballet 179
Bartenieff, Irmgard 38
Bartenieff Fundamentals 104
Baskar, Shanta 15
Batsheva Dance Company 41–42, 79
Batson, Glenna 136
Bausch, Pina 23, 46, 115, 165
becoming 140

Bel, Jérôme 47, 110, 113, 176
Benjamin, Adam 178
Beyoncé 122
Bharatanatyam *see* Indian Bharatanatyam
BIPED 53
Birmingham Dance Network 70
black artists and companies 99–100, 107
Black Mountain College, North Carolina 105
Blasis, Carlo 117
blogs 88
Blue-Eyed Soul 178
Bodenweiser, Gertrude 104
body awareness 38–39, 41
Bourne, Matthew Christopher 44–45, 142
branding 72
Brannigan, Erin 164
Broadway musicals 19
Brooks, Meglin and Matluck 110
Brown, Carol 162
Brown, Trisha 20, 159
budgets *see* funding
bullying 10
Burrows, Jonathan 106, 120
Butcher, Rosemary 109, 159
Butoh 28–29

Cage, John 50, 53, 106; *see also* Cunningham, Merce
Cambodia, Khmer Royal Ballet 24, 48
camera movement 167
Camp, Julie Van 65
Candoco (dance company) 132, 178
case study approach 146–147
Cekwana, Boyzie 116
Certeau, Michel de 160
Chandralekha Prabhudas Patel 31
Charmatz, Boris 110, 163
Cherkaoui, Sidi Larbi 32, 45, 111
children: body awareness 38; community groups 14, 176–177; and contemporary dance 179; dance games 43; *see also* young people
Childs, Lucinda 27
Chinese traditions 130–131
choreographer, role of 98–99; *see also individual choreographers*
Choreographic Coding Lab (CCL) 173–174
Choreographic Lab 134–135
choreography, origins 96–97
choreutics 103
Chunky Move 172–173
cinema 163–165
Cirque du Soleil 18
Claid, Emilyn 73
Clarke, G. 18
classical ballet 9–10, 157; costume design 49; myths and fairy tales 22; and other cultural dance forms 24–26; *see also* ballet
climate justice/activism 159
Cloud Gate Dance Theatre of Taiwan 29–30
Code of Conduct and Safe Dance Practices 10
Colker, Deborah 18
collaboration 16, 37, 57–58, 77, 114, 174
collage 45–46
collectives 70
commercial sector 18–19
community cultural groups 14–15
community dance 174–180
community youth groups 13–14
Company Käfig 80
conceptual choreography 47
contact improvisation 59
contemporary ballet 110–112
contemporary dance: and Asian traditions 28–35; technique 12; *see also individual choreographers; individual companies*
contemporary dance companies 16–17
content 43–48
context 64–66

controversy 126
copyright 121–122
costs *see* funding
costume design 48–49
Countertechnique 82–83
COVID-19, 60, 72, 122
creating 11
Critical Path (dance research lab) 134–135
Critical Response Process 89–91
critical thinking 89, 90–92, 110, 138
criticism 62–66
cross-gender dance form 142
Cullberg Ballet 44
cultural dance groups 14–15
Cunningham, Claire 132
Cunningham, Merce 16, 23, 27, 38, 48, 108; and Cage 50, 106, 108; digital software 169–170; motion capture 170; multimedia work and collaborations 53
Curry, John 18
Cvejić, Bojana 119–120

Dadaists 109
dance criticism 62–66
dance for camera *see* Screendance
Dance for Parkinsons 174
dance houses 70–71
Dance Nucleus (dance research lab) 134–135
dance theatre genre 46–47
Dartington College 105
Davida, Dena 109
Davies, Siobhan 119
De Keersmaeker, Anne Teresa 119
de Mille, Agnes 122
Dean, Christopher 18
decolonizing the curriculum 83–84
deconstruction/reconstruction model 43
DeLahunta, S. 120
Deleuze, Gilles 140–141
Deren, Maya 164, 168
Dewey, John 105
Diaghilev, Serge 24, 25, 98

diaspora communities 14, 127
diasporic artists 113–114
digital apps 34
digital archives 119
digital platforms 7, 60, 72–73, 120–121, 122, 168
digital software 169–170, 172
diploma degree 149–150
direct casting 8
disabled dancers 177–178
diversity 133, 174
Dixon, Steve 169
Doctoral studies 151–152
Doherty, Oona 76
Dorner, Willi 159–160
Dublin Fringe Festival 76
Duchamp, Marcel 109
Duffy, A. 84–85
Duncan, Isadora 22, 49, 98, 157–158
Dunham, Katherine 99–100, 107
Dunn, Robert 108–109
Dunne, Colin 114
duty of care 176–177
DV8 (physical theatre company) 133

Eckman, Alexander 17, 45–46, 52
eclecticism 27, 37
Edinburgh Fringe Festival 76
editing 5, 167–168
Ek, Mats 44
electives or co-curricular dance 13
embodiment 140, 141–142
emotions 14
English National Ballet 16, 32
entrepreneurial approach 84–85
eukinetics 103
European Dance House Network (EDN) 71
Evans, Robert Alan 179
experimentation 71, 76
expressionist dance theatre 23

'fall and recovery' technique 40
Farrugia-Kriel, Kathrina 111
feedback 87, 89, 90; *see also* ORDER (Lavender)

female innovators 98–100; *see also individual female dancers*
festivals 19, 74, 165; *see also individual festivals*
Feuillet notation 97, 117
film *see* cinema
filming dance 166–167
films, choreography 19
Flexn 76–77
floor sensors/lasers 172–173
Flying Low 39, 80–82
Fokine, Michel 24–25, 33, 98
folk dances 14
form 38–43
Forsythe, William 4, 17, 38, 41, 111–112, 120–121
Foster, Susan Leigh 1, 78
framing 166
France 110, 113
Franko, M. 117–118
freelancers 17–19, 70, 71–72, 73–75, 98
Friedes Galili, Deborah 79
Fuller, Loïe 52, 98–99, 164, 169
funding 70, 71, 76, 86

Gaga 41–42, 79–80
gallery spaces 163
game structures 43
Gardner, Howard 141
Gardner, Sally 100–101
Gat, Emanuel 43
gender fluidity 111
gendered body, the 142–143
genre 16
Germany 23
Gibbs, Graham 88
Gibson/Martelli 171–172
gig economy 70
Gilmore, Natasha 179
Giselle 22, 44
Glass, Phillip 42, 50
Graham, Martha 16, 23, 48, 106, 141
Gray, Reggie 76–77
group choreography 43
Guattari, Felix 141

Guerin, Lucy 176
Guggenheim, New York 20

Halprin, Anna 180
hand-held camera 167
Hanna, J. L. 143
Harvard Dance Centre 80
Haseman, Brad 87
Hay, Deborah 120
Hip Hop 80
Hiroaki Umeda 53
HIV/AIDS 180
Hollywood 24
Horst, Louis 106, 107
Hume, David 139
Humphrey, Doris 22, 23, 40, 99, 107
hybridisation 15, 126

ice dancing 18
icosahedron 104
illumination 59–60
immersive and experiential practice 147–148
improvisation 40, 42, 59, 77, 81, 136
inclusivity 174
incubation 58–59
independent choreographers 17–19, 71, 73–75, 136
Indian Bharatanatyam 4–5, 14, 15, 31
Indian classical dance 31–32
Indian classical music 51
indigenous dance 30–31, 65
Indonesian choreographers 129–130, 142
innovation 4, 15, 21–22, 110
inquiry *see* research and inquiry
institutes of higher learning (IHL) *see* universities and IHL
intentionalism 139–140
intercultural contexts 112–116
intercultural exchange 112–114
interdisciplinary creative practice 148
internet: marketing 72; *see also* digital platforms
Isadora (digital software) 172
Italian Futurists 164

Jackapura Munyarryun 30
Japanese Butoh 28–29
Javanese dance 129, 142
jazz age 21–22
Jeyasingh, Shobhana 4
Johns, Jasper 27, 53
Jones, Bill T. 170–171
Jooss, Kurt 102, 105
journalling 59, 88
Jowett, Deborah 65
Judson Dance 26, 27, 105, 109

Kant, Immanuel 139
Kathak 31, 32, 113
Kazuo Ohno 28
Kearns, L. 90, 91
Keersmaeker, Anne Teresa De 47, 106, 122
Khan, Akram 4, 17, 32, 44, 45, 113, 142; and independents 75; lighting design 52
Khon *see* Thai classical mask dance (Khon)
kinesphere 103
Kloppenberg, Annie 77–78
Klunchun, Pichet 32–33, 47, 113
Koplowitz, Stephan 161, 162

Laast, Anthony van 19
Laban, Rudolf von 22, 38, 40, 102–104, 118
Laban Movement Analysis (LMA) 22, 104
Labanotation 22–23, 118
laboratories 134–135
Lafrance, Noémi 162
Lavender, Larry 91–92
Lawrence, Kate 20
Lawson, Brian 160
Le Roy, Xavier 110
Lee, Rosemary 175–176
Lefebvre, Henri 160–161
Lengger Lanang 142
Lerman, Liz 89–91
Lester Horton technique 127
lighting 52, 169

liminality 126–127
Limon, José 23
Lin Hwai-min 29, 130–131
Linyekula, Faustin 163
live streaming 7, 60, 72
lived experience 180
logistic planning 55–56
London 19, 163
London Contemporary Dance School 165
Louppe, Laurence 75
Ludus Dance Company 178

Mabingo, Alfdaniels 83–84
Macaulay, Alistair 111
Mafe, Dan 87
male choreographers 110
mapping 145–146
Marin, Maguy 110
Mark Morris Dance Group (MMDG) 50–51, 174
marketing 72, 74, 77–78
Masilo, Dada 45
Master's degree (MA) 151
Mazo, Joseph H. 24
McGregor, Wayne 28, 110, 111, 169–170
McPherson, Katrina 166, 167–168
mentorship 70
Merleau-Ponty, Maurice 140
mid-scale dance projects 74–75
Midsummer Night's Dream 46
Millennium Dance Complex 10
Miller, Bebe 120
mirroring 43
modern dance: asymmetry 40; early innovators 163–164; post-war 106–108
Monk, Meredith 158
Morris, Gay 106, 107
Morris, Mark 50–51
Motion Bank (research project) 120–121, 173
motion capture 53, 170–172
movement generation software 53

movement vocabularies 23–24, 28, 40–42, 50, 78
multidisciplinary focus 53–54
multi-modal planning 57
Murphy, Graeme 18
music, and choreographers 50–52, 105–106
musical theatre 19
myths and legends 7, 43; *see also* narratives

Naharin, Ohad 41–42, 79
narrative research 145
narratives 43–48, 107
national dance companies 16
Netherlands Dance Theatre 17
Nettl-Fiol, Rebecca 72, 79
networking 85–86
New Adventures 45
New Dance 109, 159
new technologies 53
New York City 70; Dance Theatre of Harlem 115; *Flexn* 76–77; Judson Church 26, 27. *See also* Judson Dance
Newson, Lloyd 133, 169, 178
Nigeria 113, 116
Nijinska, Bronislava 110
Nijinsky, Vaslav 25–26, 33, 50
Nikolais, Alwin 50, 53
non-dance 110
notation 97, 117, 118
Nugent, Ann 112
Nunes Jenson, Jill 111
Nutcracker ballet 44

Obarzanek, Gideon 172–173
One Dance UK 86–87
Onikeku, Qudus 113, 114–115, 116
ORDER (Lavender) 91–92
Overlie, Mary 38–39

Page, Stephen 114
Paris 24–25
Paris Opera Ballet 16
Parkinson's Disease 174

partnerships 74
P.A.R.T.S. dance training institution 83
Passing Through 81
Paxton, Steve 109
performative practice 135–137, 144
Petipa, Marius 50, 51
phenomenology 59, 136, 139, 140–141
Phoenix Dance Theatre 115
physical theatre 133
Pite, Crystal 17, 52
pop-up companies 27
postmodernism 20, 26–27, 49, 143
power 160
practice-based research 136–137
preparation 54–58
presenting 11
preservation 116–121, 135
Primus, Pearl 99, 100
private dance studios 9–10
process 54–61, 175
ProDance Leeds 70
producing 86
production elements 48–54
professional company training programmes 8
prompts 57

qualitative research 144
quantitative research 144

raga (mood) 51
Rainer, Yvonne 143
Ramayana story 44
Ramirez, Sébastien 179
recreational dance classes 8
reflective practice/reflection 13, 59, 62, 87–89, 92, 136–137
repetition 45, 46, 47
research and inquiry 56, 134–152
resilience 87, 92
Rianto 142
ritual practice, dance as 40
Robinson, Sir Ken 10

Rosenberg, Doug 165
Royal Academy of Dance (RAD) 9

Saire, Philip 179
Sankai Juku Company 29
Sarco-Thomas 81–82
Sawhney, Nitin 45
scale, and social hierarchy 160
Schön, Donald 136
school education system: accredited courses 11–12; electives or co-curricular dance 13
Sciarroni, Alessandro 179
scores 119–120
Screendance 165–168
Sehgal, Tino 20
self-promotion 72–73
self-reflection *see* reflective practice/reflection
Sentler, Susan 136
shape and structure 39–40
shared experience, artwork as 140
Shechter, Hofesh 17
Sheets-Johnstone, Maxine 135–136
signature artists 98
silent film action 164–165
Singapore 15
site-specific dance 20, 158–163; and activism 159; and architecture 160–161; creating 161–162; gallery spaces 163; urban sites 159–160
skills, transferability 73
social change, choreography for 126–133
social issues 14, 15
social media 9, 21, 34, 62, 72
soundscapes 51
South Africa 116
South Asian Kathak 4–5
space(s): internal (mental) and external (physical) 160; outside/inside 161
spinning 32
St. Denis, Ruth 24, 98
Stock, Cheryl 112–114

storytelling *see* narratives
strategic planning 55
Stravinsky 50
street dance 9, 49, 76
Strictly Come Dancing 19
Studio Wayne McGregor 28
subjectivity 139
Supriyanto, Eko 129–130
Swan Lake 17, 22, 44–45, 46
Sydney Dance Company 18

tai chi 30
Taiwan, Cloud Gate Dance Theatre 29–30
tala (rhythm) 51
Tanztheatre Wuppertal 23, 46
task-based creation 56–57
taste, philosophers on 139
Tate Modern, London 163
Tatsumi Hijikata 28
Tchaikovsky 50, 51
teaching: key influences 101–106; *see also* a/r/tography; training
television shows 7, 19
Thai classical mask dance (*Khon*) 32–33, 48, 113
Tharp, Twyla 17, 27, 42, 50
theatre dance 117
time 40
tone 57
Toole, David 178
Torvill, Jayne 18
training 70; curriculum, decolonizing 83–84; and diversity 133; skills, transferability 73; *see also* teaching; *specific approaches and skills*

UNESCO 10
universities and IHL 148–152
urban contemporary/Hip Hop 80
urban environments 7, 159–160, 161

validation 61
Van Camp, Julie 65
Van Dijk, Anouk 82

Vertical Dance 20
video recording 59, 72, 118, 166
Viewpoints 38–39
Vimeo 168
virtual reality 171–172
vocabulary and language 97, 110
vulnerable adults 176–177

Wagner-Bergelt, Bettina 46
Wallas, Graham 54
Wang, Honji 179
Warhol, Andy 27, 53
websites and web design 72, 122
Weiss, Frieder 172–173
Western classical music 51
Western theatre dance, notation 97

WhoLoDancE project 171
Wigman, Mary 22, 23, 46, 102, 105–106

X6, 109, 159

yoga 31
Yoruba culture 114–115, 116
young people: African American dancers 128; community groups 176–177; dance groups 13–14, 178; *see also* children
YouTube 7, 121, 168

Zambrano, David 39, 80–81, 83
Zoom 41

For Product Safety Concerns and Information please contact our EU
representative GPSR@taylorandfrancis.com
Taylor & Francis Verlag GmbH, Kaufingerstraße 24, 80331 München, Germany

www.ingramcontent.com/pod-product-compliance
Lightning Source LLC
Chambersburg PA
CBHW050525170426
43201CB00013B/2082